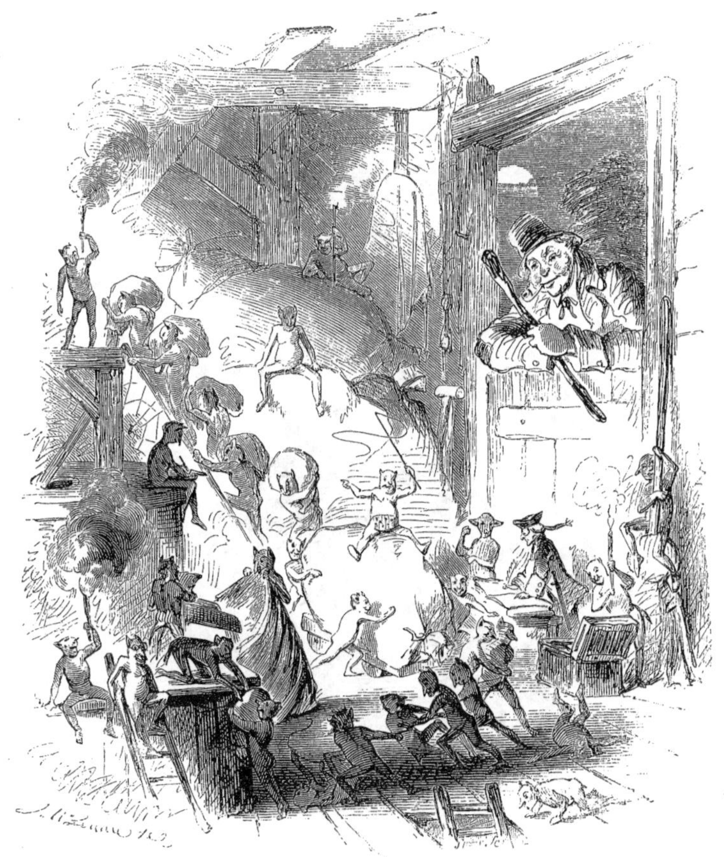

NED. GERAGHTY'S LUCK.

BASKET OF CHIPS

BY

JOHN BROUGHAM

NEW YORK

Bunce & Bro.

A

BASKET OF CHIPS.

BY

JOHN BROUGHAM.

NEW YORK:
BUNCE & BROTHER, PUBLISHERS,
126 NASSAU STREET.
MDCCCLV.

W. H. TINSON, Stereotyper. BAKER, GODWIN & Co., Printers.

To

MY EXCELLENT GOOD FRIEND

AND FELLOW-COUNTRYMAN,

DR. WILLIAM B. EGAN,

OF ILLINOIS,

THIS LITTLE VOLUME

IS MOST AFFECTIONATELY

INSCRIBED.

PREFACE.

My Dear Public.

My publishers, with that delicious *sang froid* so characteristic of the frigiferous class, have just intimated to me that they are "waiting for a Preface."

For a *Preface!* good gracious! was there ever such an absurdity? A Preface! why, the very term sounds to me far-off-ish and antediluvian. I had fondly imagined that, like the prologues to plays, Prefaces belonged now to the cocked-hat and shoe-buckle period.

But it appears that I am mistaken; my publishers want a Preface, and publishers are unappeasably despotic.

I am well aware that nobody reads the confounded thing; and with that assurance and the thermometer so pertinaciously at 80, that there's a tidal mark on the glass wall of the instrument, you may imagine, my very dear public, with what amount of enthusiasm I set myself down for the undertaking.

Now, I have a kind of general idea what a good Preface should be, just as I have a tolerably shrewd notion of what a good dinner should consist. But unfortunately my resources, both mental and monetary, restrict me to the simple but unsatisfactory consciousness of the abstract knowledge.

A properly organized Preface should be more suggestive, than indicative, of that which is to follow, just as a tastefully ordered table with its plate and glass, its bouquets and snowy serviettes, prepares, instinctively the fortunate invitee, for a grammatical repast.

Indeed a *Preface might* even go as far as the ante-prandial "half dozen of Massachusetts Bays," with which the convives at Delmonicos are wont to stimulate the epigastric relations, smacking their lips upon the after-taste of the accompanying single glass of Chablis, with the double relish of present enjoyment and appetizing anticipation.

But inasmuch as I have no intention of inviting you to such a

"FEAST OF REASON,"

but simply ask you, in the earnestness of the broadest kind of hospitality, to drop in and take *Pot Luck*—why there is no necessity for so elaborate a preparation.

A Preface is usually either apologetic or explanatory, or both. Now, I have nothing that I am aware of to apologize for; and the book I sincerely hope will explain itself.

It was *not* the urgent solicitation of flattering friends, which gently forced me to this evulgation. No, I have no hesitation in acknowledging the compromising fact, that I was partly propelled thereto by considerations of a merely mercenary nature; added to which, I must do myself the justice to say, that I was also influenced by the hope that my Publishers might also be recompensed for the compliment they paid me in imagining that the *scraps* now set before you, would satisfy the least exigeante appetite.

"A BASKET OF CHIPS," is a somewhat dry and unpromising repast to ask any one to participate in, to be sure, and the unsavoriness of the name will, no doubt, be eagerly laid hold of by some of the critics. I know *one* who will hardly let the opportunity escape for saying a smart thing or two. Perhaps it might be as well in explanation of the title, to say that the random sketches contained in this volume, are but the *sawdust* and *shavings* accumulated during intervals of more laborious carpentry.

There! I wonder if that will save me? I'm really afraid not.

At all events I can at least be permitted to indulge a hope that the accompanying "Chips," may help to light a gloomy hour, and haply not decrease the brightness of a cheery one.

J. B.

CONTENTS.

PAGE

Some Passages in the Life of a Dog 9
The Opera of "La Fille du Regiment"—done into English. 80
Love and Loyalty—an Episode in English History . . 86
Pauline 103
O'Dearmid's Ride 115
The Coming of Kossuth 123
The Fairies' Warning 128
The Killing of the Shark 137
Every-Day Drama—The Pigeon and the Hawks . . . 143
Kit Cobb, the Cabman—A Story of London Life . . . 148
The Phantom Light—A Tale of Boston 167
Revolt of the Harem—Simplified 170
Fatality—A Condensed Novel 176
Dramas of the Day—Revenge; or, the Medium . . . 191
Ned Geraghty's Luck 200
The Eagle and her Talons—An Eastern Apologue . . 213
Peace and War 216
Summer Friends 217
Love's Mission 218
Evenings at Our Club 219
Romance and Reality 245
Jasper Leech—The Man who never had Enough . . . 264
Nightmares—I The Lamp Fiend 272
II. Political Ambition 279
III. Murder 288
The Bunsby Papers.—The Opinions and Observations of Jack Bunsby, Skipper, and of Ed'ard Cuttle, Mariner . . . 301

SOME PASSAGES

IN THE

LIFE OF A DOG.

CHAPTER I.

Being a strange, self-willed, and slightly egotistical old dog, I shall make no elaborate apology to the snarling puppies of the present time, for thus presenting the memorials of a long, quiet, and observant life, to the consideration of that insolent and overbearing portion of animal existence called man, singularly blind as it is to its own incongruities of nature, and stupidly vain of its very imperfections.

Were I here philosophically to consider the matter, with what ease could I demolish man's pretensions to assumed superiority. Surely it is not the accidental circumstance of a few mere superficial inches in his formation, that gives him the right to lordly domination; or many a long-eared donkey would be his superior. Can it be possible that he prides himself upon a poor shivering frame, shrinking from contact with all vicissitudes of weather, save when he dons our natural clothing for protection and ornament? No, his own conduct gives the lie to that; for it is not of his awkward and unsightly form that he is proud, but of the quality of the sheep's wool which envelops it. The result of a long experience in the man-world has convinced me, that it is to external embellishment they pay the greatest deference, and that in the great battle between broadcloth and brains, the former in almost every instance obtains the victory—a fact which I shall sufficiently prove as I "unfold my tale."

The human inconsistency most especially vaunts itself upon the possession of an exclusive faculty, which it calls "reason," and which I dogmatically assert is but an extension of that "instinct," which with us stops before it takes a selfish and deceitful character. And is it not better far, to be bounded by the limits of a heartless intelligence, than to rejoice in the dangerous possession of a greater range of thought, peopled as it is with spectres of perfidy, mistrust and dissimulation? Look at the dog species. Degraded though it is in creation's living chain by presumptuous mortality, when did a dog ever exercise the powers of his mind in secret machinations against his fellow? When did one of our tribe ever despise another for the roughness of his coat? When did a dog ever wag a hair ot his tail, without he felt a positive and real pleasure in the friendly demonstration? On the other hand, how often has man's much prized immortal essence—reason, been employed to the secret destruction of his very kinsman? Is not a tattered garment a bar to social recognition, in almost every circle? How many hands have been grasped with apparent cordiality, when the hearts to which they belonged throbbed with hatred?

In fact, truth and fidelity are the attributes of our instinct, while man's boasted reason is allied with lying and deception.

Why, therefore, should dogs, even if they were dissatisfied with their condition, which they are not, envy or even covet the possession of such a dangerous faculty—a faculty which must bring distrust and discomfort to its possessor; for he who occupies his thoughts in scheming against others, must dread the application of the same system against himself. Be satisfied and thankful, therefore, oh, ye most fortunate dogs, that ye were not born of that perfidious race. Heed not their self laudations, and foolish assumptions of superiority. Remember that we resemble the royal lion by nature, while they are only one step removed from the obscene and chattering monkey.

Suffice it to say, that *we* well know which is the inferior species of the two. But let us not, therefore, imitate them in their stupidity, and puff ourselves out with ridiculous vanity, for that which we had no act or part in, more than the disgusting worms, which in the end will fatten equally on both.

Selfishness is the immediate staple of an autobiography. Therefore I must be pardoned if I still make the personal pronoun predominant in my narrative. The early part of my existence was passed in the usual checkered routine of puppyhood, alternately petted or punished by the juvenile members of the family, my treatment on all occasions entirely depending upon the capricious and variable temper of those changeable humans. Nor indeed could I really tell which was the greatest torture to me—the absolute punishment for some pretended fault, some failure in my efforts to work my original nature into that of a monkey or a man, by attempting to assume their ridiculous attitude, or the uncomfortable caresses, the pulling and mauling I received during their more merciful moments.

How many a time have I been rudely swung up from my cozy basket, where, snugly snoozing on my mother's breast, with my nose buried in the flossy, silken fur, I was haply dreaming dog dreams, to be exhibited amongst a group of these young human savages. Then commenced the lugging and tugging and screaming, each striving to nurse (?) the darling pet, who repine and patient, although, of course, intensely provoked, submits to the excruciating torments of human kindness with the best possible grace, as he knows very well, first indications of annoyance will be the signal for an ill-tempered pet from some graceless pride of the family, whose ebullitions of temper are considered so amusing by his natural instructors and guardians, that the unworthy display is stimulated by encouragement until faults are smiled into vices.

Strange, indeed, was it to me, to behold the pertinacity with which even the elder, and one would suppose by consequence the wiser portions of my patron's family—strove to force upon my natural instincts, and intention, acting entirely at variance with the original dignity of doghood; hours upon hours have I sat painfully perched upon my hinder legs, with my back against a corner of the room, to my own innate disgust, but to the great gratification of my instructors whenever I made the most successful attempt to get away from my individual nature. At this late period of my existence, and inasmuch as the principal persons who flourished contemporaneously with me, are at rest, I have no hesitancy in saying that I would most assuredly have rebelled against the silly and hurtful indignity, but that I found this plan of education was general, and indeed, that if my master's own children were obliged to return to this course of training, this perpetual struggle to cast native impulse into the iron mould of expediency, within whose cranks and corners the original form is lost, so that I at last became resigned to my fate; shrewdly suspecting that my punishment was only second-hand, and that the difficulties the children encountered in being compelled into the prescribed world-standard, was only reduced one stage lower in the process of my own education.

In taking an occasional retrospective glance upon this comfortless period of my existence, it has often struck me with what a singular avidity the human beings by whom our species are surrounded, endeavored upon every occasion to imbue us with a species of their own ferocious inclinations—as a matter of illustration let me mention a single incident.

We had sojourneying with us a charming cat, who, with her highly amusing and frolicsome little family, formed the nucleus of a very sociable party. The kittens being exactly my own age, I naturally began to form an attachment for their society, evidently very much against the wishes of our mutual parents, who very seldom met in the course of our casual acquaintance without interchange of compliments in the shape of a growl on one side, and an emphatic "spat" on the other. Often have I puzzled my little cranium to discover the cause of this confirmed animosity, when one fine morning it was developed in a very summary manner.

Upon the occasion to which I allude, I, with my feline friends, were enjoying, to the topmost extremes of our animal spirits, a most exciting race after a vagrant spool of cotton, which we alternately pawed and watched amicably from each other, panting with the very joyousness of the excitement, when two of our young human torturers of the male species suddenly interrupted our harmless play. One of them seized me, and the other possessed himself of a nice innocent little kitten, and then commenced the most unworthy employment of striving to irritate us against each other, by poking our heads together, and various other aggravating proceedings, until at last the poor little thing, inadvertently, I thoroughly believe, scratched me slightly on the nose; this roused up my ill-temper, and I am ashamed to say, that instead of snapping at the vile hands which had placed us in antagonism, I forgot my doghood, so much as to enter into a fierce personal encounter with my little associate, the consequence of which, was a rough-and-tumble fight, fitted only for the arena of a bear-bait, or the Halls of Congress; and never shall I forget the demoniac delight with which the instigators of the outrage looked on and shouted, at this pretty fair example of what humanity calls "sport," both in youth and adolescence.

This first conflict disrupted the bonds of fellowship which had hitherto united our respective families; and from that time forward similar occurrences so subverted the original friendliness of our dispositions, that in a short time we scarcely ever crossed each other's path without getting up a squabble upon our own account, and needed no "pressure from without" to urge us into animosity.

I have observed in the course of my experience among the humans, that the egotistical authors of histories like mine, invariably enlighten the benighted world with interesting accounts of their juvenile existence, each foolishly supposing that his individual early life and adventures are of especial importance; forgetting, in the immensity of his self-esteem, that millions upon millions of his stupid species have passed precisely through the same routine. As well might an insignificant grain of sand upon the sea-shore exclaim, "how fortunate am I! how gifted with peculiar blessings! Behold how the ever-rolling tide bathes me at the appointed time with its refreshing coolness! See how the varying seasons dispense upon my head their respective delights! The spring breezes fan my cheek; the summer flowers fling their odors upon my atmosphere. The golden autumn clothes me with its softened radiance. The benignant winter covers me with its protecting snow." Poor, silly grains, both.

But, as I was about to observe, you see I am a rambling, discursive, independent kind of an animal, and must make up my sentences in my own dogged way, inasmuch as such personal commencements seem to be the expected form in such cases as my own; I, therefore, obey the conventional rule of usage, although in direct opposition to my real inclination.

My name is Carlo; it was also the name of my respected sire. Indeed, my lamented mother told me, that it was the privilege of our exalted breed,—capriciously called "King Charles," although I need not tell the intelligent reader, that our ancestry dates much further back—for the then head of the family to preserve the hereditary name. As I was the eldest hope, I was, therefore, as a matter of course, called Carlo; and consequently looked up to, and petted by the elegant society in which my youth was passed, as the possible living link which bound together the long and brilliant ancestral chain.

I have but an indistinct recollection of my father, for he unfortunately died while I was yet a puppy; but that remembrance suffices to call up before my mental gaze, a fine, portly dog, scrupulously sleek, silky, and of decidedly elegant manners. With respect to his moral character, I have in vain questioned my poor, dear mother, but she invariably evaded a direct reply. My impression is, however, that the human society into which the accident of circumstance had thrown him, by pernicious example, had the effect of undermining the native excellence of his principles.

As for my maternal parent, she was indeed most beautiful; filial affection would fain give a true description of her loveliness of form and truly exalted nature, each attesting the indisputable nobility of her birth; but no language can do the theme sufficient justice. She was exactly sixteen inches and a quarter long, her color was a brilliant black and tan, not a single white hair visible. Her magnificent orbs, astonishingly large and lustrous, now sparkled with an eagle's fire, now melted in softened tenderness, like the benignant glances of a cow. Her nose was valuably small, piquant, and *retroussé* almost to a fault; her redundant ears, in long, silky curls, swept down to the very carpet: while her brilliant tail, feathered like the chapeau of a General, was a very miracle of beauty.

Such is a most insufficient portraiture of my immediate maternal ancestor. I have had many brothers and sisters, but only two were suffered to live, of whom I may have occasion to speak hereafter. The inexorable dictum of the exclusive society of which we form a part, decrees destruction to the majority of our devoted species, in order to enhance the rare value of the residue; a circumstance strikingly illustrative of the short-sighted stupidity of the human kind in general, which estimates the value of a thing, not by its intrinsic worth, but by its scarceness; and greedily covets the possession of that which is absolutely useless, if it be only difficult to obtain.

It was on the very same day made ever celebrated in the annals of history, when the justly famous Dog of Montargis astonished the canine world by his heroic deeds in the Forest of Bondy, that I first saw the light—not that I mean to arrogate to myself any peculiar excellence from this simply fortuitous circumstance. It was only a curious coincidence, and therefore I mention it with, I trust, becoming modesty. By a remarkable ordering of consentaneous events, it so happened, also, that a favorite cat belonging to the family, blessed the world with a numerous and interesting progeny; and the chimney of a house on the opposite side of the street to that which we inhabited, caught fire, but was speedily extinguished.

Like Alexander the Great, therefore, my entrance into this changeful and uncertain existence was accompanied by portentous and extraordinary omens, indicating, I diffidently submit, a coming destiny rather more distinctive and important, than that of doghood generally.

CHAPTER II.

It has just struck me, that it is quite time to say something about the particular family by whom I was surrounded in my youth, and whose family, in a great degree, tended to the formation and development of my individual character.

The head of the house was a gentleman of the greatest possible respectability. The outer world, of which he was an acknowledged ornament, looked up to him with deference, and pointed to him as the very embodiment of propriety. Of course, he went regularly to church every Sunday; took an active part, as far as zeal and oratory went, in all charities, whose claims upon respectability were duly endorsed by his own clergyman; deprecated with upturned eye the increasing iniquity of the external world. So thoroughly was he grounded in essentials of religion, that he absolutely knew all the response by heart; and when the place of worship was enlightened by the presence of some high or fashionable church dignitary, audibly joined in the service, without once referring to his morocco-covered gilt-edged prayer book. The weekly locality of all this pious enthusiasm was a magnificently appointed pew, which, as its late occupant had failed in business, he was enabled to secure for a mere trifle, compared with the original outlay, so that he could indulge in the reflection that in the matter of religion itself, he had exercised those habits of business, which taught him to take a proper advantage of the inferior tact, prudence, or fortune of his fellow man.

The name of this exemplary character and correct business man was Glosely—Adonijah Glosely. His family consisted of his "lady," Mrs. Angelica Glosely—who must have a special paragraph devoted to her peculiar characteristics presently—two sons, and one daughter.

One of the sons, Hector Glosely, was eighteen years old, rejoicing in high collars, in the matter both of coat and shirt; the other, Rufus, was a boy of about eight; while the only daughter, Priscillina Augusta, was a blooming, thoughtless, naturally good-hearted school-girl of fourteen. Here was a stock in trade for domestic harmony and household comfort, if properly managed. How it was dissipated and destroyed, my narrative will show.

I promised Mrs. Angelica Glosely an especial paragraph, and I must now endeavor to depict her most contradictory and antagonistic traits. In appearance she was decidedly the reverse of prepossessing, but her lack of personal attractions was amply compensated for by an overweening vanity and supreme selfishness; her creed consisted in the perfect consciousness of her own great excellence, and the corresponding unworthiness of all the world beside. Every groan which she upheaved for the sinfulness of humanity, was a trumpet blast in proclamation of her impeccability. With a countenance expressive of the most intense humility, she admitted with the Rubric that mankind were all "miserable sinners;" but she by no means included herself in the category. With apparent sincerity she inveighed against worldly vanity, while she looked exultingly around the velveted worshippers to watch the effect caused by the display of her own magnificent attire.

In the meantime, her domestics at home were but scantily fed, the household requirements being reduced to the utmost limits, not from a praiseworthy regard for economy, but that the abstracted sums so clipped from the poor drudges' appetites might be expended upon indispensable finery. In fine, she was a pattern of fashionable wives and "professing" Christians. Her faith was self—her hope, the opinion of her modish friends—and her charity a newspaper paragraph.

The characters of the younger branches of the family must develop themselves.

It was near the close of a lovely afternoon, late in the fall, when the regal and benignant summer, like some potentate of old, arrayed in gorgeous robes, lies down to die in sovereign splendor, that my mother and I were reclining upon our especial cushion, at the feet of Mrs. Glosely. My mother was quietly slumbering, all unconscious of passing events, haply used to the many contradictions and perversities amongst the human society in which she had placidly passed her hitherto existence. She heeded them not; but me, only just admitted within its extraordinary circle—curiosity and wonder kept me a constant and unwearied listener.

"Angelica, my love!" said the correct husband to his irreproachable spouse—there was no one else present, "You will permit me to have the arrangement of all matters connected with the welfare of my sons myself." This simple observation, spoken in the mildest and most dulcet tone, certainly did not sound very alarming; but in spite of the soft smile, the heart was bubbling with indignation. Strange effect of education and association upon the human being, thought I; and as unnatural as though a ferocious watch-dog were to smile—for dogs do smile—and wag his tail, at a midnight burglar.

"Very well, sir! very well!" quietly responded the lady. "Have your own way; of course you will, in everything; it is proper you should, fit and proper, very proper." This was a great peculiarity of hers, I found, repeating any word or sentence, which she imagined possessed an atom of point, retaining in the meantime the same expression of face, until the one painted by the next thought, supplanted it.

"Madam," rejoined the gentleman, and with a still sweeter smile; for the angrier he was the more polite he became. And this little domestic jar had been going on for several minutes. "Madam, you will confer an extreme obligation upon me if you will relinquish the discussion."

"Why, sir, may I presume to inquire, if it will not be taking too great a liberty?" Ah! how ceremonious aggravation is.

"May *I* not be permitted to have some interest in the matter—some little interest—as their mother, only their mother to be sure, that's nothing with some people: nothing, positively a mere nothing."

Mr. Glosely had taken up a book, with the evident resolution to silently endure the assault of words; which action upon his part elicited nothing but an indignant "h'm, indeed!" from the lady, and a sulk of some moments, duration ensued: during which time, I shall take an opportunity of relating, as briefly as possible, the cause of the discussion.

You must know, then, that Mr. Hector Glosely, who had just been hastily ground through one of those intellectual mills, called Colleges, where he was mainly distinguished by his anti-scholastic predilections for a little game of brag, or a "quiet dash" at "the Tiger;" and it was shrewdly suspected that he knew a great deal more about the mysteries of the card table than the metaphysics of Aristotle—had of late been the occasion of some uneasiness to his respected parents—forgetting that no real care had ever been expended upon his mental culture, and, indeed, that the growth of nature had not only been neglected, but by the modern system of training so warped from its primal intent, that scarcely a trace of his original impulse was discernible.

He had arrived at the atrocity of a latch key, and occasionally exhibited great ignorance, or was guilty of much prevarication, with regard to the time of night he came home.

The father and mother, strict and irreproachable, have just had a conversation as to the means of counteracting the evil effects of such conduct, which has, from the complacent self-esteem of both, eventuated in a scene of polite, courteous, but implacable recrimination.

For the last five minutes he has had the book before him, but never saw a letter on the page; while she was keeping up a petulant and perpetual tattoo upon the carpet.

At length the natural spirit of wrath rebelled against the restraints of ceremony.

"Confound it, madam!" he roared, dashing the book upon the floor. My mother woke up with a sharp bark, which she continued for some time with a vague idea that some calamity had occurred. An authoritative ring, sharp and aristocratic, announced some distinguished visitors; but not a muscle moved in the imperturbable face of Mrs. Angelica.

In a few moments Patrick announced Mrs. Whipley Syllabub, and the Misses Whipley Syllabub.

If it were not that Glosely was so very correct a character, I could have solemnly declared I heard a remarkably profane expression; but his face resumed its accustomed smiling serenity as Mrs. W. S. and her two lovely daughters sailed majestically into the drawing-room.

"How do you do, my dear? I'm so delighted! This is kind of you, Angelica, my love. Yes dear. How charmingly our *dear* friends are looking." All was rapture, happiness, good nature, and cordiality. The clearest observer could not detect a ruffle upon the surface of Mr. and Mrs. Glosely's domestic current.

My mother, however, barked a low but significant bark, which I understood perfectly.

As my mother was a most intelligent animal, and never omitted an opportunity to inculcate within my opening mind lessons of correctness, she therefore seized upon the present opportunity to give me some wholesome advice and instruction.

"Observe, my son," said she in a whisper, "one of the most prevalent traits in the human character—Duplicity. Who amongst us could suppose that those people, to whom our master and mistress are now speaking in such honeyed accents, were the same of whom they spoke so disparagingly before they entered?"

"But, surely they are not all thus perfidious alike?" I asked my intelligent parent.

"Nearly all, my dear," she replied. "Indeed, the exceptions are simply those few individuals whose natural excellences are too strong to be influenced by the pernicious effect of example, or the injurious tendency of human education. But let us remain silent, and listen to their conversation."

It was just at this moment that Mr. Gloseley having casually looked at his watch, started up in great apparent agitation, exclaiming—

"Dear me, can it be possible? My dear Mrs. Whipley Syllabub, your most interesting conversation has positively so enchained my attention, that I had nearly forgotten a most particular engagement. You know, my love," turning to his wife, "that law business—Jones, you recollect?"

"Certainly, dear," replied Mrs. G., with the most angelic sweetness, "That cannot be neglected; and I'm sure our sweet friend will excuse your not remaining."

"Oh! don't mind me an instant; business, of course, must be attended to," remarked the fascinating visitor; and so Mr.

G., having politely saluted the party, and affectionately kissed the placid and passive cheek of his wife, bowed himself out of the room.

Now I happened, at the same time, to stray into the passage, where I overheard him say quietly to Patrick, "Pat, send a bottle of claret into my own room, and tell me when these interminable bores are gone!"

My mother is quite right, thought I, as I returned and nestled by her side; most grateful to nature that I had the good fortune to belong to a single-minded, true, and faithful species.

Master Hector and Miss Augusta now came in, and the young ladies, after a most profuse and affectionate interchange of civilities, formed themselves into an animated coterie of their own; and were soon buried in the profound mysteries of bonnets, mantillas, &c., every atom of each individual dress being admired and commented upon. The young gentleman alone, whom the faintest possible indication of a moustache rendered quite offish and reserved, looked with philosophic contempt upon the frivolous group.

The old—I really beg their pardon—I mean the mammas, were talking scandal in an undertone; and the daughters talking fashions in a loud key—practising, I presume, for the Opera—for I'm told that the perfection of aristocratic demeanor at all places of public entertainment, is to try and disconcert the artist, by such exhibition of nonchalant indifference.

The confusion of tongues, consequent upon this division of the discourse, rendered the conversation more curious than instructive or entertaining to us. We, however, managed to catch glimpses of meaning through the beclouded mass somewhat as follows;

"Have you heard of Mrs. T.'s affair, my dear?"

"Oh, yes! singular, wasn't it?"

"Where did you say you bought it, love? At Beck's?"

"No, indeed! at Stewart's, of course; and it cost nearly a hundred dollars."

"In my opinion, she was very much to blame."

"But, my love, you know *he* was never at home."

"Dear papa made me a present of it."

"Is it true, my love, that he gambles?"

"Certainly, dear; and I have heard from good authority that she—drinks."

"What a lovely pattern! Won't you give it to me? Do, there's a dear."

"With pleasure, love. Let me look at these diamonds? How magnificent."

"Yes, they are said to be expensive. Pa gave them to me on my birth-day."

"Is it a fact that he has suspended business?"

"Oh, yes, and can't pay ten cents in the dollar."

"Do, Gus, see what a beautiful chatelaine! Isn't it sweet?"

"Yaas."

After about an hour, as I considered, rather unprofitably spent, but which the parties interested appeared to enjoy amazingly, Mrs. Whipley Syllabub gathered her splendid crape shawl around her imposing shoulders; and with the conventional "dears," "loves," and "sweets," and an impressive "won't you call again very soon?" from Mrs. G., the bell was rung, and the highly complimentary and apparently affectionate visitors swept ceremoniously from the drawing-room.

There was a short pause; not a word was spoken until the carriages rolled away from the front door, when Mrs. Gloseley exclaimed, dashing aside the beautiful bouquet which was just presented to her, "What! in the name of wonders, does your father mean, by permitting these parvenues to visit our house?"

"Nay, mamma," interposed the amiable daughter. "I'm sure they are really very nice people." I loved her for the kind-hearted observation.

"Nice? nonsense, my child; they have no position. I do believe our's is the only place in society they ever approach."

"Oi only wondah at the audacity of the people," drawled Hec, twirling the place where the long coveted moustache ought to be, but was not. "They are insufferably vulgah creatures; and if the governah insists upon receiving them heah, I shall have to move."

"Why, brother, how you talk," said my pet. For although a mere puppy, I began to feel a dog's attachment for that girl. 'Tis such as she who almost redeem the native wickedness of the human race. "I'm sure," she continued, "they are infinitely more respectable acquaintances than the ill-bred, noisy, and characterless individuals who turn your house into a sort of lunatic asylum, occasionally."

"You, just shut up," rejoined the elegant hope of the family. "It's absolutely essential for a fellow who wants to know anything of life to submit to miscellaneous companionship; and, once for all, if I am to be restricted in my choice of acquaintances, I shall most assuredly institute an exclusive establishment."

"Don't be angry with me, brother," she hastened to observe. "You know I love you too much to find any fault; I only thought you reflected a little too harshly upon papa's friends. There, let us make it up;" and the affectionate girl threw her arms around the unworthy young reprobate's neck, and gave him such a kiss as angels bestow on sleeping children.

It was received as ungraciously as though it were a most intolerable annoyance. Rudely disengaging her clinging arms, he exclaimed petulantly:—

"Don't be a fool, sis; if you knew what a time it took me to fix this neck-tie, you wouldn't be so inconveniently enthusiastic."

CHAPTER III.

Horace has gone to exhibit his elaborate neck tie and thin legs on Broadway. Mrs. Glosely is examining the "*Courrier des Dames*," and the girls are busy at something they facetiously call "work;" that is to say, fashioning impracticable birds out of various colored worsteds.

Mr. Glosely, enveloped in his comfortable dressing-gown, has re-entered the drawing-room, having been duly acquainted with the departure of the Whipley Syllabubs; when clatter, clatter, dash another aristocratic load up the door, for by this time it was high 'Change amongst fashionable visitors, that is, the very heart of the day.

"Out! out!" cried Glosely to the "obsequious lacky," as distinguished novelists of the "patchouli" school usually designate the humble fellow mortal, whom fortune chooses to fulfill the character of domestic.

"A moment, dear!" interposed Mrs. G. "Had we not better ascertain who it is?"

"Very good, my love," replied the amiable spouse. The servant was still there.

"Bring up the cards, Pat." However, my friend Pat was scarcely removed from the vicinity, when, with a *tête-à-tête* frown, he continued:—

"Mrs. Glosely, how often have I to point out to you the great annoyance it is to countermand any order of mine to the servants?"

"Nevertheless, Mr. Glosely," she replied, with no less dignity, "I shall continue to do so when you speak foolishly."

"Madame, you forget yourself," he rejoined, slightly elevating his, as yet, placid voice.

"Sir, are you aware that your children are in the room," she answered with an educated sneer. "Don't let my individual wretchedness extend to my family."

By the by, I never could make out what made Mrs. Glosely so wretched. She had everything that she could desire; no one dared to contradict her, and her life appeared to be one constant round of amusement. Through the week at Opera, Theatres, Balls; and on Sunday at the most *recherché* church. Yet she never seemed to be satisfied, always seeking after something, only to be wretched again immediately after its attainment. As for Mr. Glosely, I don't know how his life was passed away from his domestic hearth; but if the real unhappiness of that small portion of his existence were any indication, he must have been the most ill-fated of mortals. I scarcely ever saw him smile, except amongst his visitors; and as to his married life, such was the idea I had formed of its dreadful misery, that when I first began to have a dawning of sense, sufficient to see my way slightly into causes and effects, I inquired of my mother what awful crime had these two people committed in society, that it should force them to endure such a hateful, mind-irritating, companionship? Well I remember how my mother laughed at my ignorance and simplicity, when she informed me that mankind had invented this torture for the double purpose of reducing the natural affections down to its own prudential level, and also that there should be some distinction between the "Smiths," "Browns," and "Joneses," which otherwise would be so mixed up together, that there would be no disentangling them.

The foregoing is simply the result of a momentary reflection, and therefore must not be supposed to have occupied any "valuable time," as mortals insist upon calling those passing hours of existence, which are wasted with as little thought as though Death and Eternity were travelling onward with them.

But here comes Pat with the cards. Whom do they announce?

Mr. Glosely takes them from the silver salver, and reads with unmitigated abhorrence—

"Mrs. Charity Skindeep."

"Oh Lord!" exclaimed Glosely. "Pat, another bottle of claret in my room!"

"You know I must receive this horrid woman," whispered Mrs. Glosely. "I think the least you could do would be to share the annoyance."

"Excuse me, my love. What! to listen to a long rigmarole about Patagonian Missions, and Sunday Schools for Omnibus Drivers. Out, Pat, most emphatically." And so he rushed up the back stairs, where I would have given my breakfast to have followed, and seen how he employed himself; but my mother told me that she had frequently done so, and always found that he occupied the time reading very small notes, smoking cigars, and occasionally kissing a strange daguerreotype, which was so small that he carried it in a locket, fastened to his watch chain. I found out all about those notes and that locket some time afterwards.

"Girls," said Mrs. Glosely, "hand me a prayer-book, and for gracious sake don't let this mischief-making woman see you smile!"

Smoothing her features into a rigid, stony quiescence, with her prayer-book, beautifully bound, and redolent of "Jockey Club," not open—that would have been too evident a tableau—but closed by her side, as though she had been just seeking blessed consolation from its scented pages, she collected herself for the threatened assault.

A moment after, Mrs. Charity Skindeep stalked into the room, creating a cold atmosphere in the wake of her rustling heavy silk dress, that made my mother and me shiver as she swept by us.

There was a frigid interchange of conventionalities, which, being duly performed, the new visitor enthroned herself in the most advantageous easy-chair; for your pious people, I have always observed, take the pleasantest places by a sort of prescriptive right.

"I am glad you have called, my dear Mrs. Skindeep," placidly murmured Mrs. Glosely, "I am just in the frame of mind to enjoy the calm delight of a hopeful conversation; 'tis not an instant since I occupied a few transitory moments, I trust, with profit to myself, and to those dear children, by reading in this comforting volume."

So saying she carelessly turned over the gold edged leaves of the book, and cast a benignant glance towards the ornament in the centre of the ceiling.

So absorbed was she, probably in contemplating the readiness of the falsehood, she was not aware that the action of opening the book dislodged from thence a slip of thin paper, doubled up, which, unfolding itself in its downward progress, exhibited on the carpet the plain and unmistakable enormity of—

A Play Bill!

"What is this?" screamed Mrs. Charity Skindeep. She knew very well what it was; but it was an opportunity, and those individuals never miss one.

Mrs. Gloseley, suddenly called from the investigation of the chandelier, glanced downwards; and there she saw the passport to perdition.

Fear seized upon her; fear, not for the imagined sinfulness, but for her position as a committee woman of the Society for the Instruction of the Poor; when a ray of joy suddenly flashed upon her darkened hopes:

It was for the Museum!

Taking it up quietly in her hand, Mrs. Skindeep, shrinking therefrom as though it were gifted with dangerous vitality, and every letter could bite, she pointed out the privileged locality from whence it was issued.

Looking at the terrible paper through her glasses, but not as yet condescending to touch it, Mrs. Skindeep suffered her indignant frown to subside into a sort of endurable expression, as she said, only a trifle less sharply—

"Ah! I see; it's only a Museum. I must entreat your pardon, dear Mrs. Glosely; but for an instant I was under the apprehension that it was actually a *play bill.*"

"What an overwhelming difference there must be between these two places," said I to my mother, as I witnessed the emphasis of abhorrence with which our visitor uttered these two words.

My mother, poor dear soul, only winked her eye; she was evidently sleepy. Be it as it may, the discovery had the effect of bringing the conversation into a calm channel once more; and before many minutes had elapsed, Mrs. Charity Skindeep was eloquently describing the effect of missionary labors upon the inhabitants of Nova Zembla, and dilating upon the very encouraging results which had followed the dissemination of Doctrinal Theology amongst the benighted omnibus drivers.

After a pleasant, and somewhat piquant, conversation, in which every individual of their acquaintance, together with many to whom they were personally unknown, were morally dissected, analyzed, and anatomized, with the delicate dexterity of pseudo pietists, Mrs. Charity Skindeep at length touched upon the immediate cause of her present visit.

Now the multifarious nature of this benevolent lady's businesss transactions were so well known, being Honorary Secretary, Committee Woman, and Contribution Seeker for nearly every description of eleemosynary Society in the country; besides corresponding with nearly all the parent, branch, and foreign offshoots of beneficence in the habitable globe, Mrs. Glosely, it was evident, was only puzzled upon which particular good work her visitor was now intent; it was, therefore, with a feeling somewhat akin to satisfaction, that she beheld the inevitable note-book produced, and, with due solemnity, Mrs. Skindeep opened her case.

"You know, my love," she commenced, in her blandest manner, "what universal and untiring interest our Association takes in obtaining funds for the amelioration of the condition of the poor sempstresses?"

"A most praiseworthy design, my dear Mrs. Skindeep," replied Mrs. Glosely, "and one in which I myself have taken a very active part; although, of course, from the insignificance of my position, necessarily a very humble one."

That was a very dextrous parry, thought I; how will the other get over it?

With the graces of a practised fencer, the skillful assailant smiled benignantly at the slightest rebuff, and then returned to the assault instanter.

"I knew it! darling; I knew it! Indeed, where is the scheme of benevolence which does not enjoy your active co-operation," she placidly rejoined; "but as yet, my dear friend, you must be aware that no positive good has been done. The Joint Stock Ladies' Gratuitous Work Society, although the poor creatures we employ have scarcely a moment to themselves, has not yet yielded any absolute profit.

To be sure, the Lady Manageresses get their household work done up for nothing; but the profit which was expected to accrue from the public, and which was to have been expended in a service of plate for the Reverend Josiah Doolittle, has, by some means or another, disappeared. I myself, as one of the Auditors, went over the accounts most rigidly, and must say that I saw no money wasted, except a small doctor's bill for one of the sewing girls, who happened to be consumptive, but who fortunately died before she became an expense to the Society."

"It was very remiss of the overseers to admit so sickly a person amongst the workpeople," said Mrs. Glosely, with very business-like indignation.

"I told them so, my dear," replied the Lady Manageress and charity monger, "and moreover, gave them distinctly to understand, that they should be answerable for the health of the people employed; our funds are too small, and for too sacred a purpose, to be trifled with. I am gratified in being able to state that I find the system works well, a deduction being made in the small, very small pittance given, for every absence no matter how occasioned. We have, consequently, no more sickness—that is to say, no more complaints, which you know is the same thing. When any of them happen to be taken seriously ill, they stay at home; then their places are supplied and, as a matter of course, we hear no more about them. It is thus that our sphere of usefulness extends itself, and, with our limited means, we are enabled to do so much good."

Happening to take a look towards Priscilla, I saw the sweet little dear's eyes fully laden with tears, which she suffered to run down upon her beautiful worsted birds and flowers without restraint. With a deep sigh of pure Christian sympathy and affection, she raised her long dewy lashes, and half concealing her lovely face with the flood of beautiful hair which fell upon each shoulder, she ventured at length to remark—

"How many poor girls are there employed in that Society, Mrs. Skindeep?"

"Some seven and twenty," slowly syllabled the subtle visitor, with a keen anticipation of juvenile pocket money.

"How long do they work?"

"In summer, my dear, from six o'clock in the morning until six o'clock in the evening, with an interval of half an hour for breakfast, and a whole hour for dinner," replied the matter of fact and unimpressible contribution seeker.

"And are they sewing all the time?" inquired Priscilla.

"Certainly, dear; and I do assure you they are very conscientious and industrious. Indeed, it is impossible for them to be otherwise, for there are vigilant eyes always on them."

"Do they live long?"

"Why, to be sure they do, love," replied the benevolent machine, with something which looked like astonishment, but which was really contempt for so silly a question. "I have known some of the healthier ones live for three or four years."

"Poor creatures!" cried Priscilla: the tears were there again, making her human eyes angelic. "How glad they must be to die?"

For my part, although I grieved to see my darling pet made unhappy even for an instant, yet I felt certain they were indulging in romance. It never entered into my imagination, then, that human beings could indulge in so abominable a traffic, as to speculate thus with the lives of their "dear sisters;" and, worse than all, to gloze over the murderous concern with the miserable pretence of philanthropy. However, I grew wiser in time.

Meantime, Mrs. Charity Skindeep, to whom Priscilla's last

observation was altogether incomprehensible, concentrated to the business point. Poising listlessly her gold pencil case, and displaying within her splendid ivory-covered tablets a long array of recognizable names, each with a respectable sum appended thereto, the same being a perceptible and most impudent decoy, she fixed her dull snaky eyes upon Mrs. Glosely, and murmured, with a curious admixture of sanctity and blarney—

"Our Society truly languishes for support. A few hundred dollars, judiciously applied, and our most desirable end may be attained. Our kind and considerate friends in your immediate neighborhood have given freely, amply, of their respective means; the merest trifle will be acceptable. Pray don't let any false delicacy prevent you from giving what you feel you can afford. Heaven forbid that I should venture to solicit aid, where it would in the remotest degree embarrass the donor!"

An excellent diplomatist was Mrs. Charity Skindeep; that last insinuation brought out Mrs. Glosely's plethoric purse upon the instant.

The triumphant glance of the Corresponding Secretary contradicted the humility that still dwelt upon her well-trained lips; observing yet, a slight hesitation in her victim's manner, and rightly divining the cause, she whispered confidentially, "I shall put down a nominal sum on the list; your actual contribution need not transpire."

"Don't let it be less than any of the other contributors, in the Newspapers, dear Mrs. Skindeep," said Mrs. Glosely, handing over a small amount.

So Mrs. Skindeep received five dollars for the Ladies' Gratuitous Sewing Society; but, by some mistake, the papers of the next day made it fifty.

With the blandest of smiles, the Secretary deposited the

crisp five dollar bill within the folds of her "portemonnaie," and turning to Priscilla, she observed—

"My dear young friend, whose commendable sympathies are thoughtfully excited for these poor creatures, in whose cause I am an unworthy, though zealous, laborer, will, I have no doubt, assist us with a trifle."

"No, madam!" replied the meek child; "I should feel that I was doing very wrong to help on a system, which, as far as I can judge, tends more to the benefit of the lady speculators, than to the amelioration of the unfortunate work people. I am young and inexperienced, and may be wrong; but I don't like the idea of making a business traffic, a kind of day-book and ledger concern, of the most sacred and impulsive of the Christian virtues."

"But, my dear, have you not the excellent example of your worthy parent before you, who has but this instant registered her approval of the special mission in which I am thus interested."

"Dear mamma, I know, will forgive me," exclaimed my darling, kissing her mother fervently. "Her indiscriminate benevolence of heart (the poor child could see nothing wrong in either of her parents, or rather the intensity of her filial affections haloed their very faults) renders her only too ready, at all times and for all purposes, to contribute to the extent of her ability."

"Let me entreat you but to think of the deplorable condition these poor people would be in, did we not offer them so desirable an asylum," replied the wily Skindeep.

"Ah! their condition must be wretched, indeed, to be obliged to adopt the terrible alternative," said Priscilla; "and that is one of the principal faults in the modern modish systems of improvement. Modern philanthropy thinks its duty is sufficiently done, if the object of its interest be removed one step higher in the scale of human comfort, or rather I should say, if it were rendered a thought less miserable. I have my own notions upon this subject; but a want of confidence in myself, and proper deference to those who are more experienced, keeps me silent."

"My dear friend," exclaimed Mrs. Charity Skindeep, turning to Mrs. Glosely, with a self-satisfied shrug of her already high shoulders, "your sweet daughter is quite a Red Republican in her notions. I wouldn't be surprised now to hear her advocate the ultra agrarian principles of some of our most furious Fourierites, and advise our associating with all manner of low creatures."

"Priscilla is very young, my love!" responded Mrs. Glosely, in a deprecatory tone, "and, moreover, the child has peculiar notions. We allow her to indulge in them, for they can do no harm."

Now, puppy though I was, yet I had sufficient perception to see that Mrs. Glosely was blessed with the companionship of an angel, and didn't know it. A diamond of priceless value enriched her life's cabinet, and she looked upon it as though it were valueless paste, like herself. Alas! for the blindness of humanity.

Dear Priscilla made no answer to the sarcasm of the Charity-Monger, or to the foolish observations of her mother, but silently proceeded with her crotchet-work. Quietly I stole over, and very impudently peered into her face; to say the truth, I feared that she was weeping again, but upon looking at her eye, I saw a proud consciousness of superiority there, but so tempered with Heaven's gentleness and the simplicity of guileless innocence, she looked like a sainted Queen.

Meantime, the two types of earthly vanity and affectation held a short whispered conversation.

"Certainly, my dear love!" said Mrs. Skindeep, to some

desire of the other, "with the most unfeigned pleasure; it may disabuse the dear young lady's mind of some false impressions that the worldly-wise may have implanted there."

I began already to observe—and, by-the-by I may as well now inform my reader, if any one has taken the trouble to care what may fall from the pen of a puppy—that in the course of my narrative, I shall have occasion, now and again, to push aside from the regular current, wherever a discursive creek presents a chance for a mind wandering, or perhaps jump bodily ashore, right bang away from the absolute stream of my story, and take an independent ramble through the open country; pledging myself, however, to get back again to my starting point with as much celerity as my individual powers of locomotion can command.

I am about to make one of those diverging excursions now.

I began, as I said before, to observe that amongst the crowds of visitors that I have seen at our house, there seems to be, whether from the imperative results of association, or from preconcerted arrangement, or from the proneness to imitation which mankind possesses, in common with his younger brother, the monkey—a distinctive characteristic, plainly indicating the position, profession, and especially religious—or pretended religious—for by externals it is difficult to distinguish between the two; indeed, like a well-executed counterfeit, the imitation sometimes passes current before the real gold. What let me into this small path of observation was, noticing the choice of words, as well as the sing-song slightly nasal modulation, *assumed*—it isn't natural, or everybody would speak through the nose; therefore, I say assumed—by Mrs. Charity Skindeep; and inasmuch as all the regular and irregular "Professors," the representatives of the thousand and one especial lights, self-appointed, to show benighted humanity the only road to blissful immortality, affect the same style of intonation, I naturally concluded that the peculiarity is a certain type of one extensive class. As I grew older, and acquired more experience, I found the same evidence of a distinctive individuality pervade every associated class in the entire community. Military men are unmistakable; all professions, and even some trades, are distinguishable by the same means. Lawyers, perhaps, are the most perplexing; artists you can tell at a glance; politicians are equally characteristic; and could anybody ever mistake the decided "sporting gentleman," or the conductor of a railroad? It is no part of my design to endeavor to account for these gregarious resemblances, being merely an observing, and not a philosophical puppy; nor do I pretend to say that such matters are apparent to the mass of human beings, which is composed of those several distinct bodies, and which is not proverbial for remarkable self-knowledge. I only jot down the remarks which would strike a dog of ordinary capacity, and average amount of instinct.

To return to Mrs. Skindeep. "Certainly, my love! with great pleasure," she repeated. "If the young lady will condescend to accompany me, my carriage is at her service; and I shall endeavor to point out to her the means, under Providence, that we have at our disposal, to subserve the great causes of benevolence and philanthropy."

"I shall accompany you with great readiness and delight, Mrs. Skindeep," remarked Priscilla.

An irresistible desire seized me to be a party to the forthcoming investigation, and I immediately made known my wish to my darling; but inasmuch as my natural language was unknown to her, I was obliged to demonstrate as well as I could, by other means, my inclination.

She, dear soul, by some intuition evidently saw my intent,

and taking me in her lap, said, "I think that I shall take Carlo with me, mamma!"

So, supremely happy in being permitted to accompany her, I testified my gratification as only dogs can, while preparations were being made to set out upon the proposed ride.

CHAPTER IV.

Leaping gaily up the carriage steps, I followed my dear young mistress, testifying the deep sense I entertained of the gratification it afforded me to accompany her by the only means in my power, that is to say, by executing a number of extraordinary jumps and gambols, which I meant should convey to both the ladies the expression of my gratitude and joy. I found, however, that my language was, as usual, unintelligible; for no sooner had the carriage started, than Mrs. Charity Skindeep fired a volley of small interesting screams, which increased to a positive yell, as in one of my ebullitions of happiness I happened to jump against her immaculate skirts.

"Stop, John! coachman, ah!" she shrieked; "the animal is mad, he must be put out; I won't go one step further, ah!" and again she waked the echoes of the immediate neighborhood.

The carriage was stopped accordingly, and a long discussion took place, as to what was to be done with the dreadful dog. Bless their innocent souls, I wouldn't have hurt a mouse at the time; but what with Mrs. Skindeep poking at me with her sharp pointed parasol, and some young asses of the human species who yelled around the vehicle—"A mad dog, hi, hi! pitch him out; we'll finish him,"—I do verily believe that if that dreadful woman had had her own way, I should have gone mad to a dead certainty. At all events, it would have been all the same, for, as is the invariable custom of mankind, the investigation as to my sanity would have taken place, if at all, after I had been knocked on the head.

However, thanks to my dear guardian angel, who firmly insisted that I should remain where I was, I escaped the imminent danger that threatened me.

"Give yourselves no trouble, good friends," said she; "I'll take him on my lap. Here, Carlo!"

With a bound, I reached the sanctuary for persecuted puppyhood, and gratefully muzzling my nose within her dear hand, rolled myself up into as small a compass as I could, and kept remarkably quiet for the rest of the drive.

Meantime, Mrs. Skindeep condescended to allow her fear, or affectation, to subside, and ultimately offered a kind of lisping apology.

"My dear girl," she whimpered, "you don't know what Æolian nerves I have the misfortune to possess; the faintest breath of circumstance makes them vibrate painfully. I am absolutely so full of sensibility, the slightest shock thrills through my delicate system; and it is truly astonishing how patient I am, considering how much I have to endure."

A little more than the usual obstruction on the principal thoroughfare, just at this juncture, had the effect of trying her patience very considerably. With an exclamation of annoyance she pulled the check, to inquire the reason of the delay.

"An accident, madam," said the coachman.

"Good Heaven, what?" cried Priscilla.

"Dear, dear! how very provoking just at this moment," cried Mrs. Skindeep.

"What is it?" inquired Priscilla. "Is there anybody hurt?"

"Oh! it's only a laborer that they are carrying on a sort of litter, my dear," said Mrs. Charity Skindeep, looking out of the carriage window.

"How very shocking!" replied my darling, who evidently sympathized with the poor sufferer.

"Pshaw! there are plenty more of them, love; he was drunk, I suppose."

"Ah, no!" replied Priscilla; "see, the poor creature has his working clothes on. Look how tenderly his comrades handle him, and whisper to him; and see the look of courageous endurance that's in the sufferer's wan countenance. Ah! Mrs. Skindeep, it is not always at the cannon's mouth that heroes are to be found."

"I don't understand you," cried Mrs. Skindeep pettishly; and she didn't, but I did. "I only wish they had the dirty looking creature out of the way, before my carriage was blocked up in the plebeian crowd."

At last the mass gave way. The carriage drove on, nearly running over one or two of the assistants, and I was beginning to wonder what had become of Mrs. Skindeep's sympathetic nerves, when it suddenly re-appeared. Heaving two or three very voluminous sighs, she faintly whispered to Priscilla.

"Have you a flacon, dear! or perfume of any kind? Caroline, Residue, or even Patchouli? I know I am going to faint. Dear! dear! these terrible nerves of mine—the least excitement is sure to overcome me; and, my love, that dreadful adventure just now. If it had frightened the horses, what would have become of me?"

I then thought my mistress and myself might have shared her consideration.

We now entered one of the narrow, confined, and prison-like streets, in the poorest quarter of the city; and suddenly stopped with that short, sharp plunge of the horses, which is so indicative of an aristocratic *ménage*, at a high, stern-looking brick house, the windows of which—although God knows they did not open upon a desirable prospect, the opposite side of the street being occupied by a hack stable, with a small forge on one side, and a very miserable kind of a groggery on the other—were sedulously blinded half way up by parallel slats, so that the inmates had no choice but to follow implicitly the instructions perpetually spoken, and printed before them, to turn their eyes from things terrestrial.

"You are not going to take that dreadful animal with you, Miss Glosely?" ejaculated Mrs. Skindeep, in school manner solemnity of intonation.

One appealing look from me, and she replied, "Certainly, Madam; if you have no objection, I always take Carlo wherever I *go*."

"But, my love!" rejoined the other with renewed asperity, "it is not allowed; our regulations are very rigid, and according to the rules"——

"Very well, my dear Madam," said Priscilla, mildly, "I'll leave him in the carriage. To be sure, he has a naughty trick of tearing cushions, and"——

"For your sake then, my love," interrupted Mrs. Skindeep, with sudden blandness, "we'll look over the regulations this time."

My lovely Priscilla gave my ears a gentle pull. I know what she meant; she spoke truly also. Indeed, she always did, the angel: for if I had been left in that carriage, I wouldn't have left a morsel of lace upon the trimmings, even at the risk of an additional poke from Mrs. Skindeep's parasol.

CHAPTER V.

If the exterior of the "Ladies' Provident Sewing Society" looked unpromising, the first glance at its internal organization confirmed the disagreeable impression. The portion of the building occupied by this sagacious and benevolent institution was a large, bleak, and dreary-looking room in the rear of the main edifice, for in the due exercise of profitable philanthropy, the best part of the establishment was rented out to carnal, but remunerative tenants, so that the sounds of the billiard table and of the tenpin alley, blent with the boisterous shouts of drunken revelry, frequently obtruded themselves upon the silent sisterhood, slowly offering up their lives a sacrifice to the smiling demon of hypocrisy.

The above-mentioned room I had sufficient time to examine, for I remained at the door, fearing to venture amongst those bowed heads and rapidly moving fingers. No sound, save the breathing of victims, with ever and anon a hastily swallowed sob of agony, sent up from the heart to seek the ear of sympathy, but as quickly hurried back at the dread certainty that there are none to hear.

From my station at the entrance, I looked round upon the scene. On the starved-looking pillars—on the naked walls—everywhere the eye could reach—were stuck prudent maxims of the "Poor Richard" stamp, such as "A penny saved is a penny gained;" "An ounce of experience is worth a pound of advice;" "Waste not, want not;" "Sweet is the bread of industry;" "Idleness is the parent of vice;" together with some dozen or two of similar import; while the business-like character of those stimulants to perpetual labor was slightly modified by a judicious admixture of the most dolefully pious phrases. "The wages of sin is death;" "The sinner must dwell in burning Hell;" &c., &c.

Not a glimpse of the hope which attends upon the true heart, not the faintest gleam even of that soul-sustaining happiness to come, which haloes the martyrdom to duty. To be truly religious would but induce reflection, and meditation is akin to laziness; therefore, as the policy of the Institution was to make money, and not happiness, its motto was, "work," or be damned.

By this time Priscilla and Mrs. Skindeep had completed the circuit of the room, and I could see by the dewy lashes that veiled the sorrowing eyes of my darling, that she estimated at its proper worth the philanthropy of the concern.

Not so Mrs. Skindeep. With a self-satisfied sweep of her rich, though sober colored, silk dress, and a hard, sharp, fiery glance around, she said, "I believe, my dear young subscribing visitor—I presume to hope I may now call you so—that the advantages and great benefits derivable from this associated enterprise, is made sufficiently evident by its practical working. You perceive, my kind young friend," and she cleared her throat, and elevated her voice, to its most impressive height, "There are numbers of young persons"—I have remarked that your model "Lady Bountifuls" always call poor people *persons*—"here industriously employed, who would otherwise be most probably treading the downward path that leads to perdition; for here the vanities, mockeries, and sinful desires of the world are destroyed by the absorbing influence of continuous industry. Ah! it is indeed a blessed and consoling reflection, that through our unworthy, but zealous means, so many brands have been saved from the burning."

I here observed several of the younger girls, whose poor prisoned hearts must have fluttered wistfully during the intervals of sunshine that struggled into the room, like caged birds, bend down their heads still lower, methought in shame, for their own miserable natures. Two of them were whispering together, unobserved of course, by Mrs. Skindeep, or the half revivified mummy of a superintendent, when I crept close and listened; but it was not shame for their original iniquity, or gratitude for their redemption therefrom, through the instrumentality of the "Institution." One simply murmured to the other—

"I wonder she don't try and get off a new speech."

The matter of course, predetermined, parrotty nature of the whole arrangement, was admirably illustrated by that poor child's simple sentence.

By-the-by, this latter episode took place during one of Mrs. Skindeep's pauses; for the speech itself, delivered with oratorical display, occupied some half an hour altogether: but inasmuch as it contained no essential element of Faith, Hope, or Charity, and furthermore, as I paid not the slightest attention to the string of stale common-places of which it was composed, I have neither the inclination nor the ability to give it to the world. It concluded, however, with a strictly conventional "form" of prayer, the whole assembly putting itself into a kneeling posture, with a consentaneous action, which showed that each individual knew the exact moment to be devotional—in attitude.

For my part, as the miserable scrubby mat at the door was damp and uncomfortable, I unceremoniously took possession of Mrs. Skindeep's unoccupied skirt, most sincerely wishing that if ever the theory of Metempsychosis should be exemplified in reality, fate would not degrade me into the genus homo.

Prayer ended, work was instantly resumed. Busy fingers again plied countless needles, and I could not but observe that there was a something approaching to the ghost of cheerfulness in the resumption. Even that short interval, for Mrs. Skindeep never wasted the "Institution's" time, was a relaxation; or was it, that although breathed by selfish lips, and coming from no deeper inspiration, the thoughts of many there, if not all, for a few brief moments sent Heavenward—brought back with them those blessed Angels of Content and Hope, whose mission it is to lift the humble heart above the world and all its miseries.

With a cold salutation to the mummified overlooker, who returned the courtesy by a nervous jerk, meant to imply the deepest humility, Mrs. Charity Skindeep folded her benignant arms, and marched out of the dreary place, followed in Priscilla, whose progress I considerably impeded in my anxiety that we both should escape together, for a vague suspicion seemed to have fastened itself upon my mind, that either she or I were destined never to get out into the cheerful air of Heaven again.

However, when I discovered that we really were at liberty, there were no bounds to my delight. Once in the street, I ran several mile heats round an imaginary race course; barked viciously at Mrs. Skindeep, and seriously damaged the ivory top of her parasol; hunted my tail vigorously for many minutes, resting now and then to inquire of myself how it was that my head could not by any means overtake it; coming to no satisfactory conclusion, then fruitlessly running after it again. Bless me, how many sane human beings have I seen do the same thing, metaphorically, in the great woild since that time!

I now approach the first unpleasant adventure in my most variable life, which, like the earliest unpleasant occurrence in the existence of all creatures, leaves the most indelible impression upon the memory.

Most probable some of my bipedal contemporaries would make the matter a peg upon which to hang subtle philosophic theories, or profound physiologic deduction; but being a matter of fact Dog, I shall simply content myself with the relation.

Upon our return from visiting the philosophic sewing concern, Mrs. Charity Skindeep relapsed into dignified sulkiness, induced by her failure to obtain the smallest contribution from Priscilla. Argument and artifice were wasted. "No," replied the young lady, "no!" Not to perpetuate such an unnatural imprisonment, the reflections of those incarcerated for crimes against society, must be sufficiently cheerless; but what are they in amount of mental agony compared with the thoughts of those who, in their youth and innocency, are thus debarred from the universal privileges of breathing the free air of Heaven?

Mrs. Skindeep, muttering something about "stiff necks," settled hers into poker-like rigidity, and gathering up her skirt, edged herself into the corner of the carriage, whether to avoid contact with me or the little sinner by her side, I cannot say.

As we were thus silently progressing homeward, a sudden plunge of the horses, and the sound of many voices, announced to us that something unusual had transpired. Upon looking through the window, I beheld a sight calculated to strike terror into the most courageous Dog. A huge animal, wildly furious, was scattering the crowded thoroughfare before him. Never shall I forget the fearful aspect with which my fears and my inexperience clothed that terrible creature! It appeared to my excited imagination as though puffs of fire came from his distended nostrils, as, with head down and tail erect, he dashed through the flying people, goring some, trampling down others, and filling the scene with dire and unpicturable confusion.

Since that time, however, I have discovered that the beast (it was what bipeds call a Bull) is a quiet, unobtrusive, patient, and labor-enduring animal enough when confined to his proper sphere; but, I presume I shall incur the risk of distorting the truth, when I say that, at the period to which I allude, it was actually not unusual to see droves of those creatures driven through the most public streets—many of which, goaded by inhumanity, and frightened into fury by the common confusion of city traffic, would madly rush through the surrounding pedestrians, scattering dismay and death in their path.

But to return to our own experience in Tauromachy. Our carriage being directly in the animal's track, he made a terrific assault upon the horses, one of which he gored in so dreadful a manner that, becoming perfectly unmanageable, he plunged suddenly round as though to escape the furious assailant. The consequence was, that the fore wheels locked against the side of the vehicle, and in an instant it was overturned.

Mr. Skindeep's vociferous screams gave very tolerable assurance that she had escaped without material damage; but my darling young lady was silent—oh! so silent. She was evidently hurt, although to what extent I was ignorant for a long time.

As for me, I retained my presence of mind very well under the circumstances; indeed, I have since remarked, that there is scarcely a contingency in the world of chance that the elasticity of a dog's temperament will not adapt itself to: I am sure that if previous to this accident, any body had told me that I could have endured it at all—used as I was to the silken appliances of a luxurious existence—I should have thought that he overrated my poor philosophy most outrageously. Alas! I have had worse buffetings of fate than that to succumb to—but I must not anticipate.

There was immediately, as usual, a great crowd of obtrusive sympathizers with our misfortune, collected; each one in his anxiety to do something, interfering with the efforts of the rest, so that it was some time before any thing was done at all. In the meantime, the people had so gathered round the two ladies, that I lost sight of them, and, wild with apprehension, blinded and confused by the result of the accident, I rushed madly about in the endeavor to discover where my young mistress was. In the magnitude of the misfortune it was evident that I was thoroughly unnoticed, and inasmuch as the crowd began to separate in groupes, I ran after each in turn, animated by the one hope of finding her: but in vain. I was distracted—lost!

I know not how long I was in this state, for the individuality of events were mixed up together in my agitated mind, and all was chaos. I have a faint recollection of being taken gently up by a poor, half-starved looking man—such an one as my early education had taught me to snarl and bite at, but whose arms I now gladly nestled within, for they were at least a protection—I had looked in his eyes, and saw a mild fire within them, which rekindled hope.

The poor man trembled to his heart as he carried; he was very cold: for, though it was in kindness that he placed me on his bosom, it was I that imparted warmth to him—not he to me.

And his half whispered words puzzled me as he hurried along—they spoke of gratitude and thankfulness to Heaven for having sent *me* to bring some relief. How could I relieve any one? of what import was I? This poor wretch fancies he has found treasure, thought I. How astonished he'll be when he finds that I am only a Dog!

I knew not then, that in the hands of the Most Merciful the meanest instrument may be made the medium for diffusing happiness.

CHAPTER VI.

NEVER shall I forget the scene that met my startled sight, when we arrived at the miserable apartment where the poor man who found me—lived—I was going to say—but there is something suggestive of food, clothing and shelter in the word, which renders it inapplicable in the present instance—where he, and his, wasted slowly and silently away. I had never seen poverty before; knew not what it was: to be sure, I had heard, between the Parson and the Doctor, as they complacently picked their walnuts, or sipped their Burgundy after dinner, theoretical conversations, profound projects, and elaborate plans, for its amelioration; over which they prosed and dozed, until my lady, voting such discussions a bore, would change the subject with a yawn, for something a little less soporific.

Meantime, reclining upon my velvet cushion, the solemn words of the speakers, and the rich gurgle of the wine reached my ears at the same moment, generally accompanied by a luscious smack of enjoyment from the Parson and a passing apostrophe to the delicate flavor of the vintage from the Doctor; so that I could not tell which occupied their minds most—the deplorable misery which was absent and unfelt, or the orthodox indulgence which was present and actual.

But here it *was* in all its stark reality, stern and unmistakable. Even now I can describe that scene to its minutest detail, for it made an impression upon my memory, the vicissitudes of time have not been able to eradicate.

It was evening. Already had the gas in the various stores been lighted; yet, at the open attic window, a young girl was sewing by the faint reflection which still lingered in the eastern sky. Her eyes, close to her work, were never raised, even at our entrance; to take them off a moment would be to lose sight of all. A woman, of middle age, worn to a very shadow, thin, gaunt, and weird looking, was busily occupied cooking a mess of something, in so small a measure that you would suppose it to be an infant's meal; and yet it was all the dinner which those three poor creatures had. Ah! how I wished then for the Parson and the Doctor, that they might continue their theories upon that floor, and observe the gradually fading light in those staring eyes, while they *talked*.

How the bitter wind whistled through the crevices in the roof, through the broken glasses in the small window, and up the narrow stairway like a funnel! and yet they did not shiver thereat! Custom had habituated them to exposure. As for me, fresh from the warm atmosphere of Mr. Glosely's luxurious establishment, every blast of the keen breeze penetrated to my very heart, and I trembled with cold and apprehension.

The man evidently fearing to disturb the poor girl at her blinding labor, was silent for a few minutes until the last gleam of twilight passed away, and, with a deep sigh of exhaustion, she relinquished her work.

"Rest, rest for a few moments, my darling," said the shadow at the insufficient fire-place; "our dinner is nearly prepared —if we can call it by such a name."

"No, mother," replied the other, in a voice rendered tremulous by fatigue; "I have not time just yet. This is, you know, a sample of my work, and if I do not take it back in time, the money which I had to leave as a deposit will be forfeited. Remember, if it be satisfactory," she added, with an attempt at cheerfulness, "I shall have enough of work to sustain us for some time, and that will be a great consolation; so light the candle, dearest mother, at once, I must not lose a moment!"

If the dreary apartment looked desolate in the gloom of the dusk, it appeared trebly so when dimly lighted by one thin, consumptive candle, whose faint gleams, vainly struggling to extend themselves into the dark spaces beyond, invested the surrounding objects with a ghostly character; so that to me, the whole scene was strange and supernatural.

It was now for the first time that the man spoke, and I felt that he trembled to the very heart as he did so.

"Mary," said he, "your health is of more value than aught else in the world! Pause, my dear girl, if it be only for a few minutes. See, I have found that which, no doubt, will bring us some present means." So saying, he carefully unfolded the breast of his coat, and set me down on the bare floor.

"What a beautiful creature!" cried his daughter, as I ran towards her, intending to designate, by my affectionate manner, how my natural instinct led me to approach, with confidence, the kindly-hearted.

Suddenly, in the midst of her caresses, she chased away with a profound sigh, the momentary joyousness that overspread her pallid features, saying, as she placed me again in the man's arms:—

"This is folly! What have I to do with pets? Nothing but work, work, work, unvarying and unceasing!"

Now it was that I discovered the meaning of my protector's mysterious expressions, as he carried me along.

"Doubtless," said he, "this animal is of great value to its

loser, and will be advertised. If a reward be offered, Heaven knows it will be welcome; if not, why it will be only in consonance with my usual ill-fortune.

The poor family at length sat down to their slender meal, and the pale girl's first thought was to place a portion of hers aside for me; this, however, although I estimated her generosity, and acknowledged it as well as I was able, I could not touch, it was so coarse, and unlike the profusion of delicacies with which I had been feasted at home. How I wished then that I could have conjured up the many excellent meals that I had wasted in mere wantonness! However, I consoled myself with the reflection that it was not so much my fault as it was theirs, who flung so recklessly before me, to be spoilt and rendered useless, food, which, if divided amongst the *poorer* fellow creatures, would keep many of them from the bitterness of want.

It would be useless for me to attempt any description of the horrors of that terrible night. A bitterly cold north-easterly storm beat against the crazy tenement; gust upon gust burst through the open crevices, sweeping around the wretched room with uncontrolled mastery, penetrating through the scanty covering of the poor, shivering inmates, until their very teeth chattered as they slept, and each painful breath was ushered into the world with a shudder. Sleep for me was out of the question. Separated from the warm, comfortable, quilted satin basket couch, on which I usually reclined, I felt as though I had been suddenly transported to Siberia, or some such icy region; and when I reflected that this night, so unendurable to me, was only one of the many, those poor people were destined to exist through, I wondered within my inmost heart what terrible crime they had committed that they should be made to suffer such great punishment.

Experience has since made me acquainted with its name

and nature. It is called *Poverty;* and it is of so equalizing a nature that, in the eyes of human kind, it matters not whether it be induced by reckless folly, or compelled by predestinate circumstance, those who are found guilty of that heinous offence, are effectually, and without distinction, shut out from the sympathy or consideration of the majority of their fellow creatures.

Morning, however, dawned at last, and with its earliest beams awakened the comfortless sleepers. The day's very earliest sufficiency of light saw the pale girl—still paler, from the unrefreshing rest—at work, plying that eternal instrument of death to thousands, the needle. Meantime the elder female attended to the brief domestic duties—for, though hopelessly wretched, the apartment and all within it were scrupulously clean.

After two or three hours had elapsed, the girl exclaimed with a throb of satisfaction—

"It is finished at last! Mother, keep up your spirits—quick! my bonnet and shawl—I shall take it to the store, and bring you back that, which will provide us with present necessaries."

"I shall go with you, darling," said the father. "Perhaps this little dog has been advertised; if so, I shall surely get something for its restoration."

Their small toilet was soon made, and with his devoted daughter on his arm, and me, carefully hidden in the folds of his coat, he proceeded on his journey. Few were the words exchanged between the two, for privation is not garrulous. At length, we reached an extensive and gaudily decorated store. Huge piles of clothing of every description filled the ample counters and the numerous shelves, while round a glowing stove, nearly red hot, were gathered some dozen of shopmen and clerks, for business had not yet commenced.

A deep blush suffused the white cheek of the young girl as, amidst rude glances and whispered observations, unchecked by the sacred suffering that was evident in the pinched features of both father and child, she timidly inquired for the superintendent, from whom she had received the work.

"I have brought home the half dozen of shirts which were entrusted to me," said she, in a voice tremulous with modesty and hope.

"Name?" replied one of the group, a paunchy, red-faced, weak-eyed individual, with a rude manner, and insolent tone of voice.

"Withering," said the father, seeing that, from a sensation of shame, the girl hesitated to answer.

"Let me look at them, Withering," said the superintendent, while a meaning squint, at the anticipation of a good joke, passed around the loungers. "Won't do!" he continued, with a savage expression of face, "stuff—entirely spoilt! This is the consequence of giving work to those who know nothing about it."

And with well-simulated rage, he seized one of the shirts, and tore it up the seam—taking care, however, to do the garment no actual injury.

But oh! to see the effect of these words and of that action upon the poor pale girl, and the stricken man beside her! She spoke not a word, but with one look of combined anguish and resignation, which should have softened a heart of iron, she slowly turned to go out, staggering against her father as she did so; he, however, gazed sternly upon the legalized robber, saying—

"Where is the money which was left as a deposit?"

"Money!" replied the other, "what money? Do you suppose that miserable sum will pay for the material ruined?

No! the amount is forfeited, of course," and he turned on his heel and walked away.

"Do you call this just or right?" cried the exasperated man.

"It's our way of doing business," coolly replied the superintendent.

"I call it swindling—wicked, uncharitable, unchristianlike, and dastardly swindling!"

"I don't care a curse what you call it!" said the other, contemptuously; "we don't know any thing about charity or Christianity here: *it's our way of doing business*, and that's all about it!"

"If there be law—" oh! the explosion of laughter that burst from the paunch of the ruddy superintendent, multiplied by that of the hilarious assistants.

"*Law? you* talk of *Law!*" sputtered he, through his exceeding great merriment, measuring the miserable looking outline of the poor wretch the while, with a glance of the most ineffable disdain. "*Try it!*" and out they all roared again in concert, as though the present capital joke was only one of a series.

With a heavy heart, as was evident from his despairing look, the wretched man turned to leave the store, his poor stricken child leaning heavily on his arm; when, to my great astonishment, who should walk in but Mr. Glosely. Sleek, self-sufficient, and scrupulously clean, he had quite a clerical aspect; his shiny black clothes and irreproachably starched cravat, redolent of respectability, and strikingly suggestive of rigid morality.

As I was naturally delighted to recognize any member of my former home, I gave very audible proof of my joy by barking vociferously, and making great efforts to escape from the man's arms.

"Put down that Dog, you scoundrel!" cried Glosely, in a voice of thunder. "Are you not ashamed to thus endeavor to commit so bare-faced a robbery, in the open face of day?"

"Robbery, sir?" replied the wretched man, as he tremblingly placed me on the floor; then he tried to speak, but his voice receded into his throat. He clasped his hands over his eyes, and, except the loud sobs that came up from his heart, he was silent. Not so his daughter; it was her turn now to be courageous. With a defiant glance, such as an Angel might have cast upon the Fiend, she turned upon the man of respectability.

"Sir," said she, "this is my father—nobler in heart, and soul, and rectitude, than a community of such men as you! How dare you accuse him of a crime, without giving him the time for explanation? But in the security of your position, you can insult wretchedness with impunity."

"Bless my soul, what a lecture!" sneered the redoubtable merchant, the white rage creeping over his face. "May I be permitted to ask how the animal came in your possession?"

"He found it, sir."

"Of course, he did!" replied the other, with a most insolent expression. "Suppose I choose to doubt that, and have the matter legally investigated?"

He saw the advantage of that insinuation in an instant. The idea of public degradation appeared to flash across the minds of both father and child; for, right or wrong, it would seem that poverty has but little chance against the machinery of petty law-mongers.

As for the poor girl, the filial affection that nerved her to the protection of her father's name, could sustain but a slight conflict with her physical weakness, the revulsion drove the life-blood from her heart, and she fainted.

"Come, none of that nonsense here!" cried the brutal superintendent, rudely shaking the child.

"Mercy—mercy!" almost screamed the miserable father, "don't you see, coward ruffians as ye are, that my poor heart-stricken darling is all but lifeless! common humanity might prompt you to lend her some assistance."

One of the young men whose face I liked, brought a glass of water; and in a few moments more, she was unwillingly woke again to the terrible realities of life.

"It's only a trick, a common imposture," said the respectable Mr. Glosely. "Begone!" continued he, with an authoritative flourish of his hand; "although the good of society would prompt me to make an example of you both, yet a very reprehensible benevolence impels me to overlook your offence;" and, with upturned eye and Pharisaic expression, he stalked away from the spot, absolutely deceived into the belief that he had exercised an uncommon degree of Christain charity in suffering these poor people to depart without being subjected to the blasting effect of a public investigation.

For my part, I must conscientiously say, that the result of this interview was so totally different from what I, knowing the man's honesty, expected, that I was quite bewildered, and most sincerely wished that mankind were sufficiently educated to understand my own language, in order that Mr. Glosely's mind might be disabused of the false impression; but when I saw the father and child slowly and silently prepare to depart without one step towards acknowledgment by him, who, if I were of any value, which my *amour propre* forbid me to doubt, owed them an obligation, I could not resist the impulse to evidence my gratitude by springing towards them, and looking my thanks in the sweet, pale girl's face: an act of courtesy, and indeed of justice, which Mr. Glosely appeared to take in considerable dudgeon, for he called me sharply to him, and rebuked me very profusely for taking so unwarrantable a liberty.

Oh! how I grieved when I saw the two unhappy beings take their departure, knowing, as I did, that the necessary subsistence for the whole of the day depended upon the small sum which they expected to procure from the store.

Meantime, Mr. Glosely lavished many caresses upon me, and, calling his porter, sent him instantly to the nearest eating-house for some delicate slices of meat.

"Poor Carlo!" said he, "no doubt those miserable wretches have starved you. Quick! John, mind you bring the nicest cuts you can; for this is a dainty Dog, I assure you."

It was not long before the porter came back with a most liberal distribution of excellent food, which, being placed on the counter, I was lifted up, and, by a curious coincidence, I made a most hearty meal—for I was hungry—close by the parcel of shirts which that labor-wasted girl had expended many sands of her rapidly wending existence in working.

As Mr. Glosely was watching with earnestness the avidity with which I demolished the savory food, his eye caught the strange packet, the contents of which he carefully examined. Now, thought I, for another explosion of anger; but, on the contrary, to my utter amazement, Mr. Glosely exclaimed:—

"What beautiful work! Who brought these?"—a question which was answered by the superintendent with a wink, and a peculiar movement of his thumb to his nose.

"The old plan, eh?" said Glosely.

"Spoilt, you know—stuff ruined!" replied the other, with a hearty laugh, as he held up the mutilated garment.

"You are a capital fellow!" said Glosely. "How many of those have came in this morning?"

"Only six dozen," said the superintendent.

"And all paid for in the same way?"

"Yes."

The truth flashed upon me in an instant. Wealth was speculating on human life, and the drops of mortal agony from the very heart of Poverty, were being transmuted into devilish gold. How sincerely then did I lift up my *soul* (for I deny the mortal monopoly), in thankfulness that beneficent Nature had made me a Dog!

CHAPTER VII.

GREAT was the rejoicing when I reached home, after my terrible adventure. The interview between my mother and me can, of course, only be described to Dogs; for, inasmuch as it consisted simply of an outburst of real affection, without any reference to contingent advantages, it would not interest humankind.

My darling little Priscilla, however, heaped numberless caresses upon me—even the sanctimonious Mrs. Glosely condescended to an emotion—but Master Horace, now fast growing out of boyhood and its truthful impulses, looking superciliously through an unneeded eyeglass, evidently feeling that it would compromise his budding manliness to pay the slightest attention to so trivial a circumstance.

For my own part, I can conscientiously say, that I never was so happy in my life—a happiness made even more intense by the occasional recollection of the poor wretches with whom I had passed the night, and whose bleak and miserable habitation I shuddered to think of. In the warm radiance of Mr. Glosely's luxurious apartment, as I scampered over the thickly piled velvet carpet, or played at hide and seek with my now sedate parent, through and about the heavy satin drapery of the window-curtains, every now and then, the unspeakable wretchedness that I had recently witnessed would flit across my mind; then I would gravely pause, and look round upon the family group! my eye would probably rest upon its respected and respectable head, as he leaned back in his comfortable chair, enveloped in brocade, nicely scrutinizing the contents of a wine-glass, his face beaming with sensuous enjoyment; and I wondered if that poor, pale, starving girl, ever came between the glass and his lips: but the sigh which invariably followed the delicious draught was dedicated to enjoyment, not to retrospection.

Although Mr. Glosely very seldom regaled the ears of his domestic circle by relating the occurrences of the day, he departed from his usual taciturnity upon this occasion, and, to me, it was extremely curious to witness the ingenuity with which he totally subverted or exaggerated the absolute facts of the case.

Priscilla it was who elicted the narration by asking how I was restored.

"I recovered the Dog myself," replied Glosely, between sips of his favorite Burgundy.

"Indeed, Pa," said Priscilla; "oh! do tell us the particulars."

"He had been stolen, you know, by a tall, ill-looking ruffian."

"The bad creature," ejaculated Priscilla, "to steal our beautiful Carlo! He ought to be ashamed of himself."

"He ought to be hanged!" said Mrs. Glosely.

"Tell us how it occurred, dear Papa!"

"It was quite providential," piously groaned the exemplary parent. "Just as I entered the store this morning, my people were thrusting forth a man who had all the appearance of a burglar, a most ferocious-looking scoundrel, who had evidently sneaked in to carry off whatever he could lay his hands on. He was insolent, and refused to go; whereupon I laid hold of him by the shoulder, and was about to hurl him into the street, when the breast of his coat becoming loosened in the struggle, to my utter amazement, what should I see but the Dog. It is perfectly evident to me that, from natural instinct, the animal discovered, and by some means obtained entrance to the store, although he had never been near the place."

"It is perfectly wonderful, the instinct of animals," gravely remarked Mrs. Glosely.

"Poor, dear Carlo! what a night he must have passed!" said Priscilla. "How he could have managed without his basket, I cannot tell."

"Dogs know a dodge or two, I tell *you!*" said the would-be slang, Master Hector.

"Of course! I seized the animal," resumed Mr. Glosely, "and turned the vagabond into the street. It would have been a great inconvenience to me, at that time, or I should most assuredly have given the impudent fellow a month in the Penitentiary; although I have no doubt but that would have been no novelty to him, for he had all the appearance of a confirmed jail bird."

"You were very wrong to to let him go," said Mrs. Glosely: "who knows what outrages upon society that creature may work, now that he is at large! It is a false clemency which lets the criminal loose upon the world."

"Nay, Mamma," replied Priscilla, "how do we know what circumstances, what privations, may have driven the unfortunate man to the commission of those acts?"

"My dear child," replied Mr. Glosely, impressively—interrupting at the same moment Mrs. Glosely, who was about to speak—"such language is dictated by a false philanthropy. Wickedness is progressive, and the earlier it is restrained by judicious, but inflexible punishment, the sooner it will be checked. If we do not reprehend follies, they must, in time, become faults; if faults be not corrected, they increase to vices; and vices unchecked, soon grow into crimes; therefore, you see the wisest legislation would undoubtedly be that which tended to crush the very germ of guilt, before it could have time to fructify."

It was astonishing how imposing Mr. Glosely looked, and how satisfied he felt as he delivered that dogmatic opinion. It so happened that at a mass meeting for the mutual protection of storekeepers, a few evenings before, he delivered a set speech upon the same subject; the effect of a portion of which he thought he had a good opportunity of trying upon the family party.

Mr. Glosely's history of my recovery having been received with the usual exclamations, he relapsed into the quiet serenity of selfish gratification, prolonging the exquisite indulgence of taste, by sipping slowly and daintily of the delicious vintage, a certain exact and never exceeded quantity he thus lazily absorbed every day; for, like all selfish people, he was very precise, and particular in his dietary proceedings.

It was during one of those moments of tranquil enjoyment that Pat entered with a note for Mr. Glosely, which had been left at his store; but, being marked *immediate*, was, contrary to the usual custom, forwarded to his residence. With a gesture, Mr. Glosely indicated that it should be left on the table, where it remained unnoticed until he had smacked his lips, and heaved a sigh of resignation over the last aftertaste of his prescribed quantum. With an expression of the intensest annoyance to be thus intruded upon in his hours of relaxation, he tore open the unseemly scrap of paper, which, for fear of contamination, he held gingerly between his thumb and finger. Glancing hastily over its contents, he flung it down again, contemptuously exclaiming—

"Who brought this?"

"Mr. Richards, sir," replied Pat.

He was the young gentleman who sympathized with the poor father and his child at the store.

"Show him up."

In a few minutes Pat returned, ushering in Mr. Richards; the latter looking as though he was to be arraigned for some terrible crime; his face was scarlet, and his entire deportment indicative either of extraordinary bashfulness or the consciousness of having committed some great enormity.

"Sit down, Mr. Richards," said Mr. Glosely, in a voice and manner wherein condescension and pride were very curiously blended.

Mr. Richards complied, feeling tolerable certain, I was assured by his nervousness, that those preliminary coughs ot Mr. Glosely's foretokened something disagreeable. Having cleared his throat sufficiently to prepare his auditor, Mr. Glosely solemnly, slowly, and emphatically, as though he were delivering the sentence of a criminal court, proceeded thus—

"Mr. Richards, I think I have, sir, time and again admonished you, that, upon no circumstance whatever are any letters, messages, or missives, of any description, or from any person, to be sent from the store to my private residence!"

"I would not have presumed, sir," replied the other, timidly, "but that the messenger said it was an affair of life and death."

"That does not signify, sir," said Mr. Glosely, coldly, closing his eyes at the same time, "unless it should concern my own family or interests; then, Heaven forbid," he continued, looking at the chandelier, "that I should abandon the requirements of duty for my own comfort!"

He was interrupted by a sob of distress; on turning to discover from whence it proceeded, he saw his daughter in tears.

"What is the matter, my darling?" said he anxiously; foi

although one might suppose that self and the world had shared his heart between them, he did love his children with a father's love.

She simply pointed to the letter.

"My dear child," said Glosely, taking the letter up in his hand, putting his whole stock of parental tenderness into his tone and manner—"You must not allow your sympathy to counteract your reason and prudence. You are young, impulsive, and credulous: with you, whatever seems to be, is. You are not aware of the many shifts and tricks resorted to by those who, rather than labor for an existence prefer to live idly upon the benevolence of the unthinking, who thereby encourage what they should discountenance, and perpetuate laziness and mendacity."

"Did you say the fellow who brought this was waiting?" he continued, addressing Mr. Richards, but with a marked difference of intonation.

"Yes, sir," replied Richards. "He told me that he would wait at the store until I returned."

"Indeed! then, sir, if you find him there when you go back, give him in charge to a policeman. He is evidently used to this style of composition, I know by the style; I have seen hundreds of them in my time." Mr. Glosely then proceeded to read the poor fellow's letter, commenting with considerable hilarity upon what he called the professional characteristics. "*Honored sir!* ha! ha!—that's the way they always begin: 'I would not have dared to intrude upon you'—certainly not! they never do—'but that my dear child is, I fear, upon the point of death.' Of course! the usual routine. They generally have a daughter or a mother at the point of death; but, confound 'em! they never die," and Glosely had a good laugh at the joke.

"'The shock she encountered this morning at finding that

what she had done for you was unsatisfactory, was too much for a system already bowed down and crushed by the pressure of adverse circumstances.'

"Very good, upon my word! I wonder the scoundrel didn't say I killed her, at once.

"'In my deplorable necessity, oh! sir, pray forgive me for soliciting a trifle, not as a remuneration, but as absolute charity; and the blessings of a distracted father will be for ever yours.'

"Come, that's pushing the agony a little too far!"

"'Your most obedient servant,

"'JOHN WITHERING.'

"Away, and do as I told you!" said he to the young man, at the same time flinging the letter into the blazing fire.

"Dear father," interposed Priscilla, "pray don't come to a conclusion too abruptly. Consider *if* this man's story should be true, what a terrible thing it would be to refuse some small assistance."

"There—there, have done!" cried Mr. Glosely. "I know better about these things than you. Go along, sir! and keep quiet all of you, for I am going to take my nap." So saying he placed his slippered feet upon the cosy footstool, and nestling himself into the most comfortable position, gradually subsided into placid slumber.

No sooner was Mr. Glosely wrapped in sleep, than Priscilla whispered something to her mother, to which the other responded with a look of intense astonishment, nothing more. What it was, I had no opportunity of discovering at the time; but am tolerably certain that the dear soul wished some one to go and personally inquire into the truth or falsehood of the letter-writer's account. She appealed also to Horace, but he appeared to decline, and shortly after went away; but not where she wished, I saw by the disappointment in her expressive features.

The next morning, I had no sooner jumped out of my basket, than, what was my astonishment to see Priscilla attired to go out! As well as I could possibly express the wish to her, I asked her if I might accompany her? The dear soul understood my intention, for she said, with a smile: "Yes, Carlo, you can come, too;" and so bounding, frisking, and barking, with a degree of joyous and unthinking levity quite derogatory in a dog of my pretensions to discretion, I rushed into the street. A few backward and forward scrambles, however, soon made such inroads upon my scant breath, that I was glad to subside into a respectable jog trot, and so follow at her heels, demurely.

I began to wonder, within myself, where on earth she was going; for, instead of our usual pleasant ramble amongst the up-town parks, we were progressing through the confusion and turmoil of city traffic. At this time in the morning, however, reputable industry alone was astir. The fashionable vicinities did not display their impertinent bewhiskered *habitués;* consequently, without a movement of hindrance or a glance of rudeness, we continued our way, until we arrived at Mr. Glosely's store.

It was surprising to see the effect caused by our entrance. The store loungers were stricken with immediate activity; goods of every description were violently seized from their respective shelves, and flung down upon the counter, as if they had been doing something wrong; hastily they were torn open, as though it were immediately essential that they should be exposed. Hieroglyphical marks were closely scrutinised; then they were indignantly cast aside, and others hurled upon them: and all this affectation of industry, because a little girl and a dog suddenly appeared amongst them!

Priscilla inquired for Mr. Richards.

Blushing still deeper than he did last evening, Mr. Richards left his hat on the desk where he had been writing, and approached.

"Good morning Mr. Richards," said she, in that frank, friendly tone of voice, which puts one at ease instanter.

Mr. Richards' face was now as white as paper.

"I wish you to do me a favor," she continued.

Mr. Richards' face was now redder than ever, as he answered, bowing low:

"Certainly, Miss, anything, a—I"——

What could have been the matter with Mr. Richards?

"I want to know, Mr. Richards," said Priscilla, mercifully —for she must have seen, and pitied his embarrassment—"if you can tell me the address of the poor man who wrote to papa yesterday?"

"Yes, miss, I can," replied Richards; his manner now tolerably collected, but his color still changeable. "After I left Mr. Glosely's I went there myself last evening."

With an impulse she could not resist, evidently, Priscilla seized the young man's hand, exclaiming—

"Thank you!—thank you! for my father's sake. I know he must have wished you to do so, although he spoke so crossly."

You should have seen Mr. Richards' face then. Priscilla had his hand imprisoned in both of her palms and the contact seemed to thrill him like electricity.

In an instant she became aware of the impulsive impropriety she had committed, so she dropped Mr. Richards' hand so abruptly, that it fell to his side like a piece of lead. Now it was Priscilla's turn to blush, which she did most beautifully, down to her pretty little throat.

Mr. Richards, however, very properly relieved her

embarrassment by relating, in a calm and truthful manner the result of his visit to poor Withering, which detailed a picture of suffering and privation Priscilla's golden experience had rendered it impossible for her to imagine could exist in the midst of a Christian community.

He concluded by observing—

"I am not rich enough to do what I could have wished, Miss Glosely; but I have prevented the pressure of immediate necessity: and the terrible haste with which the poor man seized upon my little alms, and rushed bare-headed from the place, was evidence enough that it was most truly and deplorably needed."

"And the young girl"——

"Is in extremely bad health," continued Richards. "She was lying down, silent and unmurmuring. The place was so dark that I could not see how she looked, but there was something in her breathing that struck me with awe; however, I am going again this morning. I've got something for them. Those wild boys sometimes do a good thing, and last night when I told them the state these poor people were in, they clubbed together the money they had set by for the evening's amusement; and so we've got a little basket full of nourishing things, and a couple of bottles of wine."

"When are you going, Mr. Richards?" said Priscilla.

"As soon as I possibly can," he replied.

"Let it be now," exclaimed my dear pet, "and I shall accompany you."

"It will be a kind, good action, Miss Glosely, and worthy of you," said Mr. Richards, as he turned suddenly round, but not so quickly as to prevent my seeing two big, honorable tears filling up his eyes.

As for Priscilla, she wept like a little angel; and there was astonishing activity in the store.

"It must be confessed," thought I, as I accompanied Mr. Richards and Priscilla upon their errand of mercy, "mankind is not altogether bad! a few such hearts as are possessed by those two young people would go far to redeem a whole multitude. It is, indeed, a beautiful thing to see youth occasionally exhibit glimpses of the true unostentatious spirit of philanthropy;" and, for the first time in my life, I began to entertain doubts as to the superiority of my own species.

However, consolation visited me very shortly in the reflection that the couple before me was by no means a sample of humankind generally, as far as my limited sphere of observation went; for individual dogs do not, like individual men, fancy the circumscribed circle in which they move to be the universal world: therefore it is, that I am extremely cautious always, before I come to a dogmatic conclusion.

By this time we had reached the miserable hovel in which the man and his daughter dwelt. Terribly strange and fearful was the aspect of the wretched vicinity to the unaccustomed eyes of Priscilla. Groups of desperate-looking vagabonds gathered around every corner—for every corner, nay, almost every second house contained that fructifying element of poverty, disease, and crime, soul and body destroying Liquor—and some there were, even at that early period of the day, madly seeking oblivion from the poisonous and deadly fire. Priscilla shuddered, and closed her eyes as she passed those plague spots, exclaiming—

"How dreadful this place is, Mr. Richards! Who could believe that, in this age of civilization—in the very heart of this city of intelligence and wealth—such shocking scenes would be permitted to exist?"

"It is terrible, indeed," said Mr. Richards; "and yet one can scarcely take up a newspaper in which there are not reports of Bible Society meetings, in which a vast amount of learned casuistry is displayed, and much valuable time wasted about the spelling of a word, or the punctuation of a sentence! In my mind, there's a great deal too much attention paid to the "letter," and too little to the "spirit." Here is a matter for them to spell over, and find out the meaning of, and endeavor to put into proper form. It cannot be possible but that, by a vigorous and united effort, those to whom we look for guidance on our immortal way, could cleanse this polluted stye. I know not by what means; but surely, if they devoted as much time to meetings and consultations upon the subject, the result would be infinitely more beneficial and satisfactory than registering cannibal converts, or disputing about the termination of a syllable."

"These men—these horrid looking creatures, that we see hanging about—what are they?" inquired Priscilla.

"Perhaps criminals, perhaps merely the children of poverty; for the charitable world makes no distinction between the two," replied Mr. Richards. "They are forced into companionship, and respectability looks with an equally prejudiced eye upon both.

"But see! this is the place at which those poor people reside. You need not fear, for the law has its eye upon us, and our safety, in the shape of that burly policeman, you can just see turning the corner. His keen glance has not been off of us since we first entered the neighborhood; for all who tread those purlieus are objects of suspicion. I'll warrant now that a hundred motives for our being here has crossed that fellow's thought, but the right one; that never could suggest itself to his vice-experienced mind."

They had to disturb three or four squalid females who had gathered around the door, to gossip about the affairs of their neighbors. It was evident that there was sickness of a serious nature in the place, for these women were whispering silently, and with evident sorrow in their pinched and wasted features. Sorrow for what? That the mercy of Heaven was about to diminish the sufferings of one of their sisterhood! The love of life must, indeed, be strong, to cling thus in the midst of wretchedness and degradation!

Oh! what a scene was presented to us, as we entered the room where the poor sewing girl lay, feebly battling with the destroyer, resigned, and but too willing to quit the cold companionship of earth, and its respectable villainies, for the bright Heaven that already was opening to her. Her face, pale and almost transparent, was fast losing the grosser features of earth, and looked angelic; her eyes, now preternaturally large and lustrous, would have indicated bodily health, but that they were contradicted by the pinched nostril, and the white shrunken lip; her hands, delicate as alabaster, were clasped across her breast, and a sweet smile of heavenly hope was resting upon her mouth.

Her father, tearless, but with a voice broken by sorrowful emotion, was on his knees, reading to her, when we came in. Respectfully Mr. Richards uncovered his head, as did also Priscilla, and silently waited until he should make an end.

He was reading the prayers of the Church for the sick. Attention, Joy, Hope and Consolation, were expressed in the poor sufferer's wan face; while in mute despair, the wretched mother sat, with her head resting on her clenched hands, motionless, and grief-stricken.

Religion, heartfelt, and real in its truth and purity, was in that miserable chamber; its soothing influence enabled the sorrow-laden man to bear his burden patiently; its blessed promise of an after-joy, more bright than mortal thought can compass, dulled the present agony of that dying girl, and Earth, and all its countless woes and trials, was lost in the glorious anticipation of an eternity of happiness.

He ceased to read, just as symptoms of weariness crept across the features of the sufferer, and she closed her eyes.

"Is there any hope?" whispered Mr. Richards to the distracted father, then, for the first time, made conscious that there were any strangers present.

"No, Sir!" he responded, with an expression of the profoundest grief; "my darling must leave us—and why, why should I be so selfish as to wish otherwise?" He continued: "In the grave she will, at least, be free from insolence and want!"

"This young lady," said Mr. Richards, leading Priscilla forward, "hearing of your terrible distress, and of your daughter's illness, has brought a few things that may be of use."

"Heaven will reward her for it!" cried the sorrowing parent; "but alas! it is too late. A few days back, perhaps, it might have stayed, for a little time, the dreadful stroke."

These words sent a pang to Priscilla's heart, and a fervent prayer sprung up from its inward depths, that Heaven's justice might not reach *him* who was answerable for that soul's departure.

"What does the physician say?" asked Mr. Richards.

"The physician?" and the man smiled—a terrible smile—as he spoke. "Why, he said that he'd give me a prescription, but that as I hadn't means to get it prepared, it would be useless. He felt her pulse, looked at her tongue, muttered a few commonplaces, recommended nourishing things, looked at his watch, was really sorry he couldn't do anything, and left."

"But it may not be too late," exclaimed Mr. Richards: "let me run and find some one."

"Ah! Sir," said the other, solemnly pointing to the already changing features, "there is the surest truthteller: she is dying! Why should I disturb her last moments by useless questioning, and, it may be, quackery?"

At this moment the eyes of the poor patient sufferer half opened.

"Father—mother!" she articulated, with difficulty, "kiss me, for the last time on earth! The cold reaches my heart; but there is a Glory before my fading sight. God forgive me, that I have repined at the darkness of my earthly lot, when the recompense is so Heavenly beautiful! The sight is going from my eyes, but I hear words of triumphant joy, as though from Angels' voices. Hark! they call me; a moment, and I come. God bless you, dear father!—mother, do not weep for me, but rejoice; for my soul is happy—happy!" and thus her world-purified spirit sprang forth, all Angel, and wended towards the regions of everlasting joy.

Her name was duly inscribed upon the Register, together with the information that she had died from Consumption; but on the tablets of eternal Wisdom and Justice it was written, *Murder*—and there are many such in this virtuous seeming world of Respectability.

THE OPERA OF "LA FILLE DU REGIMENT,"

DONE INTO ENGLISH.

THE Twenty-first Regiment marching one day
In an orderly way,
To sack and to slay
An inadequate mass for their limited pay,
For though victory may
Be the sunniest ray
That over a Maréchal's caput can play,
I'll venture to say
Till the world turns grey,
The dollarum dibs will hold paramount sway.
Well, this Regiment marching in valiant array,
With colors so gay,
They
Happened to meet with an overthrown chay,
With a baby inside of it, trying to pray;
So the *enfant trouvée*
They carry away,
And adopt as their daughter, *sans cérémonie.*

Dear Reader, you'll please to remember this case
Of abduction took place
A long time before the first scene of the *pièce*;
And though Sulpice the sergeant, moreover the bass,

Has had many a chase,
In trying to trace
Out her father and mother, or aught of her race,
That they might embrace
A daughter so lovely in figure and face,
But vain his endeavors; so now you may see
That pretty Marie
Is contented and happy as happy can be,
With a step as light, and a will as free
As a sweet little bird in the boughs of a tree,
Or a nice little fish in some beautiful sea,
Or a frolicsome fawn on a meadowy lea,
Or a bee
Full of glee,
Or a little fairee,
Or anything else that occurs unto thee,
That will with those characteristics agree.
And the soldiers adore their young daughter, for she
Makes most undeniable coffee and tea,
And warbles moreover magnificently.

Now our little friend Marie, a short time ago,
Contrived to enveigle a bit of a beau—
One Tonio—
A dapper young Tyrolese peasant, although
He's rather so-so,
As pecuniaries go,
And I'm angry with Marie for stooping so low;
But love's rapid flow
Will frequently throw
Strange parties together, for weal or for woe,
Let the atoms surrounding it like it or no.
Now Toney and Marie, one day you must know

Are *singing* great love to each other, when lo!
The Sergeant observed them, and he wasn't slow
In detecting how matters were going. "Oh! ho!"
Said he, rushing down with his gills in a glow,
"The pearl of the *vingt unième* musn't bestow
Her hand on a *maudit paysan*, and a foe."
But the sergeant stout
Was soon put to the rout,
Love had carried the poorly defended redoubt
Of the heart of Marie, and no menace or shout
Can send such a conqueror right about;
"For," said she, with a pout,
"If my amiable mother don't know that I'm out,
What is it to you,
Whatever I do?
So please, Mr. Sergeant, I'll follow my gout."
"*Mille d'yeux,*
Sacré bleu!
Quelle une audacieuse!"
Said the *grande militaire*, in a deuce of a stew.
In a most unavoidable passion he flew,
For Marie was true,
To her new
Amoureux,
And stuck to her point, like a gallon of glue;
So they compromised things in a minute or two.
By putting him through
An inductory few
Mere matters of form, to a soldier he grew.
And now I expect
In the *tri-color* decked,
His comrades consider that he might affect
A duchess elect,

Or a Queen, if her Majesty didn't object.
Now the fun's what I think I may venture to call
        Uncommonly tall,
When a slice of good luck nearly ruins them all,
Making Tony the brave, sing prodigiously small.
A Marchioness something, bah! what's her name?
I really forget, but it's all the same—
Suffice it to say she's an elegant dame,
        Of the old *régime.*
All powder and hoop, *à la Louis Cinquième*,
        Has come to claim
The glory and pride of the *vingt unième;*
She calls Marie her niece, and she takes her away,
And as matter of course, there's old Harry to pay.
You'll please to remember, some time has passed
        Since line the last.
        Marie having cast
Her merino for satin that can't be surpassed,
And a natural fund of good breeding amassed,
Grows into a lady remarkably fast,
And she lives in a beautiful palace among
A *magnifique*, aristocratical throng;
But you plainly perceive there is something wrong
For instead of the light-hearted *ran-tan-plan*,
A feeling of sorrow pervades her song.
        A nobleman grand
        Has offered his hand,
With the wealthiest dower that ever was read,
But Toney, the peasant, still runs in her head.
        So the Marchioness said,
"To Toney, the peasant, you cannot be wed,
For a very good reason—because he's dead;

So oblige me and marry the Duke instead."
And the dutiful darling, tho' tears she shed,
    And her little heart bled,
Prepared to encounter the nuptials dread;
And they leave her alone, and she gazes round
Those beautiful walls, and declares she's found
But little content on nobility's ground,
When her startled ear catches a well-known sound;
    With a rapturous bound
She flies to the window, and, marching by,
Her beloved old regiment blesses her eye;
    And her pulse beats high,
    And she fain would cry,
    But her brain is dry,
And the tears won't come, and she doesn't know why
    No more do I—
But oh! her delight's inexpressible, when
The company enters the chamber, and then
She embraces the flag, she embraces the men,
David and *Robert*, *Thomasse* and *Etienne*,
She kisses them over and over again,
But where is poor Toney?—alas! now her tears
Flow freely and fast—when she suddenly hears
A voice well remembered through changeable years,
And fancy her joy, when, saluted with cheers,
In an officer's dress her old lover appears.

Dear reader, there isn't much more to disclose,
The Duke has his *congé* as you may suppose,
    The Marchioness shows
    Inclination for blows,
And doesn't seem willing the matter to close;

When Toney just throws
Out a delicate hint, that a secret he knows,
A mistake into which she once happened to fall,
She thought she was married, but wasn't--that's all,
A slight error that gave them a mother apiece;
Making Marie her daughter, instead of her niece;
So she gives her consent, but I really must say,
'Twas brought about in a most scandalous way

LOVE AND LOYALTY.

AN EPISODE IN ENGLISH HISTORY.

CHAPTER I.

"DERBY still holds Latham Castle, say you, Fairfax? The Lord of his infinite mercy prompt him to instant submission, so may much shedding of blood be averted."

Thus spoke the stern leader of the Puritan armies.

"Amen!" fervently replied Fairfax, "Heaven might of a certainty soften his obduracy, but, while the sinful man worketh within him, he will, or I misdoubt me much, do battle 'till the death."

"To the death let it be then, if he so willeth; he is an audacious traitor, and a blindly obdurate upholder of the Heaven-doomed Stuarts," savagely answered Cromwell, but almost instantly moderating his angry tone into a nasal whine, as he continued, "The sword of the Lord and of Gideon is all powerful to smite, and the great work must be accomplished."

"Doubtless, doubtless," replied Fairfax, who, of all the individuals composing the Puritan camp, affected least that canting peculiarity of expression which was then so generally adopted. "Doubtless, an we can do so with honor."

"Honor!" echoed Cromwell, contemptuously; "and what think you doth honor weigh in comparison with religion?"

"Methought they were inseparable," quietly responded Fairfax.

"And so they are, but not that foolish pride of heart which would point out a line of conduct for itself, and say, to the right or the left shall I not swerve. I tell thee what, Fairfax, thou art too much hedged round with doubts and scruples, to yield heart and hand to what we propose. The Lord's will must be executed, whatever it be; answer me, hast thou courage to help the work, even in opposition to thy very conscience?"

"Conscience," replied Fairfax, seriously, "is a rigid tutor, and will severely punish those who mind not its teaching."

"Pshaw! thou 'rt craven-hearted!" Cromwell perceived by the bright flash that kindled in the eye of Fairfax, that he had gone too far, so, stretching forth his hand, he grasped his ardently, and, in a tone of frank earnestness resumed:

"Dear brother, in the cause, even as my own life art thou to me, nor would I ask thee to encounter aught that would bring a flush of shame into that honest cheek."

Generous and unsuspecting, Fairfax forgot his anger on the instant, and with hearty sincerity returned the proffered grasp. Little did he think what direful thought had, for the first time, seized on Cromwell's brain; a thought which once conceived, was nurtured day by day, until in the blood of his liege king and master, it was fatally developed. The before-mentioned conversation was one amongst the many that the designing and ambitious general was wont to hold about this time with his intimates, and those whom he could trust; wherein he darkly hinted at some startling matter which he had in view, cunningly contriving to introduce the subject by little and little, until the repetition broke the fearful nature of the undertaking.

Scarcely had they concluded, when a chamberlain

announced the arrival of a messenger from the division of the army under Fairfax's deputy, Colonel Exeter, one "Anak Wrestle-with-sin," and as he entered, he certainly appeared to merit the appellation.

He was a gaunt, bony, loosely-put-together specimen of mortality, with a face as white as chalk, excepting an extensive promontory of nose, which gradually deepened from a light peach-color to a vivid pink; he wore a very much discolored buff-leather jerkin, with sundry belts of the same material, containing a small defensive armory; enormous jack-boots enveloped his lank legs, while his high, conical hat was stuffed down to his very nose, which stuck straight out beneath the brim, and seemed to be the only thing that prevented his face from disappearing altogether. He made only one long stride into the room, and having settled himself, stuck there, bolt upright, without a single movement to indicate vitality, except the motion of his thin, white lips, as he spoke.

Cromwell first addressed him, and, as was usual with him, when conversing with such persons, exaggerated his conventional drawl: "In the Lord's name I bid thee welcome, brother in the glorious cause. Doubtless thou bringest news from the general's division."

With a twang, something like a broken-winded bag-pipe, or a donkey with the best notes out of his voice, our lank friend replied:

"News have I brought—even from the camp of the enemy. Yea! verily, from the stronghold of the evil doer."

"Of good import, I hope?" shouted Fairfax, incapable of restraint, but checked by the wily leader, who, with an upward glance of still greater sancity, and a drawl of still increasing length, continued:

"Go on, brother, and bless our ears with thy glad tidings, I pray thee."

Anak elevated his snuffle, and, eyes all but closed, proceeded:

"Praise ye the mighty One, the Ruler of Israel, for the habitation of the stiff-necked is without a master, the family of the sinner is without its head."

"What sayest thou?" cried Cromwell, interrupting him eagerly, and forgetting, for the instant, intonation, "is Derby killed?"

"No, not killed," replied Anak, without opening his eyes, "but fled, no man knoweth whither."

"The Castle is then delivered into our hands," said Fairfax.

"I said not that, General, or had I lied most foully. The woman who calleth herself by the vain and worthless title of Countess, wife to him that is fled, still keeps it, and in answer to Brother Egerton's summons, sent this heathenish reply."

Cromwell snatched the letter and read:

"The Countess of Derby has not forgotten what she owes to her lawful King, and to her liege husband, and until she has lost both her honor and her life, *she will* defend her right."

"Obstinate, perverse woman!" cried Cromwell, tearing the sheet into pieces, and motioning Anak away: who, with one turn and a stride, quitted the apartment as he had entered.

There was a pause of a few moments. At last Cromwell, fixing a steady glance upon his companion, demanded,

"Fairfax! canst thou fight against a woman?"

"Why, sooth to say, it would not like me much," replied Fairfax. "I'd rather it were some score of men,—but were it my duty"——

"It is thy duty," sternly responded Cromwell. "I, thy General, command it. Latham Castle must be subdued at all risks."

"Be it so, an thou wilt," quietly rejoined Fairfax, rising

from his seat, "I shall do my devoir, though it be hard, and to my thinking most unseemly, to do battle with a female, be she whom she may."

"Come brother, thy hand," said Cromwell, with kindly emphasis, as they parted, "'tis the Lord's bidding, and not mine; go, strengthened in the right, and Heaven itself will send its lightnings to destroy thine enemies."

CHAPTER II.

One morning, in the month of February, 1644, the family of Latham Castle was assembled in the great hall immediately after prayers, the beautiful liturgy of the Church of England being given every day by the Earl's domestic chaplain. The Countess, with her lovely sister, the Lady Elinor Beaufort, were sitting at their now customary work, preparing long strips of linen to use as bandages for such of their scant defenders as chanced to receive a wound, while three beautiful children, unconscious of the proximity of danger, played around them, without concern or hindrance.

"What a heavy sigh was there, sister sweet," remarked the Countess, "is that for the imminent peril in which thy sister dwelleth? or doth it chronicle the impossibility of the usual visit from a certain generally punctual cavalier?"

The Lady Elinor hung down her head, while her beautiful eyes were suffused with tears.

"Nay, Nelly, dear," said the Countess, tenderly flinging her arms around her sister's neck, "God knows we have enow to cause sorrow's rain to fall, without aught of our own making; forgive me, wilt not? Come, come, Radcliffe loves thee, dearly; thou art worthy of his, nay, of a monarch's love. And I do equally believe him worthy thine. So cheer thee, cheer thee, this storm will soon pass over, all will yet be well."

"Alas, my sister," said the sobbing Elinor, "bear with me, for I have a soul full of woman's fear."

"Fear," replied the Countess, with something like reproach in her accents, and more in the flash of her eloquent eye, "fear! what fear ye? not these Roundhead recreants?"

"No, no!"

"Not for thy lover's fealty?"

"Heaven forbid," fervently cried Elinor. "No, he's the soul of loyalty and truth, my very fear lies in the deep devotion of his faithful love."

"What mean you?"

"You recollect, dear Charlotte," continued she, "that when Molineux and I parted last, not foreknowing this cruel hindrance, he promised that I should see him again this very day. The castle is surrounded on all sides by vigilant and cruel Puritans. His devotedness to his royal master is well known, and should he attempt to gain an entrance"——

"He cannot be so mad," interrupted the Countess, "he would be lost."

"Then may I at once deplore his loss," tenderly rejoined Elinor; "for, if I know his heart, he will attempt it."

At that instant, several shots were heard in quick succession, followed almost immediately by a shot from the battlements of the Castle. And before either had time to breathe their thoughts, the door was burst open, and the noble Molineux Radcliffe was in the arms of his beloved one. The shock was almost too much for her, but, with a powerful effort, she checked the sensation which was creeping through her frame.

"My own, own love," said he, "look up, I'm here, my pledge is redeemed, my promise fulfilled, I'm here, here, to live or die with thee."

"My Radcliffe, my noble, my devoted Radcliffe"——

She could say no more—insensibility came to the relief of her over-wrought feelings. After a brief space, tended by Radcliffe and her sister, she awoke to happy consciousness, and seating her lover by her side, gave full scope to the intensity of her delight. With one hand in his, and her head resting on his manly breast, she entreated him to tell her how he had contrived to elude the vigilance of the enemy.

"To my own marvel, I confess, my bonny Nell," said Molineux, "when I set forth 't was with my last prayer upon my lips, thy safety, love, and that of my sinful soul."

"But see, dearest, you are wounded," exclaimed Elinor, in alarm, perceiving traces of blood upon his doublet.

"A scratch, beloved: a mere scratch," continued Radcliffe, "for which, believe me, I returned a deeper. I had passed undiscovered by the last sentinel on the rounds, and was just about to creep into the moat, when one of those prowling followers of the camp, whose business 'tis to give the *coup de grâce* to any wounded wretch whose appearance might betoken chance for plunder, seeing me move stealthly along, and no doubt thinking I was disabled, darted forward and aimed a knife at my heart. I warded off the blow, and seizing him by the throat, plunged at once into the deep water of the moat. The noise the fellow made in drowning, disturbed my Roundhead friends, who, as they saw me scramble up the moat, deliberately drew forth their match-locks, no doubt highly delighted at the opportunity to pick off a cavalier with safety to themselves. However, I ducked and dived, and in the very face of those unskillful marksmen, climbed to the outer postern, rendered invulnerable by Love. My friend Ogle, at the risk of his own life, threw a partisan—I grasped it, and reached the top in safety—rushed here to give the best confirmation of it—and methinks, if I solicit a kiss from those Hybla-shaming lips, it might not be considered too much for my heroic retreat."

Whatever might have been the result of that presumptuous demand, it was interrupted by the Countess, exclaiming, "Perhaps, Master Radcliffe would condescend to acknowledge one other individual in creation besides Elinor Beaufort." At the same time extending her ungloved hand toward the abstracted lover. Molineux knelt as he kissed the extended finger, soliciting pardon for his grave offence.

Now, the Countess had all along favored this love-suit; but the earl, to whose guardianship the Lady Elinor was entrusted, deemed her too rich a prize to be bestowed upon the cadet of a noble house—a mere soldier of fortune: for alas! poor Radcliffe ranked in the category of younger brotherhood: leading the conversation dexterously to the interesting point, she continued:

"Molineux, I know and estimate your good qualities, but my lord, who has the precious casket in his charge, has all along expressed a determination that she shall become the mistress of some noble house."

"She shall"——

"Nay, don't interrupt me, Sir Hector. Had I my will, you should not wait long before your wishes should be accomplished. That you love Elinor with a true and whole heart, I do sacredly believe, and would that it were in my sole power to pay you with her hand, no petty recompense."

"A prize, a rich and peerless prize, that kings might battle for, and be raised higher than their thrones in winning," replied Molineux, fervently gazing in her flashing eye, which kindled with responsive enthusiasm as he spoke. "I am not worthy of her now, but by the cross of my good sword, I'll win for her a name that none dare question; when that I have achieved, though all men call it paramount, yet will I shame to offer it, so great will be the disparity between my desert and her great excellence."

"Nay, my own love," replied the beautiful and happy Elinor, "whatever may befall, I can but be the gainer by linking my poor life with so much nobleness. But your wound bleeds afresh, let me bind my scarf around it. There! it does not hurt thee now, my own liege love and true knight? This scarf be my gage that *for good or for ill, in life and to death, I am thine, and thine only.*"

Molineux, fervently pressing the scarf to his breast, knelt, and kissing the hilt of his sword, exclaimed with ardor:

"*Hear me, and register my vow, oh, Heaven! when in thought, word, or act, I swerve from duty to my heart's choice, may I be accounted recreant knight, false gentleman, and base, disloyal knave.*"

"By my halidome, but this is most romantic troth pledging," said the Countess, "and I misdoubt me much that I should countenance it."

At that moment, a servant was hastily ushered into the hall, crying:

"For Heaven's grace, my dear Lady, retire to some more secure apartment. The enemy are in motion, and several howitzers and a mortar-piece are pointed directly towards this quarter."

Before the Countess could express her determination to remain at any risk, with a tremendous crash, a grenade swept through the window, exploding in the very midst, but most providentially, without injuring any of the party.

"Away, sir," she exclaimed, drawing herself up to the extremity of her majestic height, "let my brave defenders know, that a brave woman is at their head, and hark ye, if there be a coward in my suit, let him but show himself by his prating of surrender, and he shall be hanged up as a mark for the Roundheads to practice against."

As the Earl had gone to Douglass for supplies, and could not by any possibility be expected to return within a month, the officers of the small garrison held a brief council. Some advocated a steady and continued defence, but the impetuous and ardent Radcliffe was for an instant sally.

"Look, gentlemen," he exclaimed, pointing through a small, embrased window, "look, where those rascally knaves have planted their howitzers, full against our lady's own apartment. As we are true men and loyal, this is not to be borne."

With a sudden flash of excitement, he started to his feet, crying with increased energy, "Would it not be a glorious deed to wrest those villainous engines from them? See, by Heaven, they are firing them, even now. Some damnable traitor must have informed them where the Countess keeps. What say you, sirs, shall we strike one blow for the safety of our beloved mistress?"

"We will, we will!" they all shouted simultaneously, catching up the enthusiasm of Radcliffe.

"'Tis well," replied Molineux, now as fearfully calm as he was before excited. "You, Hawthorne, collect the men in parties from the opposite battlements, to the amount of five hundred. I would not have more had we a million. Then wait for me at the eastern portcullis; through the shelter of yon wreath of fog we may move down upon them unawares. *Allons! mes amis, and Heaven defend the right!*

CHAPTER III.

The diminutive but gallant band issued noiselessly forth, and fell unexpectedly upon the advanced post of the enemy. Sharp and furious was the encounter; the impetuosity of young Radcliffe, and the determined bravery of his men, animated as they were both by his voice and example, prevailed over every obstacle. After above an hour's hard fighting, they succeeded in driving the besiegers from their trenches; demolished, altogether, the embankment raised opposite to the Countess's apartment; nailed up and overturned the cannon into the moat, and carried back in triumph the mortar piece which had threatened so much injury, after having killed some three-score of the Roundheads, and all with the insignificant loss of three men. As this handful of gallant hearts entered the Keep, they were received with a shout of gratulation and welcome, which wrought them up to such a pitch of enthusiasm, that had they been called upon to face the universe in arms, led by such a captain, not one would have hesitated.

The Countess having caused them to be brought into the grand hall, thanked them with tearful eyes, calling them her children, her friends, her deliverers; not one individual of that group but mentally swore that while life's current ran within his veins, its every drop should be devoted to their gracious lady's service. Turning to Radcliffe as the men departed, "Molineux" said she, "now do I feel as though I were, indeed thy sister; mayst thou, ere long, have right to own thyself my brother; but go, receive the best reward to loyal gentleman and good soldier, the smile of thy lady-love.

She waits thee in the oratory, fearing to stay, lest the fullness of her joy overflowing into tears, might make thee deem her of too weak a nature for thy indomitable spirit."

Returning heartful thanks for the Countess's cheering words, it was not long ere Radcliffe found his beloved one, and there kneeling before the sacred altar, they mingled prayers together for the safety of their honored kinswoman. What more they said or did, who that has passed the first delicious hours of love's unchecked and blissful flow, but can imagine? Suffice it to say, that no two hearts in Christendom beat with a more happy throb than did those of Molineux and Elinor, in the very neighborhood of danger, and not knowing at what moment a savage assault might be made upon their very threshold. So rapt were they, and so regardless of external things, that, at her lover's solicitation, Elinor took up her cithern, and in an exquisitely sweet voice, whose low musically thrilling tones seemed almost to absorb the very sense, steeping the soul in ecstasy, warbled the following romaunt:

"'Tis a midsummer's eve, and the gorgeous west
Glows with the setting sun's rich behest;
Mild Zephyrus whispers his love to the heath,
As placidly sweet as an infant's breath.

"Now twilight is donning her mantle of grey,
To steal a last kiss from the parting day;
Reluctant she lingers, then follows amain,
Enshrouding the earth in her dusky train.

"A youth and maid gaze on the scene, to whom
No brightness is lost in the deepening gloom,
And the varying beauties of earth and sky,
Like a shadowy dream pass unheeded by.

"On sombre wings borne, now comes the dull night,
But their sunny thoughts from a halo so bright,
They feel not time pass, 'till the love-nurtured spell
Is broke! they must part; 'tis the deep curfew bell.

Their love 's yet unspoken, one glance their adieu,
Yet Heaven ne'er smiled on affection more true,
No hearts more devoted earth's compass within,
Than the hearts of young Raymond and fair Madelin."

Oh! how delicious beyond all form of expression are those moments when, in the confidence of trusting love, two youthful hearts hold sweet communion, uncankered by one jealous thought, unruffled by one suspicious doubt, but each seeing its own truthfulness reflected in the other—then all is JOY, all hope, all happiness!

CHAPTER IV.

FOR upwards of three weeks did that courageous few, headed and cheered by the truest wife and noblest lady in the land, hold Latham Castle against the assailants; but notwithstanding that every individual put the best face he could upon the matter, yet did they each, to himself, begin reluctantly to acknowledge that hope was almost gone; their ammunition all but exhausted, their provisions lamentably scarce, and still another week might elapse before the expected succor should arrive. Three thousand of the besiegers, according to their own account, perished before the walls of that heroically defended keep.

Fairfax, either from shame, or else called away to other duty, left the command to one Rigby, a malevolent and implacable enemy to the Earl—naturally of a merciless disposition, and consequently the fittest instrument to carry out Cromwell's cruel order.

Matters were in this desperate state within the garrison,

when they observed, one morning, a herald, with a trumpeter, approaching the draw-bridge. They were ushered into the hall of state, where, seated, magnificently dressed, and surrounded by her soldiers and household, all wearing in their looks the appearance of animated devotion, they beheld the Countess.

"Well, Sir Herald," demanded she, haughtily, "what pressing message doth this traitor now send?"

"Gracious madam," replied the herald, "Colonel Rigby commands me to say that due consideration and quarter will be given, even now, after so many murders have been committed"——

"By him and his rebel gang," fiercely interrupted Radcliffe, but a look from the Countess restrained him from proceeding.

"Go on, Sir Herald," she quietly continued, turning to him.

"The Colonel desires me to add, that if within five hours from the receipt of this summons, this castle be not surrendered without reserve, his imperative orders are, to carry it by assault, and without reservation of age or sex, to put every living creature within its walls, to death." Radcliffe gasped! a low crunching of teeth might be heard, but none spoke.

"Is that all, sir," said the Countess, calmly.

"All! gracious madam."

"May it please you retire; we have doubtless a few moments for consideration before you return?"

"Of a certainty."

"No sooner had the herald left the hall, than Molineux started up, his face livid with compressed rage, and his whole frame shivering with excitement. "Gracious lady, pardon," he exclaimed, "but that foul braggart, that butcherly traitor, has driven me beside myself; it was with much ado I restrained myself from felling this brute messenger on the instant. Oh, God in heaven," he continued, throwing himself on his knees, "grant that I may meet this base-born dastard face to face!"

"Rise, rise, Molineux," said the Countess, "this is a moment for calmness and cool deliberation, not for imprudent ardor. One word for all, my noble officers, my gallant men, what shall we do; hold on to the last, and risk this slaughter, or succumb to their debasing mercy? I need not ask the question; 'tis answered in those flashing eyes; as for me, by the grace of Heaven, and by the help of God, I will yet defend my lord's heritage. Go ye with me?"

"To the death! to the death!" was the heart-uttered response of all.

"Enough! admit the messenger." Regarding him with a look of majestic dignity, she exclaimed—

"Doubtless thy master thinks that we are in a piteous strait. Know, sir, that I have received assurance that my noble lord will be here, perhaps before thou gettest back; and further, tell the insolent rebel, Rigby, that if he presumes to send another such demand, I'll have the messenger hanged before his very eyes! away!"

That day and night all was most hopeless despondency within that poor, starving garrison, but what was their dismay, when by morning's light they found that their stay, their sole dependence, Radcliffe, was missing, and with him, full two hundred of the choicest men-at-arms. The idea of treachery was scouted on the instant; but where could he have gone to? what wild scheme could he have engaged in? The suspense did not continue long, for soon a mysterious movement seemed to take place amongst the enemy's lines, and as this was the day appointed for the final assault, all was perturbation and despair. Suddenly there was heard a distant anc prolonged shout; it reached the ears of the Countess, and falling on her knees, she exclaimed, "My lord, my lord, my loved, my honored husband! he comes, and we are saved!" Causing the guns to fire a *feu de joie*, she ordered the banner of the house of Derby to be hoisted to its topmost height. She rushed to the highest tower to catch the first glimpse of the—oh, how intensely welcome, succor. Meanwhile the enemy began to file off in an opposite direction to that from whence the shouting proceeded, in rapid but orderly retreat, the men from the battlements hailing them with derisive cheers. The siege was raised, and ere an hour had passed, all that vast array was lost in the distance. Still and still the loud hurrah of the approaching rescuers was heard, and every eye was strained in the direction. Soon a long line of men-at-arms was seen approaching, stretching across an immense extent, and looking like the advance-guard of a mighty host, but upon approaching nearer, they were discovered to be alone. The truth flashed across the Countess' mind upon the instant. "My brave, my noble Radcliffe," she exclaimed, "well hast thou won thy guerdon!"

Shortly, Radcliffe, for it was indeed he who had stolen forth with his partisans in the dead of night, and without breathing a syllable of his intention to any but those concerned, fearing that his desperate manœuvre should be countermanded, entered the portcullis with his two hundred devoted followers, receiving, as they progressed, a shout from their comrades, which proceeded even to the Puritan army, giving them increased impetus in their retreat.

The stratagem had full success, nor had the enemy time to be apprised of their mistake, for the next day the Earl arrived, bringing with him a reinforcement of ten thousand men, commanded by Prince Rupert, and an ample supply of provisions.

The meeting between the Earl and his heroic wife was utterly indescribable, and when she related the many deeds of bravery performed by young Radcliffe, and particularly the last act of devotedness by which he had preserved the castle, it need not be told that he made no further opposition to his marriage with the Lady Elinor; indeed, he himself assisted at the solemnization, which took place in the little oratory just two months afterwards.

NOTE.—February, 1644—This month was rendered notable by a famous resistance made by Charlotte, Countess of Derby, while her lord was absent in pursuit of supplies, she having held Latham Castle against six thousand of the parliament's army, commanded at different times by Fairfax, Exeter and Rigby, for one whole month, killing, by their own account, three thousand men by successful sallies and skillful manœuvering, so that her husband found his castle safe at his return.

English History.

PAULINE.

If you hav'n't yet been
    To visit Pauline,
It's representation at Wallack's I mean,
    While memory's green,
And the Trials and Terrors of sweet Laura Keene
Are fresh in my mind—brought about by the hein-
ous offences of Lester, whose *rôle* is between
A dove and a hawk, if you know what I mean,
The most elegant scoundrel that ever was seen,
A Chesterfield cut-throat so aristocratical,
Graciously rude and indeed problematical,
    Pale and Piratical;
Just such a "creature" as causes lymphathetical
Boarding-school misses to feel quite extatical.

ACT THE FIRST.

Seriatim, the plot to unfold,
Which without any doubt is remarkably bold,
    And new, we are told
(For the matter of that, it will never be old),
You'll please to imagine a brilliant and rare
    Pavilion somewhere
In France, looking out on a pleasant parterre.
    Seated quietly there

Are a daughter and mother, affectionate pair,
(Mrs. Stephens, *La Fille*, Mrs. Cramer, *La Mère*).
It's a beautiful scene—by the way it's but fair
To let it be known, as his truest well-wisher would,
All the fine pictures are painted by Isherwood.
It must be confessed that with wonderful skill
The son of a quill
Who fashioned the drama, begins it so dozily,
Quiet and prosily,
Every one thinks he'll attend to it cozily,
Placid and pleasantly,
Little expecting the row we'll have presently.
And now to continue, the pretty Pauline,
Miss Keene,
I mean,
Burst out like a sun-ray upon the dull scene,
And for a few moments it's very serene;
'Till a jockey in green—
Appropriate colors—requests her to tell
A story that sounds like a regular sell,
About Tigers and Jungles;
A Count, too, who most unaccountably blunders,
In killing the "critter,"
The way that he "fit" her.
And hit her,
And how that it wasn't convenient to quit her,
Except on a litter.
She piles it all up in a deuce of a twitter,
And then she proceeds quite correctly to faint a bit,
Thinking him dead, but the fact is, he ain't a bit.
Meanwhile the neighbors surrounding the place,
Prepare to assist in the "joys of the chase;"
And in beating around

The contiguous ground,
It's evident something alarming they've found—
A boar very likely, such monsters abound
In such pieces,—phsaw ! bless me,—I mean in such places,
There's fear in the faces
Of pretty Pauline and her Cousin and Mother,
For somehow or other
The animal's rude to the son and the brother,
By Reynold's enacted, who bravely to lick him meant,
Hadn't the best, and is in a predicament;
Up and down fighting they have on the sward,
And the brute is decidedly running him hard,
When in comes De Beauchamp or Mr. Bernard,
A little mite "scar'd."

Unsteady and shaky and queer in the wrist,
From terror, or toddies he'd taken at yest-
erday's banquet, a hundred to one but he'd missed,
When in glides the Count, and right out of his fist,
He snatches the musket,
And up to his "weskit,"
He raises and fires it, when right through the tusk it
Is safe to suppose that Mr. Boar has the bullet in,
Slap through the gullet, in
Rushes "the crowd" with "the cousin and son,"
And De Beauvale, that's Lester, says—"Very good gun;"
The meeting between
The Count and Pauline,
To duly appreciate has to be seen;
She shivers and shakes,
And quivers and quakes,
While *á la Seigneur*, the Count haughtily makes
Love in a manner, 'tis perfectly certain, ain't

Anything else but extremely impertinent;
    Using his eyes,
    To the lady's surprise
As if he had meant to anathematize
The whole of the family, says—but he lies,
As the sequel will prove he's a capital prize
    In the marrying lottery—
    Choose him she ought, or he
Knows what he'll do—then her eyes become watery,
    Seeing he's caught her, he
Grins like a good-looking vampire in fun,
    Upon every one,
    While the "cousin and son,"
Young Lucian de Nerval, looks nervously on;
For his recent delivery not at all grateful, he
Strokes his imperial and scowls on him hatefully;
And this being all that is proper to know,
The curtain descends on a brilliant Tableau.

    You'll understand here
    There's a lapse of a year,
    During which 'twould appear
The Count marries Pauline—but I won't interfere
With the thread of the narrative now waxing queer.

ACT THE SECOND,

    Discloses a small Cabaret,
A broken-down groggery out of the way,

Where pretty Pauline soon arrives with her "shay."
She's going to pay
A visit to-day,
Quite extempore,
To Horace, her husband, and wants a relay,
An order, the hostess, I'm sorry to say,
Is really unable just now to obey,
For there's not a postillion, though brave as he may,
Will venture his clay,
Through fear of becoming to brigands a prey,
Who lately in murder made such a display.
Pauline, very properly, says that she'll stay
Where she's safe, and is thinking to order a quail
For supper when Harriet comes in—(Mrs. Hale),
And they quietly rail
At their lords, and assail
Their faults and their weaknesses; each has her tale—
Pauline's enough to make any one pale,
Though it mainly embraced
Count Horace's—her husband's—equestrian taste;
It happened that she
Discovered that he
Directed *one horse* should in readiness be,
Perpetually,
All saddled and bridled, and ready to flee;
And when Max and Henri,
(Messieurs Chandler and Lee)
Once paid him a visit, why then he had *three!*
She can't make it out,
Or know what it's about,
Although of his honor she hasn't a doubt.
But there isn't much time to discuss the thing here,
For, "Talk of the fiend," the whole trio appear.

Count Henri de Beauvale, and Henri and Max,
With guns at their backs,
But its easy to see that their courtesy's lax,
For Horace attacks
The Countess for coming without his permission,
And she's in a very distressing condition;
So thinking 'tis better her grief to disperse, he
Talks blandly enough, though he feels *vice versa*,
And quelling a curse, he
Conveys her right off to the "Chateau de Burcy."

This awkward rencontre it's evident suits
Not the men in the boots,
But they are quickly consoled by a brace of cheroots;
And one of them—Max, I think—rudely salutes
Mrs. Walcott, who calls them a couple of brutes.

And now we 're transported to "Normandy's shore,"
Where the brother of Pauline has come to explore,
Some remarkable ruins he'd heard of before;
And he will not give o'er
His purpose, though thunder will probably roar,
And the threatening heavens a cataract pour.
(This scene is so real, one prudent old fellow,
Looked close, to be certain he had an umbrella).

Anon to intense and remarkably slow
Music we go
To the room of Pauline, in the lonely chateau,
Where she's sitting, in spirits remarkably low;
The little distinction 'twixt *husband* and *beau*
She's beginning to know,
And has a suspicion she's somewhat *de trop*.

For certainly though
Toute à fait, comme il faut,
Her brilliant *boudoir* can but scantly show
Available means of amusement, and so,
As in spite of herself she's beginning to grow,
Excited and nervous and very *distrait,*
She rings up friend Rea,
The Milesian Malay,
Costumed in a strikingly picturesque way,
All turbann'd and braceleted up to the life,
A kind of a hyf-
alutin, "tame tiger" to Horace's wife,
With a double bass voice and an "ell" of a knife.
She endeavors to pump him, to cross him and wind him, and
Can't get a word from the cunning East Indiaman.
Putting on airs,
She sends him down stairs,
Reads "Uncle Tom's Cabin" awhile and declares,
It don't interest her, and therefore prepares
To find from the book-case a volume that bears
A pleasanter character—doing that thing,
She touches somehow a mysterious spring,
When slowly the book-case commences to swing
Right round on its axis,
And she upon one of Count Horace's tracks is;
For, dreadful to see—there's *a hole in the wall.*
To be sure it's but small,
Though enough to appall,
'Twas so chilly—a lady without any shawl.
With the tact of a woman she fathoms it all,
Exclaiming, "Whenever *he* happens to fall
In love," as is likely with every new face,
This must be the place

Where he takes his disgrace-
ful companions, good Heavens! if that be the case,
I'll soon give him "Caudle" for conduct so base.
Meanwhile though the tempest is raging without,
Despite of the lightning that flashes about,
She imprudently will at the window look out,
Where she sees what immediately banishes doubt:
Her husband, Count Horace, with Max and Henri,
And the reprobate three
Are carrying something wrapt up in a cloak;
By the aid of a vivid electrical stroke,
She perceives *'tis a female*, a very bad joke
To Pauline, who now seizes the light with temerity,
Then with dexterity
Touches the spring, and to test its sincerity,
Down to the cellar descends with celerity;
Where she arrives just in time to take part
In a scene that, to view merely makes the blood start
Right away from each heart.
Possessing the very peculiar traits
Of a salade of horrors dressed *à la Française*,
Consisting of crimes of so fearful a texture,
That murder's the least in the awful admixture.
True it is the act ends
With a splendid effect that makes ample amends
For whatever offends
True taste, and imbues with a ray of vitality,
This gallimaufry of Gallic morality.
Perhaps it's as well to inform you that here
There takes place, another delay of a year,
Or near.
So being apprised of that fact,
I'll take you at once to

THE THIRD, AND LAST ACT,

Where Count Horace de Beauvale appears once again,
The sweetest of men,
A delicate plant from the uppermost ten.
Pauline has departed,
And he's broken-hearted,
And now he's come back to the place where he started.
To rouse up his spirits the best way in life,
By taking a wife.
Mam'zelle de Nerval he's been able to win,
It's a good speculation we know to begin,
For Lucian comes in,
And curious enough, only twenty-five min-
utes before the betrothal—as nearest of kin,
He's to give her away and to settle the pin-
Money, titles, and tin,
And the style he goes on is to Moses a sin.
He comes it so grand,
He'll not condescend to take Horace's hand,
Who won't understand,
The cut, 'till he's put all the business through.
Because, *entre nous*,
She's, as Lucian insinuates, rich as a Jew.
Now the notary comes, and the witnesses too,
And there's nothing to do,
But the contract to sign and distribute the u-
-sual kisses and blisses and compliments due.
Now heedless of guile,
La belle Fiancée writes her name on the file.
Then Horace advances in drawing-room style,
His single eye upon Lucian the while,
In a manner to rile

The sweetest of tempers right up to the bile.
'Twas as much as to say "Now I'm sure of the pile."
Lucian immediately waxes irascible,
Horace's features are pale and impassible.
"Scoundrel!" the former cries, "would you then dare
To write your name there,
And doom to despair
Another poor victim?" that makes Horace stare.
Then Lucian berates him with might and with main,
Declares he's the bane
Of his household, and if it so happened the twain
Had been married, 'twould never get over the stain.
To which Horace replies—"I'm afraid we'll have rain."
Though mad with vexation,
Concealed perturbation,
And rage at the incomplete solemnization,
Without hesitation,
Or manifestation of slightest sensation,
From Lucian he placidly asks explanation;
Who, looking all mystery, goes to the back
And leads in Pauline, dressed in very deep black.
The people all gaze in dismay and with reason,
For she was supposed to be dead a whole season.
But our hero's *sang froid*
Even this cannot thaw;
He looks at the new comer
Cool as a cucum'er,
Plainly implying he don't care a straw.
The ladies go out,
With the notary too, and the rest of the rout.
And Horace says, seemingly, not a bit nettled,
To Lucian, "This little account must be settled."
A sudden and singular duel they fight,

And further description would hardly be right.
But if you are curious to know how they do it,
Just purchase a ticket and see them go through it,
What we ourself, think of this drama so terrible,
He'll, with permission, expound in a parable.
A Lion once thought that he'd give a great feast,
To every beast
Within his dominions, some hundred at least;
So sent for his cook,
An excellent one, who'd read Kitchener's book,
And told him to furnish it on his own hook;
To spare no expense
On any pretence,
But get up a banquet in such sort of way,
As the palate to suit of each fair *gourmet.*
The cook then retired,
And duly inspired
With love for his art—in the manner desired,
Produced a repast which the Lion admired.
But lifting a cover, he cried, in a flame,
"What garbage is this?" "Why, my lord," said the cook,
With a confident look,
"It's a *thistle*, some folks, nay and very genteel,
Would rather have that than aught else for a meal."
He lifted another—'twas nothing but mud.
It fired his blood.
"Off with it!" he cried, "I have seen quite enough
Of this villainous stuff."
But the cook unconcerned at such a rebuff,
Replied, "My dear lord,
If *Lions* alone were to dine at your board,
To your own individual taste 'twould be stored.
Pray wait till the banquet is over and deign

To form your deductions from what doth remain."
The Lion consented, and found the *cuisine*,
Although 'twas the nastiest ever was seen,
The very best fare for the animal host,
And the *filthiest garbage* was relished the most.
Indeed, it was said, he himself, on the sly,
Had a little put by,
Rather liking the taste; but that must be a lie.

O'DEARMID'S RIDE.

Once upon a time, a mighty long while ago, when Ireland's green fields and pleasant valleys belonged to those who had a natural right to them—before her Saxon neighbors overspread the beautiful land, despoiling the rightful possessors of the soil, heaping mountain loads of oppression upon the poor inhabitants, and then deriding them because they could not stand as straight as they did formerly—there happened to live in the town of Clonmakilty, a well to do, industrious, and kindly-hearted weaver, whose name was Connach O'Dearmid.

Now, at this time, there was not a country in Christendom could produce such splendid fabrics of every description, from the heavily woven cloth of gold, down to the exquisite linen, whose texture was so fine that yards upon yards of it could be drawn through a wedding ring; and amongst all the looms in the land, none turned out the equal of Connach O'Dearmid's—and mind you, the weaver then, was not the hunger-wasted, gaunt, phantom sort of death-in-life object, one may now see occasionally peering from a miserable aperture called a window, in the very centre of Ireland's once proud Capital. No, indeed! He had his servants and his grooms, and retinue like a nobleman.

And if the kings and warriors had their bards to chronicle their high achievements, and inspired minstrels to sing them, so had the handicrafts' man his, to hymn the still prouder deeds of holy labor.

A fine, high-spirited, happy and contented people were they then, until the insatiable and cunning Islanders close by, after vainly endeavoring by open warfare to subdue them, secretly introduced the fruitful elements of discord, which unhappily divided those who never more can be united. Colonies of a strange and utterly antagonistic blood and breed, were planted in their midst; a new religion, brought forth and nurtured with ecclesiastical zeal, that most fatal of feuds which results from a difference of faith: is it surprising then that, robbed of their inheritance and driven into the woods and savage hiding-places, their hearths usurped and their altars desecrated—is it to be wondered at, that the poor persecuted people without shelter, without food, and most especially without education, should slowly but surely have retrogaded, when all the rest of the world has advanced, until centuries of oppression have almost depopulated an entire nation?

But to go back to Connach. He happened, fortunately for himself, to live in a time when every man held his own, in quietness and peace; there were no 'evictions,' no homesteads levelled to enlarge my Lord So-and-So's estate, no damnable middle-men and agents to plunder equally the unfortunate tenant and absentee landlord, no intriguing double-faced demagogues, no selfish semi-political priests—all the accursed spawn of Saxon interference—but contentment, like an atmosphere of perpetual summer, rested upon the land, and amongst the happy Islanders none had more cause to be so than Connach, the weaver; a benignant fate having placed him in that most enviable of all positions—cheerful and well satisfied mediocrity—too high for privation to reach, and too low for envy to assail, with just sufficient intellect to comprehend and enjoy everything enjoyable in nature, and thoroughly impressed with that instinctive religion of the heart which causes it to expand in gratitude to the benign Giver of all good—true, loving and considerate in his family relations; free, open-handed, liberal and conscientious in his friendships.

Such were the characteristics of the representative of the O'Dearmids living at this time; and with but slight modifications of temperament, such have they been through succeeding generations, even up to the present time; for amidst the chances and changes of conquest, colonization and foreign absorption, the old house, land, name and occupation has been transmitted from son to son, in regular descent, and in the town of Clonmakilty may be seen at this very day—if the tourist should ever discover it—a tolerably good sized, but curiously patched tenement, bearing an exceedingly old fashioned sign board, on which is painted "Connach O'Dearmid, Weaver."

The cause of this strange preservation and uninterrupted transmission of name, property and occupation, for such a number of years, is satisfactorily explained in a family tradition which I had the pleasure of hearing from the present representative; and as it appeared to me to be more graphic in his own diction, I shall endeavor to present it to the reader as nearly as I can in his words.

"You know, sir, I suppose, that at the time luck fell upon the name of the O'Dearmids, makin' somewhere about, it might be, a thousand years ago—but the date doesn't matther a *thrawneen;* however, the fellow that owned it thin was a bowld-hearted, rollickin', ginerous divil-may-care boy, as iver breathed the breath o' life. Well, sir, the fairies, you know, was plintier thin nor they are now; by raysin, I suppose, that the ground was trod upon by the raal ould stock, an' not by furrin schamers and yalla-headed inthruders. More's the pity! A' most every family ov dacint behavior thin had somethin' or another in the shape ov a fairy visither; some had maybe a "*Puckaun*," them's the divil's own hounds at mischief, turnin' houses topsy-turvy, an' larropin lazy huzzies; others might stumble over a "*Liprechaun*," and if they looked sharp, for them's the greatest chates out, would get heaps o' money. Thin there was *Phoukas*, *Fetches*, *Banshees* and hundhereds of sich likes; to some families they comes as warnin's, to others as luck signs.

"But I'll tell you how we got one, sir—long life to him! He's here now, listenin' to every word I say—[he reverently lifted his hat as he spoke]—an' if I tell you a word of a lie, he'll make himself known somehow.

"Well, you must know, sir, that me great ancesther that brought us the luck, was oncet riding home from havin' ped a visit to his sweet-heart, for he was a coortin' at the time. The night was murdherin' dark, an' he was a little apprehinshus ov the "good people" for the fear of threadin' on a "fairy circle," or maybe disturbin' a frolic; so he rode mighty slow across the turf, for there was no roads at the time. Well, sir, all ov a sudden the moon bruck out from the black clouds like a red-hot ball from a cannon, an' began to run wild, as I heerd me father say, right across the sky. He had scarcely gazed an instant, with terror and wonder upon the quare capers the moon was cuttin', when on turning round agin he saw a phantom horseman ridin' close beside him, that imitated every action. When he galloped, it galloped; when he reined up, it did the same. Fear nearly paralyzed him. He tried to say his prayers, but memory had gone. Still, however, he urged his horse along rapidly; and altho' the sight froze his very blood, he couldn't keep his eyes off the black rider.

On comin' to a sharp turn in the road, what did he see but a little ould woman, sittin' upon a stone, right in the road ov the horseman, by his side, now grown into a solid substance—despite of his own terror, me ancesther shouted out to his strange companion:—

"'Howld hard, you black fool! Pull in, won't you? Don't you see the ould creather in the road? You'll run over her, you blackguard, you will!'

"But not a hand did the other move in restraint. On they went, full gallop.

"'For the love of Heaven, ould woman, clear the road!' cried me ancesther, but not a peg would she stir. Another instant, and the black horseman crashed right over the pooi ould sowl, and knocked her as flat as a pancake.

"'Ah! you murdherin' villain, you've done it; I knew you would!' shouted me ancesther, burnin' wid indignation, and reinin' up his horse as soon as ever he could; so did the other.

"What wid the cruelty and the impidence of the fella, my ancesther couldn't stand it any longer; so, turning his horse round, he let dhrive at him, but unluckily one of the big, black clouds gradually swally'd up the moon, an' in the darkness, the black horseman cut across the fields and vanished out of sight. As soon as he was gone, my bowld Connach groped his way back as well as he could to the place where the ould woman was run over, an' to his great surprise found her sittin' upon the same stone as quietly as iv nothin' had happened.

"'God save ye, stranger!' said the ould creathur.

"'God save ye kindly!' said Connach, 'an' I hope yer not hurted much?'

"'I'm not hurted at all, Misther Connach O'Dearmid, the Weaver!' says she.

"'What! you know me then, do you?" says he.

"'Bether nor ye do yerself!' says she. 'It's a good fortune that you desarve, Connach, an' it's a good fortune that ye'll get, both you an' yours, to the end o' time; for you're respectful an' kind to the ould an' the helpless. You're lovin' and dutiful to them that gav' ye life an' its blessin's, you're open-handed to the poor an' the needy, an' honest-hearted to the whole world besides.'

"'Bedad I'll come to you for a characther, if ever I'm in the want ov it. Bad-cess to me, av you haven't brought coals of fire into my cheeks, in spite ov the cowld weather!' says Connack, blushin' like a girl at the ould woman's praisin' him.

"'I'll do you a greater sarvice nor that,' says she. 'I'll tell ye yer faults.'

"'Fire away!' says Connach; 'let us have them.'

"'Get down from yer horse, an' sit by me upon this stone,' says she.

"'Wid all my heart,' says he, jumpin' off in a jiffy; for he was a little sprung, you see; the curse of Ireland, sthrong drink, was even then in bein'.

"'Now for thim faults,' said he, wid a laugh, as he sat down beside the ould woman. 'How many have I?'

"'One,' says she.

"'Is that all?' says he. 'Pooh! I know betther.'

"'Stop!' cries the ould woman, 'hear me out. That one, if suffered to remain within yer heart, will soon breed *all the rest.* For it's the fruitful parent of every crime that has a name.'

"Murdher! how ye frighten me,' says Connach. 'What the divil is it?"

"'*The love of strong drink!*' says the old woman, seriously, 'You behaved kindly to me, an' urged only by the feelin's of your kindly nature. I have the power to save you, an' I will, from this hour forward, as long as time exists. It will be the fault of you an' yours, if misfortunes, other than those nature demands, should fall upon yer name; for yer faults an' vicious inclinations shall be pointed out to you, by *fairy* power.'

"'Lord save us!' says my ancesther, frightened amost out of his siven senses, 'are you a fairy?'

"'I am!' says she, 'behold the proof!' wid that the ould rags and tatthers melted away, an' instead of a dirty-looking heap of deformity and wretchedness, Connach beheld a weeny form, scarcely as big as a blade ov grass, but as bright as if it had been made out o' sunbeams, standin' an' kissin' its love to him, while the tiniest an' most musical little voice, like the ringin' of fairy bells, tingled upon his ear, so small, but so distinct.—

> Farewell, Connach! thou hast had thy warning;
> Profit by it, and be happy!

"The fairy then vanished, an' me ancesther slept upon that identical stone until mornin', but when he woke up he didn't forget the fairy's caution; for not only did he never touch liquor, but he left it in his dyin' directions, to be transmitted from father to son, through every generation, that both house and lands should go away from him who should get the name ov Drunkard.

"An', to our credit be it spoke, we haven't had one yet, though some have needed and received the fairy's warnin' for that, as well as other faults, an' it's very wonderful the various ways they took to tell us ov them, that's been runnin' through the family histhory since that time, sometimes in a parable, then again in a dhream, now one way an' now another. Me own grandfather got his warnin' in a quare way. His prevalin' fault was harshness, an' a strong inclinin' to cruel conduct. He threated me father wickedly durin' his youth, an' at last, because he married unbeknownst to him, turned him right out ov doars.

"Well, it wasn't long afther that, grandfather was sittin'

mopin' alone—for in spite ov his hard natur', he missed his child—when all at oncet, when he was tryin' to nurse up his angry feelin', who should he see come in the door but a favorite cat ov his, that had just lost her kittens, tenderly carryin' in her mouth a bouncin' young rat. Well, grandfather naturally thought the cat was goin' to make her supper off the rat; but not a bit ov it. What does my bould puss do, but takes the rat into her basket, an' pets it up an' plays wid it in the most motherly way!

"At first, grandfather laughed till the tears run down his cheeks, at the fun ov the thing, to see the rat taken so much care of; but when the cat rowled over on her side, singin' 'purr-roo,' winkin' at grandfather, an' puttin' her paw as gingerly over the rat as if she was afraid ov breakin it, he knew immediately that there was some manein' in it. It was thin that it struck him all at once, that if it was an unnatural thing to see a cat nourishin' a creather that didn't belong to her specie at all at all, it was more unnatural a mortial sight to see a father turnin' his back upon his own flesh an' blood.

"'It's the warnin!" says he.

"Tears that he had never shed afore—for he was a hard man—fell in showers from his eyes, an' he prayed for grace to conquer his faults.

"Well, sir, before the night fell, my father an' his purty young wife was in the ould man's arms, an' greater joy and happiness seldom echoed through these ould rafters; for next to never doing any wrong, the most heart satisfyin' thing in creation is, to repent the wrong you've done!"

THE COMING OF KOSSUTH.

Potential muse of burning fluid, dangerously bright,
Come burst upon creation with intense explosive light—
A flame, the deleterious gases which amalgamate
In Barnum's great extinguisher, could not annihilate.

I pant to sing the glories, if I only knew the way,
The glories in extenso of that most auspicious day,
When with one soul the multitude poured forth from every
street
Great Freedom's incarnation, in one noble form to greet.

He's here, the age's topmost man by destiny designed
To lift up from oppression the down-trodden of mankind—
To preach in tones unanswerable Liberty's crusade,
And seek for suffering Hungary some temporary aid.

Anon, he will be with us, if his mission be not o'er,
For scarcely had he landed upon Staten's lovely shore
When perilling the Empire City's pageant of the morn,
His every wish was granted by the potent Hagadorn.

Alack, to lose our holiday, Manhattan murmured then,
The sanguine Staten Islander declares he *shall* have men
As many as are wanted, and sufficient money too,
He'll surely hurry back again, there's nothing more to do.

'Tis twelve, upon the Battery, the chill December breeze
Is playing most unpiteously among the Scotchmen's knees,
The Officers and Privates all fell frozen in the throat,
And Doctor Bostick's glad he's got his regulation coat.

And there is Sandford, Senior, legal Military Chief,
And there is Sandford Junior, his epitome in brief—
While proudly caracolling ride the gallant Brigadiers,
Each with his staff so brilliant, aiguletted to the ears.

The gay and dashing Vosburgh, yclept Major of Brigade,
With the engineer in chief, who boldly volunteered as aid,
A masterly diversion through the southern gate did make,
Each ardently determined that something he would take.

Well knew they then what enemies fate had for them in store,
For in their thirst for glory, they'd encountered them before—
So when a second Bayard led the passage to renown,
Each single-handed seized and put the potent spirits down.

But hark! the cannons echo through this section of the land,
Sound, Dodworth, sound—blow Shelton, blow—blow every brazen band,
Hang out your banners on the wall, the crimson, white, and green,
For Hagadorn and Company have left the Quarantine.

Come, wake up your enthusiasm, mercantile Broadway,
Show samples of your goods in economical display—

Who wouldn't be most liberal on such a fete as this,
Fling forth your woollen merchandise, bold Chittenden and Bliss.

You'll hang in goodly company, look over *vis-à-vis*,
Your neighbors, pious Bowen and sagacious MacNamee,
What burning words of freedom on their banners you may read,
Contrasting white and black, so emblematic of their creed.

All hail, immortal Genin, who with Jenny the divine
Rang loudly at Fame's bell-pull, like—that's no affair of mine—
That you have acted liberally, nobody can doubt,
Whatever feeling prompted you—why that's your own look out

I simply wish to say, sir, that your allegoric flag
Unquestionably, "off the bush" of banners "took the rag,"
The Magyar in verdant garb and turbaned Turk were there,
With Austria and Russia, the Hyena and the Bear.

But see, the city architect has *built* a pasquinade,
Those arches to the Park, of sundry barbers' poles are made—
The Satire would be perfect, had they printed at the top,
Instead of "Welcome Kossuth," "To the Public Shaving shop."

And now, commingled shouts and shots resounding through the air,
Conclusively proclaim there's something going on somewhere—

Enthusiastic citizens, with ardor overflowed,
And occasionally "villainous saltpetre" *would* explode.

He's coming—*there he is!* oh, mark that lofty pallid brow,
Those eyes deep sunk by sorrow, though they flash so brightly now,
His heart is dead within him surely, for his country's thrall,
And that vesture of black velvet seems to shroud it like a pall.

All inwardly acknowledge, as his lineaments they scan,
If perfection dwelt with humankind, there *is* a perfect man—
Determined, though benevolent, inflexible, yet mild,
Vast on the field or forum, in his home a simple child.

Now through the crowded thoroughfares he stems the surging tide,
While Kingsland, oleagineously smiling by his side,
Is thinking rather nervously, the truth to be confest,
Of the "soaping" the Chief Magistrate must give the city guest.

To tell how men their unconsidered lungs exhausted quite,
And ladies too, God bless them, ever on the side of right,
How brightening the light of day, they every window lined,
Like blessed "interventions" between Heaven and mankind.

To tell how in each neighborhood the welcome was renewed,
How in the Park, when it was dark, the soldiers were reviewed—
And after to the Irving House politely he was led,
How very glad the hero was to tumble into bed.

How in the night, all dressed in white, the Turners did parade,
Intending to disturb the dreamer with a serenade.
All these to tell, I know quite well, would caviare be,
And so adieu, and thanks to you who like my minstrelsye.

THE FAIRIES' WARNING.

"A BROTH of a boy" as ever stood in shoe-leather was Mickey Maguire. At hurling, wrestling, kicking football, or kicking up a shindy generally, there wasn't his equal in the barony. It would really do your heart good to see him with the fun glancing all over his face, like sunbeams dancing on the Shannon's water; "batein the flure," at a fair or a "pathern," with some bright-eyed "colleen," for there was no better hand at the jig in the country round, and that the girls knew mighty well, for there wasn't one of them that wouldn't walk a long mile to dance "Planxty Molly," or the "Ould Foxhunter," with "Sportin' Mickey Maguire."

Now, you must know that our friend, Mickey, was the sole and whole proprietor of the only mill, such as it was, in the entire vicinity, consequently, at the early part of his life, the hopper was continually going, and the result was a very comfortable living for the thriving miller; but, as he increased in years, instead of growing wise by experience, and husbanding his present resources, so that, in the event of accident, ill-health, or misfortune of any kind, he might have a trifle laid bye, to fall back upon; like to many of his countrymen, he lived from hand to mouth, spending exactly what he had, be that much or little. To be sure, a little always satisfied him when he had no more; but, if it were ever so large a sum, he invariably found a way to get rid of it. It may be readily conceived, therefore, that Mickey was quite unprepared for a rainy day—indeed, he never suffered himself to think of any thing beyond the passing moment. If to-day were only provided for, to-morrow might take care of itself.

By a singular continuance of equally balanced luck, Mickey Maguire managed, for a number of years to scramble on tolerably well. The mill was his banker, and it depended upon its yielding much or little as to whether he had a "high ould time" or merely satisfied the few wants to which he could circumscribe himself if necessary.

Notwithstanding the carelessness of his general disposition, Mickey was a diligent worker in working hours. No one ever saw him lounging about in idleness when labor was in demand; and, moreover, he was possessed of a true, honest, and benevolent heart—the latch of his door was never lifted without a welcome; rich or poor, it was all the same to him, A bite and a sup, given with pride to his equals and with joy to the hungry wayfarer, was ever to be had at his table, a seat by his cheerful chimney-corner, and a smoke of the pipe, and maybe a drop of mountain dew, was always proffered to the weary traveller.

It was a thousand pities that, to his many Heaven-sent virtues, he did not add the worldly one of prudence. But he didn't, and there's an end of the matter; nor was he to blame for it either, although some felt self-satisfied, money-scraping mortals, who, fortunately for their sons and successors, happen to have that same grovelling virtue to a vicious extent, elevate their eyes, shrug their shoulders, and cry shame upon the open hand, and all the time the would-be philosophers forget that they might as well find fault with an individual for the shape of his nose, or the color of his hair, as for the peculiarities of his temperament or disposition.

Well, it so happened that, year after year, Mickey's affairs got worse by degrees, and, in the thick of his distress, what does my bold miller do but takes unto himself a wife, as he said himself, "for to double his joy, and halve his sorrow, which was two to one in favor of some comfort according to the rule of three."

How it answered his expectations, it is unnecessary to inquire into, suffice it to say that, inasmuch as she brought him nothing in the way of worldly gain saving a pair of bright, blue eyes, and a stuff gown, all settled on herself, his prospects were not materially brighted by the alliance.

At last came the year of the bad harvest; the crops all failed, and the mill became quiet and desolate; that put the finishing stroke upon poor Mickey's perplexities, and, for the first time in his life, he began to think that there was such a thing as a future to provide for.

"Musha! then it's time for me to come to my senses," said he, one day, as he took up his pipe after a most unsatisfactory meal; "many's the fine night I spint as much as ud last us a month now, and, more betoken, it's suppin' sorra I am for that same, sure enough."

"Indeed, an' ye are, an' sarve you right, too," continued his helpmate. "But, it's me that's to be pitied—me, that niver had the good of it when it was goin', and now it's gone, it's me that'll have to cry salt tears for the want of it. Ah! if you had only put by ever so little of the money that you wasted in rollickin' about an' threatin' thim that gives you the cowld showldher now, you might snap yer fingers at the harvest; an' more betoken, I wouldn't be shamin' yer name by wearin' the same gownd at market an' at mass."

"Arra be aizy," said Micky, "where's the use in tellin' me what I know mighty well already? I've been a fool, as many's the one has been afore me, but I've had my jig, an' now the piper's to be paid, out ov my bones, if not out ov my pocket."

Well, to make a long story short, Mickey went down the hill in a hurry, as easy-tempered people generally do when the light of good fortune doesn't show them their way. Puzzled, confused, and blinded, in the thick darkness of distress, he made a few ineffectual struggles towards an upward movement, only to plunge deeper into the mire of disappointment; so that, tired at last of endeavoring to buffet against the current of misfortune, he made no exertion to sustain himself, but allowed it to float him where it chose. And it is not to be wondered at that, amidst the noisy, reckless revelry of the village whisky-shop, was his general anchorage, and, indeed, misfortune's most dangerous flood-tide could not have carried him into a worse haven, for when prospects grew brighter, and plenteous harvests again smiled upon the land, the habits which he had acquired in his despondency, rendered labor distasteful, and the old mill, once more in brisk demand, was deserted for the tippling-house.

Meantime, although the grain was brought as plentifully as ever, the business of the mill was scarcely sufficient to pay the weekly score chalked up against himself and his gay companions, for again they gathered round him, laughing outrageously at his maudlin jests, and pounding the tables at his drunken songs. The labor at the mill was neglected, for, without the eye of the master, work is badly done; his home was home no longer; his wife's once beloved voice grew cold and tame to his ears compared with the wild hurrahs of his alehouse friends.

Matters had nearly arrived at a desperate state when, one summer's evening, Mickey was making triangular surveys of the road as usual, his locomotion having been rendered extremely uncertain by copious libations of whisky-punch, when he happened to strike his foot against something metallic. Stopping in the midst of a fragmentary song, he stooped down, and found it was a *horse-shoe.*

"Hurrah!" shouted Mickey, at the top of his voice, "luck's come at last; an', indeed, not before it's wanted."

For, be it understood, that amongst the Irish peasantry, the finding of so common-place a thing as a horse-shoe, under such circumstances, is considered to be the precursor of the most illimitable good-fortune, and so it was with Mickey Maguire, although not exactly in the way he anticipated.

"Aha!" he shouted, in glee; "won't this fill the ould woman's heart with joy?" for with the certainty of approaching good luck came back all his warmth of feeling for his wife; it was but the pressure of calamity that deadened it for a while. "The blessed Heaven be praised for this," cried he, as with the earnestness of a hearted belief he knelt and offered up a prayer of deep-felt thankfulness for the precious gift which he felt assured would be the instrument of his delivery from distress.

Rising up, thoroughly subdued by the grateful feeling that pervaded every sense, he dashed the tears from his eyes, exclaiming, "I'll be a man again now, wid a blessin'." Then another mood came over him, and he kissed and hugged the horse-shoe, capering about, and making the echoes ring with his voluble delight.

Many were the castles in the air poor Mickey built before he reached home, and, amongst other notable intentions, I regret to say, that almost his first resolve was to give such a jollification to the whole country round, that the whisky should flow like pump-water, until every soul at the feast was as drunk as a lord.

He had scarcely made that last resolution when he reached his door, at which, according to his own account of what then transpired, he was just about to knock, when he felt a slight tug at the tails of his great coat, which made him hold back for a second. Thinking, however, that it was only his fancy, he lifted his hand again to knock at the door, when a little stronger pull at his coat-tail convinced him that there was something mysterious in it. The most intense fear took possession of him, as he tremblingly cried :—

"May the blessed saints above stand betune me and all harum. I do believe the good people is upon me."

He had scarcely said this when a clear, shrill, distinct, although infinitely small laugh ascended from the tufts of grass at his feet, simultaneously with which, his heels were tripped up, and with another tug at his coat, down he tumbled upon a little mound of "fairy clover," his head striking against a soft stone.

The blow stunned him for an instant, but when he opened his eyes again, what was his astonishment to see the whole extent of ground in his neighborhood perfectly alive with diminutive creatures in human form, and hundreds upon hundreds of tiny voices chirped out,

"Aha! Mickey Maguire,
Luck you'll have to your heart's desire."

"Musha then may long life to yees for that same, and may yees niver want divarshin yerselves," said Mickey, taking off his hat and making a low bow to the fairies. At that instant his attention was directed more especially to three frolicsome elves, who were carrying, kicking, and pushing along what appeared to him to be three very small apples, which were at length deposited immediately before him, when the whole multitude formed a circle round, and pointed to the diminutive fruit.

"What's them for, might I ask?" inquired Mickey. Whereupon a number of the fairies took up one of the apples, and presenting it to Mickey, they all shouted—

"*Eat this pippin, Mickey asthore,*
And see what you have seen before!"

Without hesitation Mickey swallowed the little apple at a mouthful, when lo! in an instant the house and hill vanished, and in its place appeared the old mill, as it was ten years before, the sound of perpetual industry echoed around, and soon he saw the semblance of himself, but without the care-worn traces which the ill-spent intervening time had marked upon his features. The ruddy hue of health was on his cheek, and content beamed from his bright eye. A deep regret smote at Mickey's heart as he closed his eyes upon the happy scene.

"Take it away from my sight," he cried, "it's too late, too late! Oh! for the wasted time once back again."

The voices of the fairies recalled him, as they sung—

"*The other, Mickey, eat, and see*
What now is, but what ne'er should be."

Mickey did what he was told, but with a sad heart and increasing apprehension. No sooner had he swallowed the second apple, than the mill disappeared, the busy hum of contented labor was hushed; he found himself within the house, and loud sobs of grief fell upon his ear. He looked around and beheld his wife; she was on her knees, her head buried in her hands, weeping. Presently a drunken uproar was heard, the door was suddenly burst open, and he saw himself, when all manhood was obliterated, and nothing but the beast remained. He saw himself in that brutal and degraded condition men would blush into their very hearts to behold themselves reduced to, did even one sense alone remain—the sense of sight.

"Horrible! horrible!" groaned Mickey, as he shut out the fearful apparition with his clenched hands. "Oh! for the unvitiated mind of other days; but it is too late! too late!

Again the fairy voices shouted—

> "*Eat, and see now with the last,*
> *The future purchased by the past.*"

Infinite terror took hold of him, and it was some time before he could summon up courage sufficient to swallow the apple, so conscious was he of the recompense which his hitherto wasted life deserved. At last, with a sullen determination to know the worst, he gulped it down desperately. The house vanished, and he saw nothing but a black, impenetrable cloud. Striving to pierce through the darkness, at last he distinguished a point of light, which spread and spread until it made a large, luminous circle, within which he could distinguish two forms. On looking closer, he saw that it was his wife and himself, but grown very, very old. There were also joyous children, whom he knew not, filling up the happy group. The man was reading from the household book, while a warm, glowing sunset illumined the beautiful picture.

He could have gazed for ever upon that calm, glorious scene, but that the tears coursed down his cheeks so abundantly as almost to take away his sight. Suddenly, close by that lovely group, another picture started into view in terrible contrast. It presented the aspect of a bleak, desolate, and dismal heath. Through the dull, misty atmosphere he gazed, and in a few moments discovered two wretched grave-mounds, the absence of all Christian memorial indicating that they were hastily thrown up, and in unconsecrated ground.

The strong man shuddered to the heart's core, as in burning letters his own name appeared on the miserable headboard.

In dreadful agony he uttered a wild cry, and fell insensible. When he came to himself he found that he was in his own bed, and his wife beside him, staunching, as well as she could, a severe cut in his head.

Not a word did Mickey say that whole night about his adventure with the "good people." But the next morning, although suffering considerably from his last evening's accident, he made a clean breast of it, and told his wife everything, together with his determination to take warning by the lessons the fairies had given him—a determination, I am glad to record, that he kept to the uttermost; for from that time forward there was not a soberer or more domestic and industrious man in the whole country round than Mickey Maguire, the miller.

Great was the delight he took, in after years, when seated in the chimney-corner, surrounded by a friendly circle of bouncing little Maguires, and listened to by such of the neighbors as might drop in to tea with the rich miller, to relate the circumstance which caused his reformation, and which he believed as implicitly as holy writ, although Mrs. Maguire would now and then try his temper by declaring that it was very strange indeed, for she was at the window all the time, and he wasn't down a minute, before she had him lying in bed with a wet towel on his forehead.

THE KILLING OF THE SHARK.

Come all ye jovial sportsmen bold,
Who love a famous lark,
A story, I'll to you unfold
Concerning of a shark.

Concerning of a shark, brave boys!
A cruel fish is he,
And the most voracious monster
That existeth in the sea.

There were four jolly fishermen,
And they sat down to dine,
In the Astor House, so noted
For good feed and glorious wine.

No better hostelrie you'll find,
Go search the country through,
By Coleman and by Stetson kept,
And both good men and true.

Now those sporting friends they did resolve,
As sportsmen always ought,
To go and have some fishing where
Good fish were to be caught.

Good fish were to be caught, my lads,
All with a hook so fine,
Declaring too, Black-fish and Blue
They'd get on to a line.

So they got their traps all ready,
And prepared to travel on,
Unto that grand old fishing-ground
That's called high Stonington.

And taking of the Omnibus,
These jovial anglers four,
Went on board the Massachusetts,
Where they'd often been before.

On board the Massachusetts, boys!
No finer boat is found;
She's the Queen of all the noble crafts
That steamed it through the Sound.

Commanded by a sailor bold,
Within whose breast does flow,
The heart's-blood of an honest man,
The gallant "Captain Joe!"

The gallant "Captain Joe," *Hurrah!*
Three cheers, each sportsman true!
For if you're of the real grit,
He's sure to "put you through!"

It was steaming through the Sound, my lads,
A fearful storm did rise;
It blew a perfect hurricane,
And pitch-black were the skies.

But not a soul knew aught of this,
Until its rage had passed,
So gallantly the Massachusetts
Battled with the blast.

Arrived at last at Stonington,
The fishermen did find,
That for their purpose, there was still
A great deal too much wind.

A great deal too much wind, brave boys,
All for the fishing boats;
And if they were capsized they feared
They'd "sinkers" be, not "floats."

And so they did resolve to go,
The leisure time to pass,
Unto a little creek hard by,
All for to fish for Bass.

The Captain he did go with them,
Likewise a man of *nous;*
The courteous and obliging host
Of Wadawanuck House.

Not long had they been fishing there,
All in that little stream;
When they had such amazing sport
As none of them would dream.

The Captain he soon found his line
Receive a sudden check;
He pulled with might and main and caught
A bottle by the neck!

But another of the party saw,
With wonder-opened eyes;
A strange fish slowly move along
Of an almighty size.

A strange fish with a peaked nose,
A body long and dark;
And all declared that he must be
A devil of a shark!

"A devil of a shark," it was,
As ever you did see!
And, said they, if we could tackle him
What jolly sport 'twould be.

They baited a "Virginny hook,"
All with a piece of clam;
For such fixin's, it was evident,
He didn't care a *pin.*

So next time that he came along,
They tried a gob of fish;
He was cursedly fastidious,
For he didn't like that dish.

At last a gallant hero from
Hibernia's distant land,
Approached the finny monster
With his fishing rod in hand,

Exclaiming "where's the vagabond?"
In voice a little gruff,
"If I don't pin him in a crack,
Why then my name's not—— Jenkins."

Two minutes scarce had passed, when he
Cried out, "Boys! give me room!
I've hooked him in the gill, by Jove,
Where is that fellow——Smith?

"Come! help! God bless my soul, come help!
The sucker weighs a ton;
My line won't stand, I tell you,
If he once begins to run!

"Come! hang it all, I did believe,
In these here sporting slaughters,
I might count on the ready hand,
Of such a man as——'Jones.'

"And Bill! if you've a lady love,
Go back to town and court her;
On you I thought I could rely
You six-foot sculpin——'Baxter.'

"Come! there's good fellows! lend your aid,
And hook him by the fin;
I'm scuttled, if I'm not afraid
The beast will drag me in!"

So they dipped their lines around, and he
Was hooked on every side;
But still the monster's power all
Their fishercraft defied.

No joke to have a mass like that,
One's common trout-rod strain,
Like wearing a half hundred weight
Attached to a watch-chain.

At last, one bolder than the rest,
Regardless of the wet,
Jumped bang into the water,
With a knife and a shrimp net.

Resolving to give battle
To the monster where he lay,
With his fins and tail all splashing
In a most unpleasant way.

So he poked the net before him,
But he gave a mighty dash,
And knocked the whole concern
Into everlastin' smash!

Then he banged him with the handle,
All about the tail and head,
Until the Shark began to feel
Considerably bad.

But after they had worried him
For full two hours or more,
They, advantage of his weakness took,
And *shovelled* him ashore.

And never it is my belief,
Occurred so great a lark,
As on that self-same afternoon
A-killing of that Shark.

EVERY-DAY DRAMA.

THE PIGEON AND THE HAWKS.

Persons Represented.

PETRONIUS FUNK, Fictitious Auctioneer.
WYLIE,
BONNETT, } Associate Funkers.
SNEAK,
PEAGREEN, in quest of knowledge.

SCENE.

The Interior of an Auction Mart, on a small scale. A quantity of apparently Gold Watches, Rings, Pins, Pencil Cases, Guns, Pistols, and other Musical Instruments, in imposing array.

Petronius. Methinks, my friends! the world is growing wise.
Here have we labored from the early dawn,
And now 'tis past meridian. Can it be
That those accursed bars to enterprise,
The vile and reckless papers of the day,
Who strive with barbarous malignity
To check our calling, have forewarned the green
And curious countrymen against our mode
Of giving practical instruction in
The various metals, from the virgin gold
Even to inexpensive brass?

Wylie. Not so, my friend. Print as they may, the world contains a mass
Of eager inexperience, glad to gain
That store of knowledge, which alone can spring
From mixing with the actual of life.
Oft have I seen the timid youngster gaze
Upon the glittering pencil case, or haply ring,
Which jeweller's paste encircles; till the sight
Did stimulate him to possession,
Even at ten times its intrinsic cost.
The eyes to dazzle of ingenuous youth
Is my peculiar province. Many a one
Have I led onward by slow step, but sure,
Until his vest did yearn to hold a watch;
Obtained at last by means which sent him where
More general information may be gleaned—
E'en the romantic precincts of Sing Sing.
Bonnett. Mine be the task, amongst the gaping crowd,
To make fictitious bids, and upward run
The specious auction; until speculation
Nods its wise head, and piles its topmost coin,
And prudence answers, let the hammer fall.
Sneak. Still more exciting, aye, and subtler far,
In its variety of artful dodges,
My occupation is. Now in the path
Of some pedestrian, whose ruddy cheek
And eye, unsatisfied with taking in
The canvass giants, dwarfs, and waving flags,
That make attractive Anne-street's crowded corner,
Proclaim him verdant and impressible.
To cast the bogus-filled, deceitful wallet,
Find, and go halves. Now lettuce-leaf cigars,
Steeped in tobacco-juice, and spotted o'er

With acids, marketable brands to simulate,
As supposititious smuggler, I appear.
Anon the glittering ring I deftly drop,
Where it may catch the greedy eye
Of some suspicionless wayfarer, who
Inwardly nettled at my better luck,
And by unworthy covetousness urged,
Closes the bargain, and is sweetly sold.

Petronius. Behold yon sandy-haired, high-collared youth,
Whose nose is almost flattened to the glass.
Let your sonorous bids strike on his ear,
But look not at him, lest ye wake suspicion
Of our design. " Dol, dol, dol, dol, DOL."
Superior watch, sir. Didn't you say N'AF ?
"N'af, n'af, n'af, n'af; shall we say another *quat*?
Na'quat, na'quat, na'quat;" he's coming—keep it up.
Take and examine it, e'en at the door.
A double case of sixteen caret gold.

Bonnett takes watch to door examines the interior, smiles, and says aside:—

Patent escapement, capped and jewelled, too!
'Tis evident he dosen't know its worth.
I'll bet another dollar [*aloud.*]

Petronius [*letting fall the hammer.*] Sir, 'tis yours;
And I congratulate you on your bargain.

[*Enter Peagreen.*] *Bonnett* to *Peagreen.* Bargain, indeed!
I would not give it now
For double. Take this fifty-dollar bill,
And let me have the change.

Peagreen [*timidly.*] Sir, may I ask
How much they charged you for that article?

Bonnett. Charged! A mere nothing. This is not a store

Where they squeeze out the life-blood of one's purse
To feed insatiate landlords.
Peagreen. I should dearly like
Of such a watch to be the proud possessor.
Thinkest thou that I have any chance?
Bonnett. 'Tis doubtful.
But were I to advise, I'd say remain
Here for some moments; and, to lead them on,
Bid lustily for something inexpensive—
. That toothpick now, for instance, which he holds,
You need not speak, but simply nod your head.
Petronius. All ivory, and going for a cent.
Peagreen nods.
Bonnett. You're right, sir: you have made a good investment.
That string of beads might please some female friend.
Peagreen. Only six cents. Now that's what I call cheap,
And no mistake. [*He nods.*]
Bonnett. Ah, sir! I see you know the proper time
To close a bargain.
Petronius. Now for this pencil case;
All gold and real stone. Who'll give a bid?
Bonnett. A dollar.
Wylie. And a half.
Sneak. Three-quarters.
Bonnett. Two.
Peagreen. Two and a half.
Bonnett. Three-quarters.
Wylie. Four.
Sneak. Five.
Peagreen. Six. [*Hammer falls.*]
Bonnett. Nay, Mr. Auctioneer, you are too quick!
I would have bid another dollar, sir.
Petronius. Much I regret it; but alas! 'tis done.
But here's an article surpassing all,

A heavy double-cased gold hunting-watch;
Capped, too, and jewelled in some thirty holes!
COOPER, of London, is the maker's name,
Which is itself sufficient guarantee.
What shall we trumpet forth for the beginning?
Bonnett. Ah! fifty dollars.
[*Aside to Peagreen.*] Worth two hundred, sure!
Peagreen. Fifty-five. [*Hammer falls.*]
Bonnett, [*much excited.*] Again, sir!
Petronius. It is really your own fault.
You should speak quicker. We have little time
To waste on pitiful deliberation.
The watch is yours, sir! If you'll step in here,
We shall make up our small account; and settle.

Peagreen, Petronius, and others, enter back room.

Petronius. Now, let us see. Of toothpicks, twenty gross,
At one cent each.
Peagreen. Why, I bought only one.
Petronius. Excuse me, sir! that one was but the sample.
One hundred strings of beads, at six cents each;
And of gold pencil cases, seven dozen.
Peagreen. I did not intend to purchase all these goods.
Petronius. But you have done so. I appeal to those
Three gentlemen who bid against you.
All. Certainly.
Petronius. Then there's the hunting-watch; which, altogether,
To make it even money we will call
Five hundred and fifty dollars.

[*Peagreen faints. When he recovers, an arrangement is entered into, by which he is relieved of all his ready money, and finds himself in the fortunate possession of a miscellaneous assortment of tooth-picks, beads, and impracticable vencil cases.*]

KIT COBB, THE CABMAN.

A STORY OF LONDON LIFE.

INTRODUCTION.

In which the Author frankly acknowledges his Ignorance.

It is not in my power to give you the slightest account of my hero's birth and early experience; indeed it would be very hard if I were called upon to do anything of the kind, seeing that my worthy friend Kit himself was equally ignorant upon the subject. His recollection did not carry him back further than his tenth year; why it took so limited a retrospect it is impossible for me to determine; perhaps he was a *forward* boy, too strongly imbued with the go-a-headativeness of Yankeetude, to waste time in Parthian glances,—perhaps like Swift, and other great geniuses, whose juvenile dullness has become matter of history, he indulged in no precocious draughts upon memory. However, the reader may exercise his ingenuity in establishing an hypothesis, I can't say more than I know, and what's more—I won't; but should you speculate on the subject, you can bear in mind that the probability is, he must have been tolerably easy in his circumstances, for early discomfort makes a notch in the memory not easy planed off; how far that may have been the result, more of a contented disposition, than of the velvet accessories of wealth, can, I think, be safely deduced from the relation of a simple fact. He wore his first pair of shoes, strong double-soled and nail-paved, after he had attained his fourteenth year—that is to say, there or thereabout, for poor Kit never had a birthday but once, and he couldn't even swear to that, for no man can give evidence in a case which concerneth himself. That he had a father, we have only the same circumstantial proof, utterly invalid in a legal point of view, and, inasmuch as no clearer testimony could be adduced to establish the fact of maternity, consequently, according to the unerring dictum of English jurisprudence, he was an absolute nullity; to be sure he lived, and breathed, and moved, but of what avail was that—*he couldn't prove it.*

Poor Kit, he certainly was a waif upon the road of life, a stray fly in the great sugar-hogshead of the world, a thing of chance, an incomprehensible atom; for aught we, or any, know to the contrary, he might have been "evolved from contingent matter," hatched in the "Eccalobeion" or won at a raffle! No matter, there he was, an inexplicable human riddle, a fine, fat, chubby, laughing, squalling, *hungry mystery!*

CHAPTER I.

Which is to be hoped will give you a better Opinion of the Author, and of his Subject.

A cold, grey, drizzly, uncomfortable November morning began reluctantly to tint the eastern sky with a dull something which might be almost mistaken for light, holding a deadly, lively contest for precedence with sundry pale, sleepy-looking gas-jets, that reeled and flickered in their lamps, with a tipsy up-all-night sort of undulation. Silence brooded over the west-end of the town, broken only by the echoing tread of the ever-watchful (?) policeman, and now and then the sudden rattle of a furiously driven cab, containing some belated son-of-Nox, some titled ruffian, who, sheltered by a name and wealth, defies all law, owns no restraint, and breaks through every social tie, upheld by the mean-souled worshipers of Mammon. Save those, all was stillness, but in the abodes of wretchedness and continual labor, to which I am about to conduct the reader, all was astir.

Perhaps no other city on the face of the globe can parallel the utter destitution and misery, both apparent and actual, which are to be found in the very core of London, this great metropolis, surrounded by evidences of superabundant wealth, with the palaces of the nobility bounding it on one side, and the scarcely less splendid mansions of the merchant kings on the other, stands, or rather rots the parish of St. Giles, the very focus of squalid poverty, the nucleus of disease, the nurse of vice, year after year has it been denounced as the hot-bed of contagion, the "normal" school of crime. Yet, there it remains, and will remain unless the hand of heaven, by the purification of fire, averts a second plague.

In a wretched stable, in the most wretched lane of this wretched neighborhood, the sound of a merry voice might be heard, in startling contrast to the surrounding scene. The singer is Kit Cobb, now about fifteen years old, and the happy owner of a hack cab, and horse. Although the most of his hitherto life had been passed in lounging about, running of messages, pulling down shutters, with intervals of dangerous inactivity, yet he had curiously escaped the vitiating influence of the society into which "fate or metaphysical agency" had cast him.

About a year previous to this time, a large cab-owner, struck by the boy's frank countenance, engaged him as a driver, and as a reward for his integrity and industry, sold him a vehicle, consenting to receive the amount weekly, in small installments.

Last night the purchase was made, and this morning behold him. Alexander the Great, when Darius owned him conqueror—Napoleon, when with his own hands he placed the crown of Charlemagne upon his head, were not a whit more happy than poor Kit Cobb, when, in the extravagance of his joy, with eyes streaming, and a choking voice, he cried, "Horse and cab, all mine, mine!" and then he would laugh, and dance, and sing, with all his might, now squaring up at the horse and punching him as though he hadn't a greater enemy in the world, now hugging and kissing the brute's long face with most alarming emphasis.

He was fond of the animal; the truth is, it was his first affection, and I'm happy to say the feeling was reciprocated, for as Kit would rub his horse down, pluck his ears, and bestow such like evidences of partiality, the animal would neigh and sniff and wink knowingly at him, as much as to say:—

"You're my particular friend, Kit; stick to me and I'll stick to you."

And Kit held an interesting conversation with his favorite, but inasmuch as they were both rather excited, it's not worth while to relate the substance of it; indeed, it was very well for them that they were not observed by the keeper of a lunatic asylum, for no madman could possibly exceed the extravagance of Kit's demeanor, and if ever a horse deserved a strait waistcoat, it was Old Turk.

CHAPTER II.

Which is Short, but (for else the Author flatters himself) Pithy.

Gentle reader, with your kind permission, we jump two years, and find in addition to his horse and cab, Kit has persuaded an unfortunate little girl that he couldn't live without her; she, with the innocent simplicity of her sex, believed him, and they were married. Our poor friend's worldly store was but little augmented by this procedure, for his bride brought him, by way of dower, one stuff gown, one doubtful colored silk ditto, one imitation French shawl, one Dunstable bonnet, with other smaller matters, not mentioned in the category, and all settled tightly on herself; but no matter, Kit loved her with an overweening love, and when the heart is driver, prudence gets the whip. The result of Kit's domestic arrangement was, in due time, a duodecimo edition, so that there were soon three mouths to provide for, besides that of Old Turk, the most expensive of all, for though Kit might and did stint his own appetite, yet he held it part of his religion that the horse should have no cause to complain for lack of food.

Things began to look gloomy; the outgoings exceeded the incomings, notwithstanding their most stringent exertions; for the first time Kit had been unable to make up the installment of purchase-money; he became despondent, and the old horse moped for sympathy.

One morning poor Kit took the last truss of hay and feed of oats, discoursing as was his custom with his early friend, and the person who had the temerity to say that the horse couldn't understand every word, would have been looked upon by him as an intensely ignorant individual.

"Come up, you old brute," said he. "I've had no breakfast myself yet, but here's yours. We've a precious long day's work before us, and if you don't earn more than you did yesterday, it ain't much you'll get to-morrow, that I can tell you."

Old Turk sniffed, and pushed his nose out in anticipation of the coming meal.

"What a hurry you're in, you precious old rascal," said Kit, rather offended at Turk's evident want of sentiment; "let me tell you a bit of my mind before you eat a morsel," and he snatched back the sieve of oats just as Turk had licked his teeth round for the second mouthful, a proceeding for which he made his displeasure tolerable evident.

"Oh! I don't care," continued Kit, "you may blow up as much as you like, but it's my belief that you're a selfish old reprobate." The horse gave Kit one reproachful look that went directly to his heart. "There, take it," said he; "I beg your pardon. I didn't mean to insult you; pitch into it; it does my heart good to see you enjoy it," and flinging the corn into the manger, Kit folded his arms and watched his pet as he plunged into the welcome food. It was not long before he nuzzled up every grain.

"Now then," said Kit, stroking down the old horse's mane as he spoke, "I'm going to tell you something that will break your heart—learsways I think it will. I wouldn't say any thing of it before, for fear of spoiling your breakfast; but things are getting worse and worse, Turk, and if something don't turn up in the course of this very day, we—we'll have to part. You—you and I'll have to part—to *part*, Turk," he repeated sternly, one round, big tear settling in the corner of his eye, and gently pulling the horse's ears as he spoke.

The old brute, for the purpose of enjoying the luxury to an extent, placed his head on Kit's shoulder. That was enough;

7*

construing it into an appeal to his affection, he could stand it no longer, but burst into a flood of tears, exclaiming through his sobs—

"Don't, don't! Turk, you deceitful old beast, don't you go to take advantage of my weakness. I tell you my mind's made up. I—I have a w-hi-hife! now—I have! and a chi-hi-hild! They've had plenty as yet, but they don't know how I have pinched myself to get it. I can't let *them* want. You wouldn't if you were me, bless your old bones, I know you wouldn't; so let us part friends. I can't pay for you, and I must give you up again. You must go—indeed you must. Come, now bear it like a Christian. I'll give your ears another pull, if you want me. There, there, come."

And poor Kit wept like a sick child, while he harnessed old Turk for, as he thought, the last time.

CHAPTER III.

Which is essential to the Story, and contains, moreover, a Moral Lesson, though Inculcated in a curious way.

"Dear Kit, you don't eat."

"Never mind me, Betsey, love, go on—I—I'm not hungry yet; I shall be sure to get something by and by."

Now that was a lie—a deliberate lie; he *was* hungry, and would have thought no more of demolishing the entire of that meagre meal, than if it were but a mouthful, but he struggled manfully against his inclinations, and having watched his darling wife and child make a sufficient breakfast, kissed them both with his heart upon his lips, and departed upon his almost hopeless toil.

"God bless and preserve *them*," said he, "whatever may become of me; I can battle with the world's strong arm; I *will*, Heaven help me in the effort; it is not for myself I ask it. No, no; were I alone, like a stray weed on the surface of the waters, I'd make no opposition to the whelming tide, but float along wherever fate impelled me; but while these two helpless and uncomplaining creatures look to me, I *will* work, I *will* strive, for I love them so, that I could willingly give up my life to rescue them, nay, if it would ensure their happiness, I do believe—God forgive me—that I would *sell my very soul to the fiend.*"

Who can tell at what time an "idle word" may meet its recompense; or the mental invocation be answered, and the destroyer permitted to fling his specious lure upon the sea of circumstance.

Kit spoke from the very promptings of his heart, feeling sincerely what he said, but without the vaguest notion of supernal aid in this debtor and creditor age; it was merely a common saying uttered heedlessly, yet even as he spoke the words, the soul-ensnarer had begun his work. He was hailed by a sedate-looking, middle-aged, but no further remarkable gentleman, who engaged him for several hours, giving promise of a good day's work, from so favorable a commencement, and poor Kit's heart bounded again with joy at the thoughts of home, and this cheering omen of better fortune. Great cause had he for joy!

At the self-same moment that the stranger entered Kit's cab, two suspicious-looking individuals might be observed creeping stealthily up the rickety stairs which led to his miserable home; as they seemed to move slowly and with difficulty, I'll describe them as nearly as I can, while in progression. The first was an apoplectic son of Iscariot, short, squab, and intensely fat, his huge carcass decorated in the very extremity of gaudy show, his capacious chest enveloped in a flaming plaid velvet waistcoat, about which an endless convolution of snake-pattern, imitation gold chain played at hide and seek, now fantastically twining round an exaggerated breast-pin of some red material, then flitting through sundry button-holes, and finally plunging into a side pocket; his continuations, or *pants*, to use the Yankee abbreviation, were composed of light, very light blue material, and made so uncomfortable tight, as to give one a sensation of pain, while his—I was going to say feet, were squeezed into French gaiter boots, with patent leather tips. The coat was of that economically fashionable material, generally worn of nights, when rows are expected, mostly patronized, though, by ambitious apprentices, in the last year of their time, when they begin to be entrusted with the door-key, and from a laudable anxiety to go to bed early, invariably defer it until next morning. His hands—fins—flippers, or whatever they were, *au naturel*, were surrounded on all sides with kid gloves, but where he got the gloves, how he got into them, or when he did, are matters as mysterious to me as Mesmer, Hahnemann or Pusey. What *did* those fists look like? Can you fancy a pair of the largest size boxing-gloves stuffed into kid, that may give you the shadow of a notion how they showed; and then his cane of painted wood, with a magnificent leaden head, electrified into the appearance of gold so completely as to deceive nobody; you must imagine the *tout ensemble* was *imposing* in the extreme.

His follower, literally, was in every way antithetic, long, scraggy and cadaverous; he looked like a slender and consumptive ninepin by the side of a plethoric ball.

Now these men were characters, though they had none, and I wish I had time to illustrate them more fully. "Phew!" ejaculated Solomen Duggs, our adipose friend, following it up with a series of fatty suspirations. "*Dim* these *dim* stars." You will observe that he affects a modish drawl, and a singular method of tautologizing his *only* expletive; whether the latter arises from a paucity of ideas or mere affectation I cannot say.

"Phew!—stop, *le's* rest—*dim* the *dim* thing—how *dim* fatigued I *em*. Why, Badger, you *dim*, watery-blooded anatomy, how *dim* cool you look."

"I *am* cool," gruffly responded the thin-ribbed follower, "I have only myself to carry."

"*Dim* your impudence!" puffed Duggs, "do you mean to insinuate that I am so *dim* fat?"

"Not I; I only thought it would be convenient to be a *shade* smaller," said Badger, the ghost of a smile shivering on his lips.

"You lie, *dim* you, it wouldn't: I like it—phew!"—and Duggs fanned himself with his great fist.

"Oh, very well, I've done. I'm sorry I spoke. If you like it, may your shadow never be less, that's all;" and Badger fairly laughed—a breach of discipline and of decorum, which raised the ire of Duggs to such an extent, that he punched him in the ribs, which was about as much use as flinging putty against iron bars.

"Come, come, no more of this *dim* nonsense, but *le's* to business; phew!" and he fanned faster than ever. "Are you sure this is the *dim* place?"

Badger nodded, for he was an economist in words.

"Well, knock, *dim* you."

Badger knocked a small, crafty, neighbor-like knock—a miserable, mean, *dirty* "summons."

Poor Betsey flew to open the door, and started back again with astonishment and vague apprehension, as Duggs, followed by Badger, waddled in; utterly unable to speak, and gasping from an indefinite sense of dread, she gazed on the intruders.

"Sarv'nt, *mim*, don't be so alarmed; we ain't agoing to hurt you," blandly simpered Duggs, flourishing his libellous cane, while Badger, with the practiced eye of an appraiser, in one glance round the room, calculated to a sixpence the profits of his brokerage.

"Take a *cheer*, *mim*," continued Duggs; "hem,"—and he cleared his throat for his stereotyped introductory speech. "I'm extremely sorry that so unpleasant a *dooty* should *revolve* upon me as a legal functionary, but laws *is* laws, and *dooties* is *dooties*, and if I *warn't* to do it, *p'r'aps* some one else as is not so tender *'ud* be *obligated*."

"For Heaven's sake," cried the agitated Betsey, "tell me what all this is to lead to." Duggs shrugged up his shoulders, and began fumbling in his pocket, pointing at the same time to Badger, who, seated cross-legged on the bed, was noting down with callous indifference every article of furniture. The extent of her misfortune struck her in an instant, her brain reeled, the blood rushed upward from her heart, and she fell.

"*Dim* the *dim* thing," gasped Duggs, "she's fainted."

"So she has, I declare," said Badger, drily, without moving.

"Then *dim* you, come and help." Badger got slowly up, and helped to raise the poor victim, giving her a shake, and saying, gruffly, "I hate your fainters; don't put her on the cheer; we'll want that; here, drop her on the mattress, at once; there, she'll come to time enough."

"Give her some water, *dim* you." He did so; it seemed to revive her a little; she swallowed about half a glass full. Badger threw the remainder under the grate, and pocketing the tumbler, proceeded with his inventory.

"Com, *mim*," said Duggs, "don't take on so; 'taint for much—only a paltry *fip-poun ten; dimme*, I'd pay it myself, only that dooties is dooties. Can't you give it us, and we'll be *hoff*."

"God knows," said poor Betsey, her eyes streaming with tears, "I haven't five farthings in the world, but do wait until my husband comes home; he'll give it you, I know he will, for he's as honest as truth itself."

"Why, you see, *mim*, there ain't no honesty in the case," replied the amiable Duggs, speaking the truth, by mistake, "the long and the short of it is, if you haven't the *dim* money, we must take the *dim* things."

But why linger over a scene, which, to the disgrace of British judicature, is enacted daily in our Christian metropolis. Suffice it to say, Kit had neglected, from perfect ignorance, to answer a summons before the Court of Requests, summary execution was issued, and amidst the agony of grief and ineffectual remonstrances of that poor, lonely mother, the humble apartment was stripped of every article except the bed she lay on, even to the very cradle of her infant, to satisfy the greed of a stony-hearted creditor, and the most beastly rapacity of a shameful and cruel law.

CHAPTER IV.

In which Kit spurns at Fortune in a most unaccountable manner.

"So, ho! old Turk, we've done well to-day, old boy, ha! ha! I've paid my installment and have ten good shillings in my pocket. So, ho! good old fellow, who'se afraid, there's life in a muscle yet—there, there, now don't be impatient, you shall have such a feed presently, you'll feel in your stall like a bishop, only you won't have no wine—so much the better.

Water's the good, wholesome drink that nature provides for all sorts of animals, and how mankind got to like any thing else, puzzles me, but the sense is leaving us and going into the brutes—there, you're unharnessed, now give yourself a shake—that's right—now just wait until I go cheer up my darling Bessie, and kiss that varmint, young Kit."

So saying, with a light step and a joyous heart, Kit bounded up stairs, singing as he went—

"Oh, there's nothing like luck all the universe over,
Misfortunes don't always stay with us 'tis clear,
To-day we're in sorrow, to-morrow in clover,
The light follows darkness throughout the long year,
Oh! the light follows darkness"———

At that moment, with a gladsome smile on his very lips, he rushed into the room. Heavens! what a sight met his view, the quick revulsion of feeling almost drove out sense. It was as though one were suddenly to wake fresh from the glories of some blissful dream, to find a devouring flame enveloping his bed. In the confusion of his first dismay, he had a vague conception of some sweeping destruction, and that wife, child and all were lost, but when he saw that they were safe, a deep feeling of relief came over him, the blood flowed on again, and full consciousness returned.

"Great Heaven! Bessie!" he cried in dry, husky accents, "what's the meaning of this? who has been here? what has happened?"

"Oh, Kit," she replied, flinging her arms round his neck, and breaking into a flood of tears, "dear Kit! why didn't you come sooner?—they have been here—and—everything is gone."

"Who! who has done this?" said Kit, with a savage glance in his eye, but seldom lighted there, but once it was, most fearful to encounter.

"That man, you know; that grocer, dear Kit," said Bessie.

"Higgins!" cried Kit—she nodded. "The grasping cur, the sneaking, dastardly slave, to take advantage of my absence," said Kit fiercely, clenching his hands and grinding his teeth—"May"—the large tears rolled in streams down his cheeks; burying his face in his hands, he continued, "May God pardon him for this day's inhuman work—forgive me for the harsh words I've used, and avert the strong hate that in my own despite springs up within me towards him. Oh! 'tis hard!—hard to be thus dashed, dear Bessie, with a soul full of hope,—but come, it's over now, and we must make the best of it."

"Bless you, bless you," replied the devoted wife, "we will—we will, for your sake, and for the sake of our child, I can endure anything."

"Heaven reward your true woman's love, Bessie, darling," fervently replied Kit. I have enough for present want, here,"—placing his hand in his pocket to take out the piece of gold which he had carefully deposited there, when to his utter dismay he couldn't find it—he hunted through every crevice, but to no purpose, it was gone. "Fool! fool that I am," he exclaimed, bitterly. "I've lost it."

"Never mind, dear Kit," replied Bessie, tenderly, "there's enough for the boy's supper, and I do not want anything."

"What have I done?" pettishly exclaimed Kit. "Great Heaven! what have I done, that everything should so conspire against me"—at that instant they both started—hearing the peculiar chink of gold. "Ha!" shouted Kit, "there it is," and rushing over to the place from whence the sound proceeded, he saw a sight which made his brain reel, as though he were revelling in some bright dream. Seated on the cab cushions which he had brought in with him, his little boy was playing with a *bag of gold;* he had just managed to untie the string, and the precious metal poured out in a perfect shower. Kit's first thought was one of unmitigated delight, but ere an instant had passed, he and his wife looked intently at each other with faces painfully livid.

"Bessie," said he, grasping her hand tightly, and speaking through his teeth with compressed energy, "these walls are naked, you and your child are pinched by hard want, misfortune dogs our very footsteps—let us pray that a merciful God may give us strength to battle with this strong temptation." And with clasped hands they knelt in silent supplication.

The mingled aspirations of two hearts as pure as ever tenanted this mortal clay, wended upward from those miserable walls to the throne of Him who hears, and in whose own good time will answer the prayer of the wretched.

CHAPTER V.

In which Kit does an extraordinary thing, and is recompensed in an extraordinary way.

NEITHER Kit nor Bessie slept a single wink all that night; the consciousness of having so great a sum of money in their possession, which did not belong to them, effectually drove off slumber. Kit had counted it, and found there were one thousand pounds in the bag. How it could possibly have escaped his notice, as he removed the cushions from the cab, puzzled him exceedingly, but he conjectured the string had by some means got twisted round one of the buttons. Having replaced the money, he put it carefully under his pillow, and if he felt once, he felt an hundred times to see if it were safe. Bessie was equally fidgety, and at last far from being inclined to retain any, they both heartily wished it anywhere but with them—now would they fancy footsteps were approaching the bed—now Kit would jump up and put some additional fastening on the door and window, for the first time experiencing the truth of the old proverb:

"He who has naught to lose,
Need never his doors to close."

Poor Bessie, in the simplicity of her heart, exclaimed, "Dear Kit, if money makes people feel as I do, I wouldn't be rich for all the world."

Long before morning, they were both up, and when Kit cast his eyes first upon his scant breakfast and then upon the treasure within his very grasp, his heart bounded up to his throat. Bessie guessing his thoughts, with true woman's tact, diverted them into the one broad, overwhelming current of paternal love, presenting the laughing boy to receive his father's hearted kiss. "See, see," she exclaimed, "how beautiful he looks this morning. Does it not seem as though Heaven had sent one of its own angels to reward us for shunning this devil's lure—is it not a great thing, dearest, to meet his smile without a blush of shame."

"It is, it is," he exclaimed, regarding his child with the strong emotion of a father's love. "No, no, *you* shall never curse your father's memory. The anger of a just God, who visits the father's sins upon the children, shall never reach you from my misdeeds, if through his abundant mercy my soul be still strengthened in the right."

With placid minds, and even cheerfully, they sat down to their insufficient breakfast, Kit cheering his wife the while, by saying, "Take heart, love, take heart, I shall take the money down to Somerset House, no doubt I shall see the owner; he will be grateful for its return, and will perhaps reward me with a trifle—at all events, the greatest pleasures money could obtain wouldn't approach the thousandth part of the joy I feel at the anticipation of returning to that old man his, no doubt almost hopelessly lamented treasure."

Soon afterwards, Kit harnessed Old Turk, and much to the brute's astonishment, without deigning to hold with him the slightest conversation—nay, he even went so far in forgetfulness or neglect, as to leave his ears unpulled. The horse was evidently annoyed, insulted; he grew sulky, and set out with a vicious determination to kick or bite, or do something equally disagreeable; but the goodness of his disposition overcame his ill-humor, and reflecting that perhaps Kit had something on his mind, sagacious animal! he trotted along with his usual willingness.

When Kit arrived at Somerset House, he found the office for the reception of valuables found in cabs was not open, so he sat down on the curb-stone to wait, amusing himself by *hefting* the bag in his pocket, and wondering what its owner would give him for the recovery. His cab was standing in the entrance; suddenly he was startled by an authoritative voice, shouting to him to get out of the way; with habitual deference, Kit flew to lead his vehicle into the enclosure, when a splendid carriage, driven by a pair of blood-horses, dashed up the avenue, stopping short with a sudden pull.

In an instant after, one of the liveried servants touched Kit on the shoulder, and upon looking up, in the occupant of the carriage he beheld the owner of the treasure.

"Come in, come in," said the old man, and poor Kit was handed into the magnificent vehicle.

"Good fellow, good fellow, have you brought it?" said the stranger quickly, and with the slightest possible evidence of agitation.

"To the uttermost farthing, sir," replied Kit, as untwisting the string from around his neck, he placed the bag in the old man's hands.

"You're an honest fellow," said the latter, "what's your name? and where do you live?"

Kit told him.

"I won't forget; I won't forget, shake hands, I honor you!" and with a hearty grasp, wealth paid homage to honesty. "Now, good bye," continued the old man; "I've business of great importance to attend to." And without any acknowledgment except that unsubstantial handshake, poor Kit was left standing on the curb-stone, while the carriage of the ungrateful stranger whirled furiously away.

Stunned and mortified, Kit could hardly believe his senses. "What," cried he, "not a guinea, not a shilling, after restoring that vast sum! mean, miserly! Well, I've done *my* duty, and after all, I had no positive right to expect anything for it." Thus he argued in the endeavor to shake off his annoyance, but vainly; he was bitterly disappointed.

After a few hours spent in his usual occupation, utterly despondent and almost hopeless, Kit sought his wretched home, scarcely knowing how to meet his wife, or break the mortification to her; he found her in tears, which, when she saw him, she strove to restrain, but could not—in her hand was a large, lawyer-like, suspicious-looking letter, with an enormous seal, just such a document as brings a shudder through an individual in straightened circumstances.

"So, so," said Kit, "more wretchedness, more misfortune! Who is this from? some other charitable soul, who fain would help to sink a drowning wretch still deeper."

Seizing the letter he tore it open, and glancing at the contents, he gasped for breath, his eyes dilated, the big tears bursting from them in torrents; he jumped up, shouted, laughed, danced, kissed Bessie, and squeezed his child, until he fairly hurt it, and behaved altogether in a most mysterious and alarming manner.

"Merciful Heaven!" cried Bessie, a cold shiver running through her frame, "he's mad!"

"He's not, he's not!" shouted Kit, "look here, read, read," and pushing the letter towards her—between laughing and crying they slowly deciphered the following:

"*I hereby grant to Christopher Cobb, for the term of his natural life, the sum of Two Hundred Pounds, lawful British money, annually, for which this shall be deemed sufficient instrument, in gratitude for an essential service, and as the inadequate reward of exemplary honesty.*

"EGREMONT."

Reader, art thou in prosperity, be grateful to Him from whom all earthly good proceeds. Art thou in adversity, remember that He who rules the thunder is all powerful to cast from thee the bitter cup.

THE PHANTOM LIGHT.

A TALE OF BOSTON.

DARK, dark, and dreary was the night, and bitter blew the
blast,
As in a black, sepulchral shroud, all nature was o'ercast.
Amongst the leafless branches, with sad, melancholy moans,
The winter wind was wailing, like a tortured wretch's groans.

And then 'twould lull at intervals, and silence brooded round,
Except the beating of my heart there was no earthly sound.
Fated was I to endure the tempest's demon shriek of pain,
Or the silence which fell heavy, like a weight upon my brain.

At length the wind in low and fitful gasping died away,
As if merciful extinction closed a life of agony.
And of every universal sound naught dwelt upon my ear
Save the sense itself, loud clamoring some outward thing to
hear.

A reeking damp, a fevered chill, now racked my very soul;
Though cold as ice within my heart, adown my brow did roll
Large drops of sweat. I felt, I felt that cowardice was near,
And, for the first time in my life, knew what it was to fear.

The dull unchanging quiet, the unpiercing heavy gloom,
The dark and earthly chillness, was as a living tomb;
Through the chaos of my memory, years seemed to take their flight,
And the bright and glorious day was sunk in everlasting night.

I could not see my onward way, I dared not glance behind,
A vague presentiment of ill dwelt madly on my mind,
And to the very core, my cold blood shivered, but to think,
An instant might conduct me to some precipice's brink.

Now standing all irresolute, my locks I'd vainly tear;
Now shrieking wildly in the wind, with terrible despair,
I'd curse my fate, while slowly scalding tears would drop amain,
Not such as sorrows soften, but hot vapors of the brain.

Ah! little recks the reveller within the halls of bliss,
How fares the lonely wanderer on such a night as this.
Oh! for some voice of human kind, to cheer me on my way,
Oh! for the blessed morning dawn, its dullest, faintest ray.

And now, a wondrous phantasy uprose before my sight,
A faint, round, fiery glow, a changing meteoric light;
Now showing like a living coal, now fading from the view,
While around, a bluish vapor, in thin, circling eddies flew.

Close to my face the phantom glowed, and, stranger still, where'er
I moved, or back, or forward, yet, the fire was ever there;
I thought my soul must surely have departed on its way,
And this must be the corpse-light exhalation from my clay.

But scarcely had that wonder been accustomed to my sense,
When another rose more terrible, and banished it from thence.
I heard! But 'twas a sound, the very boldest might appal,
A mystery approaching, a quick, evident foot-fall.

And higher beat my fevered pulse, and brighter gleamed the fire,
When through the dark, those rapid footsteps nigher drew, and nigher,
It came! It spoke! Harsh thunder could not more my senses jar!
As in ruthless accents it exclaimed, JUST PUT OUT THAT CIGAR!

REVOLT OF THE HAREM.

SIMPLIFIED.

You'll please to imagine a hairy-faced king;
In a favorite wing
Of the gorgeous Alhambra, he's rumina-*ting.*
An unusual thing,
By the way, in a monarch, and not orthodox—he
Should do all his thinking, *en règle*, by proxy.
Well; or perhaps I had better say, Wells,
In action expressive, his misery tells.
His heart's full of woe,
His spirits are low.
(Last night, there's no doubt, if a body could know,
His majesty must have been "*how come you so?*")
In the midst of his grief
There comes a young chief,
A Moorish Adonis, or D'Orsay, in brief,
Of ducks oriental the sweetest of beaux,
In a pair of red stockings, without any toes.
And he slaps his chest,
To the risk of his vest,
(Wherat, I thought Niblo looked rather distrest),
But it must be confessed,
The emotions that fill the young warrior's breast,
Though no doubt interesting, can only be guessed.

It, however, appeared
That no danger he feared,
In the Moorish militia he'd just volunteered,
And would go the *entire* for the man in the beard.
Of course, such an offer was not to be slighted.
The king quite delighted,
To sit by his side, the young stranger invited,
And the hookah was not (*but it should have been*) lighted.
But, to honor his guest
To a nondescript nigger his wish he expressed
That, dressed
In their best,
His connubial contingencies—-that is to say
The *corps de ballet*
Should show their accomplishments, etcetera.
So Herr Korponay,
(Who does the dark gentleman) waddles away.
In scampers "the corps,"
Some fifty, or more,
And try to creep o'er
The susceptible core
Of his Majesty's heart, by well-dusting the floor.
But alas! he had oftentime seen them before;
And futile are all their endeavors to please,
The sleepy old rascal does nothing but sneeze.
He wants something new,
So all they can do
Don't prevent him from looking unregally blue.
The king in his pet,
Looked round on the set,
Like a man who had just lost a sizable bet;
When the whimsical nigger infers, "dont you fret,
Here's something *recherché*, you hav'n't seen yet."

Up the king and his volunteer visitor get,
The gong gives a bang
And the leader a twang;
And Korponay discovers Pauline Desjardin,
To the wonder of Ishmael—Monsieur Martin.
(N. B. Those will rhyme if you once get the hang.)
As you may suppose,
His majesty glows
With love, from his beard to the tips of his toes;
And foolishly goes
On his knees to the lady, his flame to disclose—
Just under the nose
Of her lover, whose feelings ain't *couleur de rose.*
He looks "deadly night shade," dementedly throws
His arms in the air, and in point of fact shows,
That the friends are most likely henceforth to be foes.
But see what a pantomime lover can do!
His soul's wild emotion sinks into his shoe,
And his griefs are expressed—in a grand *pas de deux.*
The king looks on, while they caper about,
Indicating without any manner of doubt,
This officer stout
Must be put to the rout,
Or he'll cut his most excellent majesty out.
He thinks for a minute or two, and then
He calls for paper, some ink, and a pen,
He has a sick friend
At Milliken's Bend,
And, thinks he, it's a jolly long distance to send.
This fellow shall start,
Without even a cart,
And if he's back under a year he'll be smart.
Ishmael submissively touches his hat,

But he smells a rat—
He's not such a flat—
For he knows what the wily old willin is at.
"I'm off like a shot," he infers to the king,
But at the side wing
He contrives to fling
A look, that says plain, as "the Cinti" could sing,
"I'll be dee'd if I'm going to do any such thing."
Supposing of course that the coast is clear,
Without any fear
The monarch expresses Pauline is a dear,
Conducting himself in a manner so queer,
That he must be the victim of love, or strong beer;
And Korponay looks on, but he don't interfere.
But finding in vain
Her affection to gain—
She repulses his suit, with such thorough disdain—
He orders the nigger
To shorten her figure,
By cutting her head off; remarkable rigor—
A summary knack,
A better, I think, though not much, than the sack—
At this critical juncture her lover comes back,
Pitches into the black,
And with curious facility routs the whole pack—
What the "Tall Son of York" would call "clearing the track."
As a body might say,
There's no end of dismay,
For of course it cannot be expected, that they
Could carry the day
Against all the king's troops should it come to a fray;
So suspecting there might be the devil to pay,
They sagaciously settled to run right away.

But run they do not,
And I'll tell you for what—
If they did, the spectacle would all go to pot—
And it really hasn't too much of a plot—
So just at this crisis the guards arrive
With their king, too, as hard as he can drive,
And you think they're both going to be swallowed alive.
But, not at all,
His majesty warbles uncommonly small,
And there comes at his call
Investment and pall,
A priest (for a super), remarkably tall.
As rigid as starch,
He looks up to the arch,
And blesses the crowd, to a very quick march.
Now comes a desirable intermission,
When audience, and actor, and eke the musician
Take up a position,
And Niblo *frère*
Contributes his share
To keep up the spirits of every one there.
Well,
To go back to our *mouton*, the women rebel,
For what cause, I don't feel myself bound to tell.
There's an evident mess,
And they dance their distress,
In what elegant manner I leave you to guess,
But to do something des-
Perate, when they're done bathing, their actions express.
The king's *militairy*
Arrives apropos, and of course a quandary,
And also a fairy,
Most charmingly played, by our own charming "Mary,"
Of an over-large milk-jug uncommonly chary,

Appears and down drops,
One of Niblo's best "*props*,"
Meaning the milk-jug, and out of it pops
A talisman rare,
Like a green Windsor pear.
And as speedy as light
It sets matters all right,
And the feminine soldiers prepare for a fight,
For the rest of the matter, how great their despair,
When they lost the green pear,
How shamefully tempted with presents most rare.
How the "Magic *boquet*"
(As the bills will say,
Ill-using that u in a scandalous way),
Put an end to the riot, along with the play.
How Zorah, the slave, was the genius of good,
How the pugnacious Amazons camped in a wood,
How they marched, and manœuvered, *to show that they could*,
Must be seen to be thoroughly well understood,
And when
You've seen it all over and over again,
You'll be lucky if you can unravel it then

FATALITY.

A CONDENSED NOVEL.

CHAPTER I.

NIGHT.

"Oh! the summer night
Has a smile of light,
And she sits on a sapphire throne."—*Barry Cornwall.*

"Words, words, words."—*Shakspeare.*

THE moon in tranquil brilliancy shed a soft, spiritual light upon the picturesque and happy village of Oakstown, which, like an innocent child steeped in guiltless slumber, reposed upon its grassy couch; that small, low, musical reverberation which fills the air in calm summer nights, rising and falling on the ravished sense like the undulations of some fairy minstrelsy, broke sweetly the intensity of silence; whilst ever and anon the clear, sharp bay of the distant watch-dog came ringing on the ear with startling emphasis.

It was midnight; the last peal from the village-clock had from the ivy-covered tower tolled forth the death of yesterday, the mocking echoes caught up the sound, and to the hills repeated it in myriad voices, then died away and left the scene again to silence; soft, balmy slumber closed the eyes of all—all, save one pale watcher; he, for 'twas a man, with anxious gaze peered through the doubtful light, listening eagerly and with bated breath to every passing sound. For one whole hour had this poor, pallid listener, without speech or motion stood within the half-opened window of a mansion. You would have thought him lifeless, or a statue, so little evidence of vitality did he present, and yet a close observer might have seen by the deep corrugations on that brow, by the strong compression of those lips, by the fixed, steadfast gaze with which those eyes were bent in one direction, that something uncommon had brought that midnight watcher to the open casement, when all around was stillness.

But see, his ear has caught a distant sound, his eyes dilate, he scarcely breathes as his head is cautiously stretched forth to catch its import; a signal is heard, almost imperceptible, but to the patient listener full of certified assurance; 'tis returned; a figure is seen slowly nearing the window; he reaches it, the recognition is mutual; in a low, and all but voiceless whisper, the now smiling watcher murmurs in the stranger's ear:

"Is that you, Bill?"

A nod and squeeze of the hand was the reply.

"D—n your eyes, I thought you were never coming," said our friend within.

"Hallo, Jim, none of that ere," replied the new comer; "I had to establish a crack on my own account, and a jolly good swag I got; so no more palaver—business is business, let us go to work, and *stash all jaw.*"

"Well, come on then. Have you got the barkers?"

"To be sure I have; you don't suppose I'd try a knobby crib like this, without the persuaders; do you think the gallows old cove will run rusty?" inquired Bill, the house-breaker, exhibiting an enormous pair of horse-pistols.

"He might," returned Jim, "so its best to be careful—if he stirs, shoot him, it's your only security.

"Oh, never fear me," said the other, with a significant grin. "I'm blowed if I stand a chance of being *lagged* or *scragged* if I can help it; here," he continued, cocking his pistols as he spoke, "here's my best friend in an argument, he doesn't speak very often, but when he does, he generally has it all his own way; so, now for it."

"Hold!" interrupted Jim, "there's one thing I bargain for before I admit you."

"What's that?" growled the robber.

"The valuables are in the pantry, locked up; the key is in the housekeeper's pocket; should she wake and resist" ——

"The knife," savagely whispered Bill, "the knife is a silent argufyer."

"Villain! murderer!" exclaimed the former, energetically seizing the ruffian by the arm, "not for your life. Know, man of blood," continued he, dashing the tears from his eyes, and trembling with suppressed agitation as he spoke, "I love that woman; do with the others as you please, but as you are a man, I charge you to spare her life,"—there was a pause, at length the housebreaker gave the required assurance.

"Heaven, I thank thee," fervently ejaculated the other, opening the casement—they entered.

Oh, holy and inscrutable NATURE, who dost in every being plant the imperishable germ of affection, laud be to thee, even this guilty butler, who, leagued with highwaymen, betrays his trust and yields his master to the murderous blade, has within his inmost heart, corrupted though it be, one humanizing influence. CIRCUMSTANCE, thou daughter of the sky, twin-born with DESTINY, creation hinges on thy unerring fiat, the WILL must coincide with thee, the ACT be regulated by thy inclination; thou stretchest forth the hand of man thou puts't his very tongue in motion; VICE attends thy bidding, enveloping the unrighteous with the attributes of ILL; while virtue at thy summons speeds to earth, and in holy vesture clothes the BEAUTIFUL and the GOOD.

CHAPTER II.

MORNING.

"There's no place like home."—*Clari.*

"He hath a lean and hungry look."—*Shakspeare.*

THE village of Oakstown, bathed in the sunlight of a summer morning, showed lovely as the home of everlasting joy; the merry woodland choir upraised their song of thankfulness; the gladsome sun-ray danced on the wavelets of the tiny stream, and rained a flood of softened warmth, like breath of seraphs, on the fresh cut grass with which the morning's labor had bestrown the meadows, scattering its sweetness on the breeze, and making the morning air one sweet and grateful perfume; the happy villagers thronged the various avenues, seeking their respective homes for food and rest from the first installment of the day's pleasant toil; faces embrowned with ruddy health, and all a-glow, looked gladly forth upon the liberal free air of—their sole inheritance; poor serfs of custom, hapless slaves of circumstance, did they but know their misery, shut out from scientific knowledge, far from the inspiring converse of the intellectual, and in melancholy ignorance doomed to wear out life in factitious happiness and unreal comfort.

The breakfast-room in Oakleigh Hall, presented a beautiful

picture of that homey elegance which characterize the family houses in England. Lord Elderberry, the hereditary owner of some score of miles, of which he formed the noble nucleus, reclined in his velvet chair, surrounded by all those luxuries which custom has interwoven with the wants of life, until they have become necessary to the high in station. He was a tall, graceful, aristocratic looking man; his age was about fifty, but he was so carefully toileted, that a transient observer would hardly suppose him to be more than thirty. His fair and ample brow, well chiselled, though slightly exaggerated nose, small hands and arch-instepped feet, proclaiming at once the inheritor of noble blood; his beautiful child, the sole-surviving daughter of his house, bearing also, in her every turn, the unmistakable evidences of gentle birth, sat near him, they, with a taciturn governess, and one male friend of his Lordship, made up the party. It was unusually late, yet breakfast was not yet served; indeed the table was but partially laid, and each began to wonder what could possibly have caused the delay. His Lordship was slightly, but not perceptibly annoyed. To the careless observer no change could be seen, but Mac Brose, his accommodating distant relation and humble servant, with the experienced eye of a toady, caught the shadow of an ungracious expression, and exerted his utmost to avert the coming storm, ere its arrival should oblige him to seek shelter in retirement.

"Remarkable fair day, this, my lord," insinuated he in his blandest manner.

"Very," drily responded the Earl.

"Hem!" said Mac Brose, confidentially to himself. "He is vexed; that tone is sufficient, the *deil* take their laziness," for inasmuch as his annoyance proceeded from the long protraction of the matutinal meal, he supposed the cloud upon his Lordship's brow was produced by the same cause.

The Earl sighed heavily, so heavily as to cause the Lady Emily, his daughter, to raise her head from her usual morning's occupation, that of tending her favorite exotics, when perceiving the sadness which had mantled over her father's face, she approached him affectionately, and kissing him, exclaimed, "dearest papa, you are looking quite pale."

Oh! amidst the thorny path of LIFE, its pangs, its privations, the *pointed rocks*, the *perilous obstructions*, fate flings before us as we whirl along the troublous tide of DESTINY; how sweet a comforter art thou, FILIAL LOVE.

His Lordship smiled, but 'twas as a transient sun-ray on a tomb, showing for one bright instant the external semblance of joy, while all within was dark and dismal; and yet that insubstantial gleam sufficed to calm his daughter's agitation; and when the Earl kissed her peachy cheek, and with parental fondness soothed her apprehension, she cheerfully resumed her task; her happy young heart pure and unsophisticated.

CHAPTER III.

THE APPARITION.

Morte la bête,
Mort le venin.

"Can I believe my eyes?"—*Anon.*

BETTER than an hour had passed, and yet no sign of breakfast; the intervening time having been spent by MacBrose in mentally delivering over every servant in the house, to the hottest place your memory can suggest, casting furtive glances ever and anon towards Lord Elderberry, and wondering from the inmost recesses of his epigastrium what could possibly have caused this unusual apathy.

He was *Hungry*—uncommonly HUNGRY.

At last the Earl broke silence, exclaiming, suddenly, "MacBrose; after a slight pause, continuing. "What's your opinion with regard to Apparitions?"

"Why, my lord, I—that is to say—upon my word—appar*ee*tions—*gude*ness me, the study of demonology, is one of *on*questionable ant*ee*quity from the earliest stages of the world up to the present time. H*e*story is rife w*e*th *e*llustrations. Pol*ee*bius maintains that"—

Lord Elderberry stayed him in his learned peroration, by saying with solemnity, "I saw one last night." MacBrose forgot his very appetite in more absorbing curiosity. The Lady Emily, arrested in the act of trimming a lotus, caught her father's words, and timidly crept forward to listen.

"You know, MacBrose," continued the Earl; his voice rendered nearly inarticulate from agitation, "you know the details of my early life—the mysterious loss of my first-born, my only son, the heir to my name, the last of this noble house."

"Alas! unhappy destiny," sighed forth MacBrose, making liberal use of his cambric, and inwardly exulting that distant relationship was lifted by the circumstance a thought nearer to the broad lands of Oakleigh.

The Lady Emily tried to speak, but could not; so burying her face within her hands, she knelt on the footstool at her father's feet, and nestled herself in his breast. "My child," faltered he, "my own, my only child;" and the Earl, stern, cold as was his nature, wept. The grief of father and daughter was sharp, but silent. Not so that of MacBrose; he sobbed aloud; and what's more, felt the fell acuteness of his sorrow, for he was hungered even to anguish.

After a space, the Earl resumed his natural, calm dignity, and continued: "'Tis now just fifteen years since my boy was lost; had he lived, he would have been of age to-day; after the three years which I employed in ceaseless search, believing him dead, I endeavored, as you know, to school myself, if possible, into Christian-like resignation."

"Sore blow! *sore* blow! good man! *excellent* man," sobbed MacBrose, seeing that there was a pause, and he was expected to say something.

"Time, at length, the great softener of human suffering, began to blunt the edge of my anguish; and what was at first a maddening thought that ever stood up stark and plain before me, sank into a settled melancholy. But as this day comes round, the anniversary of his birth, the greatness of my loss obtrudes itself upon my imagination with renewed violence; overpowered by such feelings, it was very late last night ere I retired to my bed; and with my thoughts full of my lost one, fell at last, from very weariness of limb, into an uneasy, broken slumber, from which I was awakened by a sudden noise, and on looking up—Great Heavens, what was my astonishment upon beholding the apparition of my son—not a sweet, smiling boy, as when I saw him last, but with his manly form developed; his mother's angel face changed into masculine severity—just as it has been my pride to picture what he might have grown to had he lived. Slowly he seemed to near my couch, and then I saw that he was meanly clad, and had a haggard, fearful look; a knife was in one hand, and the semblance of a miniature in the other; I knew it at once; 'twas similar to one in my possession; a likeness of his mother set in brilliants; his attention seemed to be directed alternately towards it and me; fear had hitherto fettered my tongue, and froze up the very current of my blood. But in the faint hope of receiving a reply, I determined to address the spectre; for that purpose I raised myself gently, and had just ejaculated, 'In the name of Heaven'—when a flash of lightning seemed to break from his very hand, a loud clap of thunder instantaneously followed, and the apparition vanished."

CHAPTER IV.

RETRIBUTION.

"Do I merit pangs like these,
That have cleft my heart in twain?
Must I, to the very lees,
Drain thy bitter chalice, Pain?"—*Morris.*

"Revenge is now the cud that I do chew."—*Beaumont & Fletcher.*

Scarcely had Lord Elderberry finished the relation when a confused murmur was heard approaching the apartment, and several voices exclaiming, "bring him along"—"we've caught him"—"villain, robber," etc.—the hubbub growing louder and louder, until Simkins, the housekeeper, bounced into the breakfast-room.

"What's the matter, Simkins?" sternly demanded the Earl.

"Why, don't you know that you have been robbed, my dear lord, she returned, "but we've caught 'em—that villain, James, to go for to have the impertinence to make up to me too—oh! the wickedness of the world!"

"Robbed?" replied the Earl.

"Robbed?" anxiously exclaimed MacBrose, for inasmuch as his posterity *might*, in a century or two have an interest in the property, it behoved him to be personally concerned.

"And by that rascal, James, too," said the Earl; "ungrateful fellow!"

"Horrible ruffian!" said MacBrose.

"Unfortunate wretch!" said the Lady Emily.

"Where is he?" demanded Lord Elderberry.

"They're a bringing him, my lord," whimpered Simkins, who, to the honor of womankind, be it said, lamented more at the prospect of the poor fellow's being hanged, and so lost to her and to respectability for ever, than for the imminent danger of his lordship's valuables.

At this moment, James, the delinquent butler, was dragged in by several of the under servants, who showed their loyalty for the Earl, and their detestation for crime, by looking awfully indignant, and grasping James tightly by the collar.

"Release him," said the Earl, in a justice of the peace tone. They did so, and the butler shook off his capturers, and folding his arms across his breast, scowled upon the group.

"Well, sir," said the Earl, regarding the prisoner sternly, "this is a pretty reward for all I have done for you."

"You are right, Earl," replied the fellow in a determined voice, "it is!"

"What mean you?" demanded his lordship.

"Patience, my lord; you'll soon know," replied the butler, casting upon him a glance of concentrated malignity.

"Come, come, fellow," interrupted MacBrose, who was playing clerk, and noting down the proceedings, "consider where you are, sir—be respectful."

"Peace, fool!" exclaimed the other, savagely.

"Mean, crawling parasite, keep to thy vocation; cringe, and fawn, and flatter, and eat your miserable meal in silence."

"I wish to the Lord I had it to eat," thought MacBrose, with quiet nerves; for he was one of those humane, milk-blooded folks, who reverence themselves too much to take offence at anything.

"Now, sir, explain," demanded the Earl, "how have I injured you?"

"How?" replied the fellow, with a flashing eye. "How! ha! I'll tell you how; great lord, *you* endowed me with this load of misery, *you* delivered me up to the tender mercy of a cruel fate. Lord—FATHER! *you* gave me life."

The Earl gasped for breath, shuddering from his very soul as the fellow continued—"Look upon this portrait, most noble lord," tearing an humbly executed miniature from his breast, and flinging it to his lordship.

"Great God! Maria!" muttered the Earl, sinking back into his chair.

"Ha! exclaimed the delinquent, "you recognize that face; you saw it when in youth, health, innocence and beauty; it beamed like a ray of light; but you saw it not when *vice, misery* and *degradation* had stamped the impress of a fiend on that angelic countenance—you saw her when she lived the minion of thy vicious passion, but you did not see her die a hopeless death, raving in mad delirium. I *did;* and kneeling beside the corpse of her that *was* my mother, I swore to be avenged upon her soul's destroyer—upon thee—ay, writhe, writhe. I've more to tell thee yet—thy son"—

"Lives," almost shrieked the Earl.

"You shall hear," quietly returned the prisoner. "You never even inquired whether there was such a thing in existence, as me, so there was no fear of being recognized. I soon obtained a situation in your household; once there, my first design was to seek your library, upbraid you with your infamy, and shoot you where you sat. Several times did I enter for that purpose, and invariably found you fondling your son—your only *legitimate* son—the heir to the house and *honors* of Oakland, when the idea flashed across my brain what glorious revenge it would be to make that much-loved boy the instrument of retribution, to nurture him in vice, to steep him in villainy, to blot out every attribute of good, *to destroy him utterly in* LIFE *and in* ETERNITY—a SON'S soul for a MOTHER'S. I stole him, kept him concealed for a time, clothed him in squalid rags, and then found means to have him conveyed to the abodes of guilt and wretchedness—ha! ha! ha! day by day, week by week, year by year, while you incessantly deplored his loss, I watched him in his progress through all the grades of infamy; schooled in wickedness—tutored by robbers and murderers, the heir of Oakleigh grew up a *fit* inheritor of his father's HONOR."

"Merciful Heaven!" ejaculated the Earl, as the suspicion flashed across his mind. "Was it he? was it my son that"—

"That aimed the murderous weapon at his father's heart? it was! ha! ha! it was," triumphantly exclaimed the fellow. I led him on to the commission of this crime. I planned it—pointed out your room, hoping he would have killed—no, not killed you; for I would have had you *know* the hand that gave the death-wound." At this moment the sound of footsteps were heard approaching. "Now," roared the ruffian "*noble* father, prepare to meet thy *honorable* son."

Several dependents entered, having in their custody the man whom the reader will recognize as Bill, of the first chapter. He gave a savage look at the butler, muttering between his teeth, "So, you precious varmint, the whole of this here vos a plant, they tell me."

"Listen," replied the butler—"listen, my lord, to the classic eloquence of your son's language. Honorable Bill, the house-breaker! let me present you to your father; ha! ha! ha!" and the ruffian's face beamed with savage joy.

The Earl groaned, and covered his face with his hands, in speechless agony.

"What's all this nonsense," said Bill; "*my* father's far enough away; he's bin *transported* this many a year."

"It's a lie," thundered the butler. "There, there he sits in that velvet chair, overflowing with parental love. *Go, go and receive his blessing before you are hanged.*"

"Will any body tell me what the fellow means?" replied Bill, looking round the group.

"Why, he asserts," said MacBrose, finding no one spoke, "that you are the undoubted son of his lordship here, whom he, from motives of revenge, stole in infancy, and caused to be brought up in iniquity, hoping, by such horrible means, to involve father and son in one common destruction."

"Oh, that's it, is it," said Bill; "then he'd best have not *hollered* so loud, damn him; I'm glad I can pay him off for getting me into this scrape. I ain't no more your son, my lord, than Oliver Crummles."

The Earl started from his chair, while the butler's face grew livid with rage.

"Proceed," said his lordship; "if there be but the thousandth particle of a doubt, you shall be saved—rewarded—go on—go on, in mercy."

"All I got to say," resumed Bill, "is, that every body knows who *my* father was; but there used to be a poor little natomy of a creature, that was sommat like me, among us. We called him Slender Jimmy. Nobody know'd where he comed from, or anything about him."

"And where is he?" said the Earl, with intense anxiety.

"Why, you see we couldn't make him useful no how; he had no taste for picking pockets, and all the whoppin' in the world couldn't drive it into him; so we let him alone until he got up to be a youth. We always knew that there was something queer about him, he had such a curious knack of reading books. Why, if you believe me, I stole nigh hand a whole stall of thim, 'cause he liked 'em, and hadn't the heart to prig for hisself. Well, at last he guv us the slip entirely, and I did hear that he listed and threw hisself away in the army."

"It must—it must be he. Oh, Heaven be thanked!" fervently cried the Earl. Meantime, the butler, frenzied at the destruction of his plans, drew a pistol suddenly from his breast, levelled it full against the Earl's, and exclaiming, "Damnation! you shall never behold him," pulled the trigger; there was a loud report, followed by a scream of agony. The barrel had burst, causing the ball to deviate, which lodged harmlessly in the wall, shattering the hand and arm of the ruffian butler up to the elbow, while a fragment of steel pierced his forehead, and sunk even to his brain. He raised himself with difficulty, and fixing his glazing eyes upon the Earl, opened his mouth several times as if attempting to speak; but vainly; shaking his clenched fist, and regarding him with a scowl of malevolence, his jaw dropped, and he fell dead.

CHAPTER V.

CONCLUSION.

"A fair commencement, better far continuation,
And the winding up the fairest of the whole."—*Knowles.*

"Ne quid nimis."—*Latin Proverb.*

But little more remains to be told. The Earl inserted a cautiously worded advertisement in the various newspapers, which very soon had the effect of discovering the individual mentioned by Bill; everything conspired to certify his identity. It appeared that after quitting the vile society in which his boyhood was passed, he gained much distinction, earning for himself the rank of ensign in the regiment into which he had enlisted, so that, had he not already a name, he would have ennobled one by his own exertions. The interview between father and son was most affecting; and as the latter had passed scatheless through so vitiating a trial as the companionship of his early years, it need not be said that he was in every way worthy to shed lustre upon the high position to which he found himself entitled.

The house-breaker was brought to trial, but inasmuch as this particular transaction was shown to be the contriving of the dead butler, and no other being proved against him, aided by the intercession of Lord Elderberry, his punishment was commuted to a short imprisonment, after undergoing which, his lordship granted him a small farm on his estate, provided that he sincerely promised to amend his life. He did so, and to his honor be it said, most rigidly kept his word. Who shall say that he has a better hope beyond this life than that reformed sinner? Doth not the holy book declare

"THERE IS JOY IN HEAVEN OVER ONE SINNER THAT REPENTETH!"

DRAMAS OF THE DAY.

REVENGE; OR, THE MEDIUM.

Persons Represented.

Copperhead,
Deyville,
Smallbrain, A Widower.
Lauretta, } His Daughters.
Penelope, }
Lunaria, A Medium.

SCENE I.

Elegant Apartment at Smallbrain's. Smallbrain and Deyville discovered.

Deyville. Nay, gentle sir! I prithee reconsider
Your last resolve; and let me not depart
A comfortless and most unhappy man.
Smallbrain. Sir, you have heard my fixed determination;
My daughter never can be thine—she loves
Thee not. If there had ever been a spark
Of fond affection evidenced by her,
Or if thy disposition was of such a sort,
That I might exercise authority,
Or gently counsel her to give her hand—

In full reliance, that thy goodness would,
In time, compel her heart to yield as well,
It might be otherwise. But I have watched,
Unthought by thee, thy every action;
And I've found thee false, deceitful, heartless, vile,
Companion of the dissolute and base.

Deyville. Nay! by my hopes of happiness I swear,
It is not so. I have been much belied.
Thoughtless and free I may have been, I grant,
But never heartless.

Smallbrain. Prithee, sir, no more!
I have had proof of your delinquency,
And, therefore, to your present catalogue,
Add not the coward's one of lying.

Deyville. Ha! if thou wert younger, thou'dst as soon have dared
To grasp the forked lightning, as have use
That most insulting epithet. Old man!
Beware how you boil up my southern blood:
It brooks not insult, even from white hairs.

Smallbrain. Thy fiery and impetuous temper proves
How right I am. Thinkest thou I'd trust my child,
The living essence of her angel mother,
Within the orbit of a star so baleful?
No! thou hast my answer, which no power can change.

Deyville. Indeed! take heed, then, I blast not thy peace,
As thou hast blasted mine.

Smallbrain. I fear thee not;
But laugh thy threats to scorn—thee and thy threats.

Deyville. Your pardon, sir! those most unseemly words
Were, from the torture of a stricken heart,
Enforced. I bow to thy decree, though harsh,
And in submission humbly take my leave.

Now nothing's left to feed on but revenge.
On which I'll banquet with the appetite of Hell.
[*Aside and Exit.*

Smallbrain. Methinks I hear that small, but conscious rap,
From her, my spirit wife, approving this.

Enter Lauretta and Penelope.

Smallbrain. My children twain, who to my heart do cleave,
Or rather, who my heart encompass round,
As shells of oysters cling around the fish—
Let me embrace thee both. Lauretta, love!
Thou counterpart of her, a seraph now;
Tell me—I won't say truly—for I know thy thought
Would never harbor a deceit: this man
Deyville, dost thou affect him aught?

Lauretta. Dear father! no. His ceaseless importunities
To me were most distasteful, and indeed
Distressing; and most gladly would I say
Come not again, but that I feared offence.

Smallbrain. Glad am I that my inference was true;
Rest in content, for he will come no more.
The flavor of the moment is still on
The lips of hungry time, when I dismissed
Him and his hopes.

Lauretta. Most kindly hast thou acted.
My father dear! 'twas but this very day
I did debate most seriously the means
To rid me of his pertinacious suit.

Penelope. And asked my counsel.

Smallbrain. Well! my madcap wild,
What answer didst thou give?

Penelope. Marry, I said,
If such assiduous cavalier had I,

And my civil conduct did not him suffice
To check impertinence, and close his mouth;
I'd fling such icy words against his head,
They'd penetrate beyond the brazen front,
And freeze the burning lava of his heart.

Smallbrain. No more of this; dismiss it from our minds,
And let us now endeavor to effect
The solemn and mysterious ceremonial,
Through which we can compel the spirit world,
And seek from them instruction and advice.

[*They seat themselves silently around a centre table. A long pause. Penelope smiles.*

Smallbrain. Why dost thou smile my child?

Penelope. To tell the truth,
Most honored father, I've but little faith
In this, to me irreverent conjuration.

Smallbrain. Speak not so lightly, child, of that great mystery
Which, upon every side, in every mail,
You see attested by the signature
Of many teachers of the sacred truth,
Who surely would not peril their own souls
By cherishing delusion and imposture.
Enough to say, I rigidly believe
That we can hold communion with the souls
Of friends departed. Wasn't that a rap?

Lauretta. Distinct and clear. My blood is chilled with awe.

[*A series of muffled knocks are heard. Tableaux of astonishment and dread.*

Smallbrain (*fearfully*). Whoe'er thou art, in whose tremendous presence,
Fraught with the mighty secrets of the tomb,
We trembling stand—I pray vouchsafe some sign,

By which we may from thee assurance have,
That thou hast power to visit earth again.

[*A puff of wind blows the window blind violently back. Smallbrain and Lauretta start with extreme terror. Penelope quietly recloses blind.*

Penelope. See how coincidences not improbable,
May twist the web of actual circumstance;
A simple puff of air thus seems a horror.
Smallbrain. Ah! but the raps, Penelope, the raps!
Penelope. Proceeded from a medium simpler still,
And more material, even from the cat!
Smallbrain and Lauretta. The cat!
Penelope. The harmless cat, who, scratching of her foot,
And in the effort spending too much strength,
Drummed on the carpet—hence those fearful sounds.

[*Smallbrain and Lauretta shake their heads. Scene changes.*

SCENE II.

Deyville's Apartment.

Deyville (*solus*). Curses on him, and her, and all the crew!
To lose her fifty thousand dollars thus;
The money I so dearly loved and wooed,
For she herself came not into the count.
Oh! for some deadly means to be requited.
Ha! I remember now, that I've been told,
The old, weak witted imbecile believes
In rapping spiritual, and consults
Occasionally, Mediums. I know one,

Accommodating and all conscienceless,
Who, for a bribe, will probably reveal
More than has e'er occurred. To her I'll hie,
And send a message, that shall turn the love
He bears his children, into direst hate—
A glorious thought, ha, to my wish
Comes Copperhead.

Enter Copperhead.

Well met my friend.
Brave accident that pulled the trigger of
My loaded thought, and shot thee here.
With thee, I fain would visit that *Lunaria*,
The *Medium* that you spoke of.
Copperhead. Art thou convert?
Deyville. No, not exactly; for I don't believe,
Pardon my frankness, in the certainty
Of your new Spiritual Telegraph.
Copperhead. Ha! ha! I thought not.
Deyville. But I have an end
To gain; say then, and quickly, if thou wilt
Assist me.
Copperhead. Speak! 'tis done ere thou dost ask.
What is it?
Deyville. I have been insulted, sir,
To the extremity of man's endurance.
Copperhead. And thy impetuous and chivalric blood,
I see, would fain appease it by duello.
Deyville. Not so, my friend. A high authority
Has shown us how to parry with a jest,
All such appeals; and at approach of hurt,
Hide a wise head beneath the cap and bells.
But you have promised me your full assistance

In that I purpose, whatsoe'er it be.
Did I not understand thee so?

Copperhead. Thou didst.
Wilt please you to put me to the proof?

Deyville. A word in secret. I will tell thee all.

[*They retire.*

A lapse of some Hours.

SCENE III.

Smallbrain's Apartment as before.

TABLEAUX OF DOMESTIC COMFORT.

Smallbrain, Lauretta, and Penelope discovered in various Household Employments.

Smallbrain. My daughters, dear! how doubly blessed am I,
To find the eve of my declining day
Made radiant by the filial love of both;
As though two suns were in one firmament,
Each shedding beams of light, and love, and joy.

Enter boy with note. Smallbrain reads.

"What's this? A spiritual communication?
Can give me proof incontrovertible,
E'en the confession of the erring party,
Of matters urgent to my earthly peace."
Who brought this? Let me see the messenger.

Boy. 'Tis a young lady, sir, who waits below.

Smallbrain. Show her here quickly. Girls, you may retire.

[*They go out.*

Enter Lunaria.

Art thou she who brought
This most mysterious missive?

Lunaria. Alas! sir, yes.
Would it had fallen to other lips to say,
What I must now reveal of her, whom love
Had so enhaloed with its dazzling sheen,
That shame was hidden in the great effulgence.

Smallbrain. Whom speak you of? How link my name with shame?
Who art thou?

Lunaria. A Medium. [*Smallbrain cowers.*] And to prove my power,
I'll tell thee who thou art. Smallbrain's thy name.
Thou hast, or thinkest thou hast, two daughters;
'Tis now some two years since their mother died,
Was mourned and honored.

Smallbrain. As was her desert.

Lunaria. So, doubtless, thou hast thought; but I, alas!
From testimony which cannot be shaken,
Even from her repentant spirit—say,
Thou wert abused by her most shamefully.

Smallbrain. Hold! hold! This blow hath crushed my very heart,
Wrung from thence all reverence and love,
Not only towards her memory, but from
Her offspring, the vile produce of her shame.
But as the most intense affection, warped
From its integrity, to direst hate
Doth turn—so I already loath the thought
Of her and hers. Nor shall my house contain
Their hated forms; but they shall hence at once,
Inheritors of their bad mother's shame.

Were this revealed to me by mortal speech,
I would not give it credence; but compelled
By spiritual knockings from the spirit's self,
It must be true. And though this heart will break,
And haply theirs, from whom I must be sundered.
What are hearts, homes, and peace destroyed,
Compared with the sublimity of Truth and Justice.

CURTAIN FALLS.

NED GERAGHTY'S LUCK.

CHAPTER I.

Brave old Ireland is the Land of Fairies, but of all the various descriptions there isn't one to be compared to the Leprechaun, in the regard of cunning and 'cuteness. Now if you don't know what a Leprechaun is I'll tell you. Why then —save us and keep us from harm, for they are queer chaps to *gosther* about—a Leprechaun is the fairies, shoemaker; and a mighty conceited little fellow he is, I assure you, and very mischievous, except where he might happen to take a liking.

But, perhaps, the best way to give you an idea of their appearance and characteristics, will be to tell you a bit of a story about one.

Once upon a time then, many years ago, before the screech of the steam-engine had frightened the "good people" out of their quiet nooks and corners, there lived a rollicking, good natured, rakish boy, called Ned Geraghty; his father was the only miller in the neighborhood for miles round, and being a prudent, saving kind of an old hunks was considered to be amazingly well off, and the name of the town they lived in would knock all the teeth out of the upper jaw of an Englishman to pronounce: it was called Ballinaskerrybaughkilinashaghlin.

Well, the boy, as he grew up to a man's estate, used to worry the old miller nearly out of his seven senses, he was such devil-may-care, good-for-nothing. Attend to anything that was said to him he would not, whether in the way of learning or of business. He upset ink-bottle upon ink-bottle upon his father's account-books, such as they were; and at the poor apology for a school, which the bigotry of the reverend monopolizers of knowledge permitted to exist in Ball——, the town—he was always famous for studying less and playing more, than any boy of his age in the barony.

It isn't to be much wondered at then, that when in the course of events, old Geraghty had the wheat of life threshed out of him by the flail of unpitying Time, Master Ned, his careless, reprobate son, was but little fitted to take his position as the head-miller of the county.

But to show you the luck that runs after, and sticks close to some people, whether they care for it or not, as if, like love, it despiseth the too ardent seeker.

Did you ever take notice, that two men might be fishing together at the same spot, with the same sort of tackle and the same sort of bait, one will get a bushel full before the other gets a bite—that's luck,—not that there's any certainty about it; for the two anglers might change places to-morrow. Ah! it's an uncomfortable, deceiving, self-confidence-destroying, Jack-o'lantern sort of thing is that same luck, and yet how many people, especially our countrymen, cram their hands into their pockets and fully expect that the cheating devil will filter gold through their fingers.

But, good people listen to me, take a friend's advice, don't trust her, and of this be assured, although a lump of luck may now and then—and mighty rarely at that—exhibit itself at your very foot, yet to find a good vein of it you must dig laboriously, unceasingly. Indolent humanity, to hide its own laziness, call those *lucky* men, who, if you investigate the matter closely, you'll find have been simply *industrious* ones.

But to return to the particular luck which laid hold of Ned Geraghty, everybody thought, and everybody of course, the worst, and that Ned the rover would soon make ducks and drakes of the old man's money; that the mill might as well be shut up now, for there was nobody to see after it; every gossip, male and female, in the town had his or her peculiar prognostic of evil. Sage old men shook their heads, grave old matrons shrugged their shoulders, while the unanimous opinion of the marriageable part of the feminine community was, that nothing could possibly avert the coming fatality except a careful wife.

Now candor compels the historian to say, that the mill-hoppers did not go so regularly as they did formerly, and moreover that Ned being blessed with a personal exterior, began to take infinite pains in its adornment. Finer white cords and tops could not be sported by any squireen in the parish; his green coat was made of the best broadcloth, an intensely bright red India handkerchief was tied openly round his neck, a real beaver hat on his impudent head, and a heavy thong-whip in his hand, for he had just joined modestly in the Bally &c. &c. hunt.

This was the elegant apparition that astonished the sober and sensible town folk a very few months after the decease of the miserly old miller, and of course all the evil forebodings of the envious and malicious were in a fair way to be speedily consummated, when my bold Ned met with the piece of luck that changed the current of his life, and gave the lie to those neighborly and charitable prognostics.

It was on one fine moonlight night that Ned was walking homeward by a short cut across the fields, for his sorry old piece of horse-flesh had broken down in that day's hunt, and for many a weary mile he had been footing it through bog and briar, until with fatigue and mortification, he felt both heart-sick and limb-weary, when all at once his quick ear caught the sound of the smallest kind of a voice, so low, and yet so musical, singing a very little ditty to the accompaniment of tiny taps upon a diminutive lapstone. Ned's heart gave one great bound, his throat swelled, and his hair stuck into his head like needles.

"May I never eat another day's vittles, if it ain't a Leprechaun," said he to himself, "and the little villain is so busy with his singing that he didn't hear me coming; if I could only ketch a-howlt of him, my fortune's made."

With that he stole softly towards the place from whence the sounds proceeded, and peeping slyly over a short clump of blackthorn, there, sure enough, he saw a comical little figure, not more than an inch and a half high, dressed in an old fashioned suit of velvet, with a cocked hat on his head, and a sword by his side, as grand as a prime minister, hammering at a morsel of fairies' sole-leather, and singing away like a cricket that had received a musical education.

"Now's my chance," said Ned, as quick as thought he dropt his hat right over the little vagabond. "Ha! ha! you murtherin schemer, I've got you tight," he cried, as he crushed his hat together, completely imprisoning the Leprechaun.

"Let me out, Ned Geraghty; you see I know who you are," squalled the little chap.

"The devil a toe," says Ned, and away he scampered towards home with his prize, highly elated, for he knew that the Leprechauns were the guardians of all hidden treasure, and he was determined not to suffer him to escape until he had pointed out where he could discover a pot of gold.

When Ned had reached home, the first thing he did was to get a hammer and some nails, and having placed his hat upon the table, he fastened it securely by the brim, the little fellow screeching and yelling like mad.

"Now, my boy, I've got you safe and snug," says Ned, as he sat down in his chair to have a parley with his prisoner.

"There's no use in kicking up such a hollabulloo—tell me where I can find a treasure, and I'll let you go."

"I won't, you swaggering blackguard, you stuck up lump of conceit, you good for nothing end of the devil's bad bargain, I won't;" and then the angry little creature let fly a shower of abuse that gave Ned an indifferent opinion of fairy gentility.

"Well, just as you please," says he; "it's there you'll stay till you do," and with that Ned makes himself a fine, stiff tumbler of whisky-punch, just to show his independence.

"Ned," said the little schemer, when he smelt the odor of the spirits, "but that's potteen."

"It's that same it is," says Ned.

"Ah! ye rebel! ain't you ashamed of yourself to chate the gauger. Murther alive! how well it smells," chirps the cunning rascal, snuffing like a kitten with a cold in its head.

"It *tastes* better, *avic*," says Ned," taking a long gulp, and then smacking his lips like a post-boy's whip.

"Arrah, don't be greiggin a poor devil that way," says the Leprechaun, "and me as dry as a lime-burner's wig."

"Will you tell me what I want to know then?"

"I can't, really I can't," says the fairy, but with a pleasanter tone of voice.

"He's coming round," thought Ned to himself, and as with a view of propitiating him still further,

"Here's your health, old chap," says he, "and it's sorry I am to be obliged to appear so conthrary, for may this choke me alive if I wish you any harm in the world."

"I know you don't Ned, allana," says the other, as sweet

as possible; "but there's one thing I'd like you to do for me."

"And what might that be?"

"Jest give us the least taste in life of that elegant punch, for the steam of it's gettin' under the crevices, an' I declare to my gracious it's fairly killing me with the drouth."

"Nabocklish," cries Ned, "I'm not such a fool; how am I to get it at you?"

"Aisy enough; just stick a pin-hole in the hat, and gi'me one of the hairs o' yer head for a straw."

"Bedad, I don't think that would waste much o' the liquor," says Ned, laughing at the contrivance; "but if it would do you any good, here goes."

So Ned did as the Leprechaun desired, and the little scoundrel began to suck away at the punch like an alderman, and by the same token, the effect it had on him was curious: at first he talked mighty sensibly, then he talked mighty lively, then he sung all the songs he ever knew, and some he never knew; then he told a lot of stories as old as Adam, and laughed like the mischief at them himself; then he made speeches, then he roared, then he cried, and at last, after having indulged in

"Willie brewed a peck o' malt,"

down he fell on the table with a thump as though a small sized potatoe had fallen on the floor.

"Oh! may I never see glory," roared Ned, in an explosion of laughter, "if the little ruffian ain't as drunk as a piper."

"Ha! Ned, Ned you unfeelin' reprobate an' bad Christian; have you no compassion at all at all," squeaked the Leprechaun in drunken but most miserable accents.

"Oh!—oh!—oh!" the poor little creature groaned, like a dying tadpole.

"What's the matter," says Ned with real concern. "Is there anything I can do for you?"

"Air! air!" grunted the Leprechaun.

"The fellow's dead drunk," thought Ned, "so there'll be no harm in lettin him have a mouthful of fresh air;" so he ripped up two or three of the nails, when with a merry little laugh, the cunning vagabond slid through his fingers, and disappeared like a curl of smoke out of a pipe.

"Mushen then, may bad luck to you, for a deludin' disciple, but you've taken the conceit out o' me in beautiful style," cried Ned, as he threw himself into his chair, laughing heartily, however, in spite of his disappointment, at the clever way the little villain had effected his release.

"What a fool I was to be taken in by the dirty mountebank."

"No, you are not," said the voice, just above his head.

Ned started with surprise and looked egarly round.

"There's no use in searching my boy; I've got my liberty, and I'm now invisible," said the voice, "but you'r lettin' me out was a proof that you had a good heart, Ned, and I'm bound to do you a good turn for it."

"Why then, yer a gentleman ivery inch of ye, though it's only one an' a bit," cried Ned, jumping up with delight; "what are you goin' to gi' me? a treasure!"

"No, better than that," said the voice.

"What then?"

"A warning."

What the warning was we shall see in the next chapter.

CHAPTER II.

"WHAT the mischief is the matter wid me at all at all?" said Ned; "sure don't I know every foot of the ground between this and the next place, wherever it is? but bad luck attend the bit of *me* knows where I'm stan'in' now.

"Howsomever, I can't stand here all night, so here goes for a bowld push, somewhere or another."

With that, my bold Ned struck at random through the fields in one direction, hoping to find some well-known landmark which might satisfy him as to his whereabout, but all in vain, the whole face of the country was changed; where he expected to meet with trees, he encountered a barren waste; in the situation where he expected to find some princely habitation, he met with nothing but rocks—he never was so puzzled in his life.

In the midst of his perplexity, he sat down upon a mound of earth, and scratching his head, began seriously to ponder upon his situation.

"I'll take my Bible oath I was on my track before I met with that devil of a Leprechaun," said he, and then the thought took possession of him, that the deceitful fairy had bewitched the road, so that he might wander away, and perhaps lose himself amongst the wild and terrible bogs.

He was just giving way to an extremity of terror, when upon raising his eyes, what was his astonishment to find that the locality which before he sat down, he could have sworn was nothing but a strange and inhospitable waste, was blooming like a garden; and what's more, he discovered, upon rubbing his eyes, to make sure that he was not deceived, it was his own garden, his back rested against the wall of his own house; nay, the very seat beneath him, instead of an earthy knoll, was the good, substantial form that graced his little door-porch.

"Well," cries Ned, very much relieved at finding himself so suddenly at home, "if that don't bèat the bees, I'm a heathen; may I never leave this spot alive if I know how I got here no more nor the man in the moon: here goes for an air o' the fire, any way, for I'm starved intensely wid the cowld."

Upon that he started to go in, when he found that he had made another mistake; it wasn't the *house* he was close to, but the *mill.*

"Why, what a murtherin' fool I am this night; sure it's the mill I'm forninst and not the house," said he; "never mind, its lucky I am to be so near home, any way; there it is, just across the paddock;" so saying, he proceeded towards the little stile which separated the small field from the road, inly wondering as he went along, whether it was the Leprechaun or the whisky that had so confused his proceedings.

"Its mighty imprudent that I've been in my drinkin'," thought he, "for if I had drunk a trifle less, the country wouldn't be playin' such ingenious capers wid my eye-sight, and if I had drunk a trifle more, I might a hunted up a soft stone by way of a pillow, and made my bed in the road."

Arrived at the stile, a regular phenomena occurred, which bothered him more and more—he couldn't get across it, notwithstanding the most strenuous exertion; when he went to step over, the rail sprang up to his head, and when taking advantage of the opening he had to duck under, he found it close to the ground.

The moon now popped behind a dense, black cloud, and sudden darkness fell upon the place, while at the same moment, the slow, rusty old village clock gave two or three premonitory croaks, and then banged out the hour of midnight.

Twelve o'clock at night is to the superstitious, the most terror-fraught moment the fearful earth can shudder at, and Ned was strongly imbued with the dread of ghostly things; at every bang of the deep-toned old chronicler, he quivered to the very marrow of his bones; his teeth chattered, and his flesh rose up into little hillocks.

There he was, bound by some infernal power. The contrary stile baffled all his efforts to pass it; the last reverberation of the cracked bell ceased with a fearful jar, like the passing of a sinner's soul in agony, and to it succeeded a silence yet more terrible.

"May-be its dyin' that I am," thought Ned; and all that was lovely and clinging in God's beautiful world, rushed across his mind at the instant.

"If it is to be my fate to leave it all, so full of life and hope, and yet so unmindful of the great blessings I have unthankfully enjoyed, Heaven pity me, indeed, for I'm not fit to go." At this moment his ear caught a most familiar sound, that of the mill hopper, so seldom heard lately, rising and falling in regular succession.

Surprised still more than ever, he turned round and beheld the old mill, brilliantly lighted up; streams of brightness poured from every window, door, and cranny, while the atmosphere resounded with the peculiar busy hum which proceeds from an industriously employed multitude.

Fear gave place to curiosity, and Ned stealthily crept towards the mill opening and looked in; the interior was all a-blaze with an infinity of lights, while myriads of diminutive figures were employed in the various occupations incidental to the business. Ned looked on with wonder and admiration to see the celerity and precision with which everything was done; great as was the multitude employed, all was order and regularity; here thousands of little atomies pushed along sack after sack of corn—there, numberless creatures ground and deposited the flour in marked bags, while Ned recognized his old friend, the Leprechaun, pouring over a large account-book, every now and then reckoning up a vast amount of bank bills and dazzling gold pieces.

Ned's mouth fairly watered as he saw the shining metal, and he heard the crisp creasing of the new bank notes, which took the little accountant ever so long to smooth out, for each one would have made a blanket for him; as soon as the Leprechaun had settled his book affairs to his satisfaction, he, after the greatest amount of exertion, assisted by a few hundred of his tiny associates, deposited the money in a tin case, whereupon Ned distinctly read his name.

While he was hesitating what course to adopt, whether to try and capture the Leprechaun again, or wait to see what would eventuate, he felt himself pinched on the ear, and on turning round, he perceived one of the fairy millers standing on his shoulder, grinning impudently in his face.

"How do you do, sir?" says Ned, very respectfully, for he knew the power of the little rascals too well to offend them.

"The same to you, Ned Geraghty, the sporting miller," says the fairy. "Haven't we done your work well?"

"Indeed, an' its that you have, sir," replied Ned, "much obleeged to you, I am, all round."

"Won't you go in and take your money?" says the fairy.

"Would it be entirely convenient?" said Ned, quietly, although his heart leaped like a salmon.

"Its yours, every rap, so in an' lay a-howld ov it," said the other, stretching up at his ear.

"They wouldn't be agin' me havin' it, inside, would they?" inquired Ned.

"The money that you have earned yourself, we can't keep from you," said the fairy.

"That's true enough, and sure if I didn't exactly earn it myself, it was earned in my mill, and that's all the same;" and so, quieting his scruples by that consoling thought, Ned put on a bold front and walked in to take possession of the tin case, in which he had seen such an amount of treasure deposited. There was not a sound as he entered—not a movement as he walked over to the case; but as he stooped down and found that he could no more lift that box from the ground than he could have torn a tough old oak up by the roots, there arose such a wild, musical, but derisive laugh from the millions of fairy throats, that Ned sank down upon the coveted treasure, perplexed and abashed; for one instant he held down his head with shame, but summoning up courage he determined to know the worst, when, as he raised his eyes, an appalling scene had taken place.

The fairies had vanished, and instead of the joyous multitude flitting like motes in a sunbeam, he beheld one gigantic head which filled the entire space; where the windows had been, a pair of huge eyes winked and glowered upon him; the great beam became a vast nose, the joists twisted themselves into horrible matted hair, while the two hoppers formed the enormous lips of a cavernous mouth. As he looked spellbound upon those terrible features, the tremendous lips opened, and a voice like the roar of a cataract when you stop your ears and open them suddenly, burst from the aperture.

The sound was deafening, yet Ned distinguished every syllable.

"Ain't you afraid to venture here?" bellowed the voice.

"For what, your honor?" stammered out Ned, more dead than alive.

"For weeks and weeks not a morsel has entered these stony

jaws, and whose fault is it? yours!" thundered the awful shape; "you have neglected us, let us starve and rot piecemeal; but we shall not suffer alone—you, you! must share in our ruin."

At these words, a pair of long, joist-like arms thrust themselves forth, and getting behind Ned, swept him into the space between the enormous hoppers—the ponderous jaws opened wide—in another instant he would have been crushed to atoms. But the instinct of self-preservation caused him to spring forward, he knew not where; by a fortunate chance he just happened to leap through the door, alighting with great force on his head; for a long time, how long he could not tell, he lay stunned by the fall; and, indeed, while he was in a state of insensibility, one of his neighbors carried him home, for he remembered no more until he found himself in bed, with a bad bruise outside of his head, and worse ache within.

As soon as he could collect his senses, the scenes of the past night arose vividly to his mind.

"It is the Leprechaun's warning," said he, "and its true he said it was better far than gold, for now I see the error of my ways, and more betoken, it's mend that I will, and a blessin' upon my endayvors."

It is but fair to Ned to say that he became a different man; gave up all his fine companions and evil courses, and stuck diligently to his mill, so that in process of time he lived to see well-filled the very tin case that the Leprechaun showed him in *the warning.*

THE EAGLE AND HER TALONS.

AN EASTERN APOLOGUE.

Fair and beautiful to behold, even as a priceless gem upon the azure garment of the Son of the Faithful, an Island of loveliness arose amidst the Southern Seas, greeting the glories of the day with equal brightness.

And the island was called Kuba, and is so called even unto this day.

Sweet and pleasant unto the sense, and delicious, as the spice groves of Araby the blest, were the breezes that inhabited the island, for it was encircled by a zone of blooming summer, and health dwelt therein for ever. And when the sons of men adventured there, in their distant voyages, they found that it was good and desirable in every way.

So they formed a colony thereon, driving out and despoiling the original owners and inhabitants, who, not being civilized, and holding not in reverence bits of carved ivory and wood, were, therefore, unfit to live and worthy to die, and so were killed accordingly.

For the nation which implanted its offshoots on the beautiful island was called Spain, a land where people hold in great and curious regard and worship, sundry inanimate, foolish and fantastical blocks of stone, wood and other substances. The which, with them, is a part of their religous ceremonial; but if indulged in by strange nations it would be called abomination and idolatry.

And even to this day the princes of the land delight in bestowing upon those images costly presents, garments of rich stuffs, gold, silver, and jewels, sufficient to make glad thousands of living hearts—but that is not the custom.

It so happened that these people planted a colony in Kuba, which in time waxed wealthy, and many were born there who did learn to love the land itself, but an atmosphere of inertness enveloped the island like the hot breath of Sahara.

Meantime the parent nation increased in tyranny, and oppression, for its own means having been nearly exhausted, it sent needy and rapacious extortioners to squeeze the people of Kuba so that their substance was enforced from them.

And there was great discontent thereat, but few there were who dared to express it, forasmuch as it was decreed that he who complained should die ignominiously by the hands of the common executioner.

Nevertheless, there were found many to lift up their voices, who perished accordingly, and there was much mourning throughout the island.

Now it came to pass that upon the main land adjacent, a mighty people had assembled from all parts of the earth, and joining together, formed one kindred.

And the atmosphere of that great land was Liberty. It was presided over by a most powerful Eagle, whose pastime was to seize upon the jewelled crowns of despots, and with one stroke of her mighty beak dash them into pieces. And the enormous strength of the bird lay in its claws, which shot forth at various spaces of time, and produced fresh talons.

For when it first built its sovereign eyrie in the land, its talons numbered but thirteen, and now you can count of them thirty and one; and the odd number vexed the heart of the Eagle mightily, and he began to yearn for another talon.

Whereupon there came to the eagle a certain Wren, saying,

"All powerful bird, I know where thou canst procure one more talon."

And the Eagle answered and said, "Where?

"If thou wilt deign to fly with me a little distance, I will show thee," replied the Wren.

"Be it even as thou sayest," said the Eagle.

So the two birds, the mighty Eagle and the small Wren, mounted upward, until the face of the world was spread beneath them like a map. And they floated through the air, until the Wren exclaimed, "Behold!" when the Eagle cast a piercing glance upon the earth, and saw the island of Kuba lying on the bosom of the ocean like a second Aiden.

Whereupon the Wren said unto the Eagle, "Even there shalt thou obtain thine other talon.

And the Eagle winked its great eye, but answered never a word.

PEACE AND WAR.

PEACE, everlastingly with those
Who still the perfect TRUTH disclose;
And, in all places, nobly dare
The mask from speciousness to tear.
Who, not by words, but actions, show
The attributes of Heaven below:
Who never with presumption scan
The failings of their fellow man.
But those who've fallen in evil ways,
By gentle admonition raise;
And thus in deed true homage give
To HIM who died that we might live—
Peace everlastingly with those
Who still the perfect truth disclose.

War to the uttermost with all
Who hold the human mind in thrall:
Be they bold villains, who appear
With bolder faces, scorning fear—
Who, in their mastery of evil,
Were there a chance, would cheat the Devil;
Or be they fat "Professors," sleek,
Soft, placid-voiced, and seeming meek.
Their aspirations worldly greed,
And selfishness their only creed—

Who, in deceit so long have trod,
They fain would hope to cheat their God!
War to the uttermost with all
Who hold the mind of man in thrall.

SUMMER FRIENDS.

As the bee is to the flower,
In the honey-laden bower,
To each leaflet in the grove,
Humming gently songs of love;
Pausing only in his flight,
Where the treasure cup is bright,
All unwilling to depart,
Till he's reached the very heart,
Sucking ever while he sings
Life from the insensate things;
As the bee is to the flower,
In the honey-laden bower,
Are summer friends.

As the shadow to the boat,
On a changeful lake afloat,
When the lake is in repose,
Like a second boat it shows;
And all fortune elevates
O'er the surface imitates
But a ripple on its breast,
Shadow trembles with unrest;

And when fiercer storms abound,
Can no longer there be found.
As the shadow to the boat,
On a changeful lake afloat,
Ar summer friends.

LOVE'S MISSION.

WHITHER dost thou go, gentle wind?
If thou hast naught to do, to thy mind,
Oh! betake thee to the west,
To the girl that I love best.
Heavy-laded with those sighs,
To the cottage where she lies;
There, without a living sound
Let them softly hover round;
Let them fan her brow so fair,
Let them thrill her silky hair,
Let them play at "hide and seek"
Through the dimples on her cheek,
Let them linger but to sip
Heaven's dew upon her lip;
Then commingle with the air,
She is calmly breathing there.
That within her gentle breast,
For an instant they may rest,
In her heart to whisper deep,
Thoughts of me while she doth sleep.

EVENINGS AT OUR CLUB,

Wherein all the interesting matters of the passing time are taken all sorts of liberties with—analyzed, criticised, eulogized, rhapsodized, parodized, philosophized, and no doubt immortalized.

THE LOCALE.

An apartment of comfortable dimensions, carpeted with that thick velvety material which yields to the pressure like the softest moss. The walls—for ours is a somewhat luxurious Coterie—hung with French paper, of a deep maroon, during the winter months, changed for the summer to a lavender grey ; but, in either case, all one color, except the line of gold moulding which defines the ceiling. The ground, therefore, contrasts with and brings into pleasant relief the few glorious paintings which adorn the room—which, by the by, do not consist of those problematic affairs, cracked and smoke obscured, dignified by the pseudo connoisseurs with the title of "Old Masters." No, indeed ; ours are fresh, vivid and truthful illustrations of our time and country. There will probably be occasion to mention them and their producers, by the by, more particularly. So to continue our description. Upon elaborately carved brackets, between each painting, rest finely chiselled busts of those worthies of the present age, who, by their various talents have done or continue to do honor to their native land. Tables of fragrant Indian wood, black as ebony, with marble slabs, whereon stand statuettes, groups of shells, and numberless rare articles of taste and vertu are scattered round. In the recesses, at each side of the fire-place, are inserted voluminous and useful libraries, where books of all kinds of reference, instruction or amusement crowd the shelves. One single piece of ornamental utility decorates the mantle-piece—a clock of black marble ; its design being of the severely classic order. There is no looking-glass, although a certain self-admiring member of the Coterie has striven laboriously to have one admitted. In the centre of the apartment there is a large, round table, covered with a plain green cloth, whereupon may be found the floating literature of the time, in all its shapes, encircling the table—from whence it is fondly hoped you, friend reader, will receive a world of amusement, mayhap a trifle of instruction—are eight chairs, snug as Morocco leather can make them, luxuriously elbowed and cushioned; each chair bearing the name of the member to whom it belongs.

Having described the locality, proceed we to its occupants. There are six individuals present. The nearest——

Hark! how lucky; here comes the President of the Coterie with a new member—thus making up the prescribed number. As he introduces him you had better listen.

[*The door opens, and Major Hilary and Frank Frolic enter.*]

The Major.—Gentlemen, this is Mr. Frank Frolic, our new member. He's a jolly fellow, I think, but his particular idiosyncrasy must develop itself; but in order that he may know thoroughly with whom he is associated, I think it right to give him some idea of your several characters: This, Mr. Frolic, is Montmorency Fitzsnob, Esq., our representative of the West End. His authority is conclusive on all super-fashionable subjects, from the cut of a coat to the selection of a bouquet. You will find him amazingly learned in the *names* of operas. He can pronounce, with extraordinary facility, the titles of the pet scenas "in very choice Italian." On all matters of etiquette he is absolute; irreproachably correct on both dress and address. He has a praiseworthy contempt for every thing that smacks of home; looks upon the majority of his countrymen as semi-civilized savages; has been to London and Paris; is in what he calls "*society*," and exhibits a nervous and unaccountable degree of annoyance at the remotest allusion to his grandpa.

Fitzsnob—(*With a fashionable drawl*).—Major, now! 'pon my life, you are too excrutiating. Where's aw the use in dragging in family mattahs. Old fellah, what's your name? Fwolic, don't mind him. He's Pwesident, to be suah; but a pwetty Pwesident he makes. He's nothing but a wegular whynocewos; a sort of Wed Wover, out of—aw—what's his name? histowy.

Major.—Come, that's a powerful exercise of lungs for you, Fitz. Now, Mr. Frolic, this is Mr. Nettle, who, I must take the liberty of saying before his face, is a strange compound of sense and sarcasm. He's neither deficient in ability, nor weak in argument, but his sentences bite like aquafortis. He's as pungent as aromatic vinegar; but unfortunately, he stings indiscriminately whatever and whoever comes near him. Nothing escapes, except that which is too well protected to receive the puncture, or too coarse to feel the smart. Never handle him without gloves, Mr. Frolic, and pretty thick ones too.

Nettle—(Sharply).—*He's a small man, with bright eyes thin lips, and a sharp nose.* That's what I call a remarkably pleasant and friendly introduction. A very agreeable impression this man must have of me, from your *flattering* description; but never mind, if he's a man of intellect, he'll be able to judge for himself; if he's a fool, it won't much matter what he thinks.

Major.—Now, Mr. Frolic, allow me to introduce to your notice, my particular friend and the especial favorite of our entire Coterie ——

Nettle.—Major, might I presume to advise you, not to compromise yourself by being responsible for any one's thoughts and inclinings but your own.

Major. Ah! I forgot. Yes; there's one exception.

Nettle.—You don't know that. Bless my soul; don't interfere with other people.

Major. Well, then, I won't. So let me say no more, but present Mr. St. Leger, a student and a thinker. His judgment is unbiased and generally clear. Lucid and temperate in argument, sophistry finds it difficult to blind him, or acrimony to raise his ire—deeply impressed with the value and indispensability of truth, you feel a confidence in his assertions, and know that whatever he commends or condemns, he does so in all sincerity of heart. His opinions, I assure you, are formed after due deliberation, and carry much weight amongst our Coterie.

St. Leger.—Mr. Frolic, I am happy to make an acquaintance which I trust will ripen into friendship. The Major, in the kindness of his heart, over-estimates my value here. It would be difficult, indeed, to realize the limning of his benevolent pencil, in all save the sincerity; that is a trait which I am proud to own. My judgment may be at sometimes faulty, but thus much I can vouch for, that it shall be at all times exercised freely and fearlessly, uninfluenced either by prejudice or partiality.

Major.—Now come we to our utilitarian friend, the stolid and imperturbable Granite. You must know, Mr. Frolic, that yonder hard-featured, porcupine-headed, middle-aged individual would have the world—had he his own way, which, heaven be lauded, he has not, nor never will have—one struggling, slaving money forge. The stars to him shine like shillings and sixpences. He reckons them up, and when he comes to the moon, it puts him in mind of a big silver dollar. What they really are, it never enters into his mind to imagine. To be sure, he has heard vague indications of their being planets like the earth, probably inhabited, and all that sort of thing; but he thinks it a shameful loss of time to inquire into such matters, and so wisely refuses to fatigue his understanding. You see him looking intently at that cosey fire, and no doubt fancy that he is enjoying the warmth thereof, inly pitying, the while, those who, in this bitter season, have insufficient. Not a bit of it. He doesn't feel the genial heat. He doesn't see the cheerful blaze. He only sees the hard, black mineral, and calculates that were the weather twice as severe, what a fine profit shivering poverty would be obliged to yield to grasping wealth. Let him remain wrapped up in his mantle of selfishness. I don't know how he came amongst us, but being here we can't eject him. Come, I won't introduce you to him. Here's a different character Mr. Rimer. He's a small poet; does nice little verses, which find their way into albums and outsides of newspapers. His language is as florid as a Corinthian capital. A good-natured, useless, harmless specimen of humanity enough; when he's not in the spouting vein, then he's uncommonly tiresome. You may probably be somewhat annoyed at first by his improvisatory vagaries, but you'll get used to it. Mr. Frolic, Mr. Rimer.

Rimer.—Sir, I am most obsequiously your obedient, humble —— Frolic? I beg your pardon. Most unavailable name. I can't think of anything that rhymes to it, but "melancholic." Excuse me; I mean nothing.

Let us henceforth be trusty friends,
Till death our mortal journey ends.

Major.—You have but one more to be introduced to; and he, I assure you, is utterly indescribable. He is as abtruse as Wieland, and as metaphysical as Kant. You perceive, by the arrangement of his whiskers, his *barbe impériale* and valanced cheek, that he's a disciple of the progressive school of modern reforming philosophers. He has successively adopted and upheld the theories of all the many visionaries who have lately endeavored to turn the current of things into other channels, from St. Simon down to Robert Owen. Poor fellow; he, like his prophets, worries himself about the stream of human events—quite forgetful that it *will* flow on, regardless of the chips that for a moment agitate its surface, and then, in their own despite, are carried along with it. Mr. Vision, allow me to present to you our new member, Mr. Frolic.

Vision.—Sir, I grasp you with the hand of fraternity. Our number is now complete; nor shall our time be lost, if a radical cure for the diseases of a corrupted society shall grow out of our deliberations.

Nettle.—Which is amazingly doubtful.

St. Leger.—That's a great admission from you, Nettle; for even when the law doubts, it is favorable to the culprit.

Major.—Pooh! never mind him. Take your seat, Mr. Frolic. If there be a weak point in argument, or an assailable place in character, Nettle chuckles at the discovery, as though he had alighted upon a hidden treasure. He is one of those sun-spot hunters, who lose the brilliancy of the orb in the intensity of their search for a defect. There is no doubt in the world but when he washes his hands he feels more gratification in rendering the water foul than in making himself clean.

Nettle.—We all know what a skillful anatomizer of character you are, or I should be tempted to retaliate; at all events, even if I were the concentration of bitterness, you would infer my medicable qualities would give a healthier tone to society than the everlasting *eau sucrée* of your *amiable* disposition.

St. Leger.—Come, come; let us change the subject. Who has read *the* book of the age—Macaulay's History?

Nettle.—Nobody but the reviewers, except, perhaps, Fitz snob, there.

Fitzsnob.—Oh! I dare say. Catch me at it. Macaulay; Who is Macaulay?

Major.—The first essayist of the time, acknowledged—and now bids fair to rank amongst the first of modern historians, if not the very first.

Nettle.—From the circumstance of having produced a ponderous mass of matter in "Ercles" vein, antithetic to pedantry and grandiloquent as a Johnsonian preface:

"Antiquity, with paradoxical ambiguity," &c. &c.

I see nothing in it at all, but the ambitious work of a mere word-maker. Have you read any of it, Granite?

Granite.—My reading is very limited. I only pursue one book a year.

Frolic.—Indeed, sir. That must be a most interesting one.

Granite.—It is, sir, to me.

Frolic.—Might I know what it is?

Granite.—The Directory.

St. Leger.—And the current literature.

Frolic.—Yes, no doubt; the prices current! But to return to Macaulay. How do *you* like his book, Mr. St. Leger.

St. Leger.—Sir, it is the very perfection of written harmony; it is readable music. It is the visible union of truth and thought, producing poetry most exquisite. At least, such are the impressions remaining with me, upon the perusal of a few chapters. And then his style. The beautiful ease and natural grace of his diction, as it ebbs and flows upon the very tide of intellect—rising and falling with his subject, as the waves obey the winds. Take my word for it, sir, it will be a great book.

Nettle.—Yes, amongst great people; but you must confess that it is "caviar to the million."

St. Leger.—Not so. This is essentially a reading age, and the mental appetite must be fed upon the living matter of the day.

Nettle.—The garbage from the foul styes of French literature, for instance.

Major.—The taste for which is rapidly declining, I am proud to say. The public palate has been palled and satiated by such foul, unwholesome food, and now begins to yearn for something healthy.

Fitzsnob.—Come, now, Major! You are a little too hard upon what's-his-name, Sue and those fellows. I think they are deucedly agweeable and piquant writers; it's so difficult to get a sensation of any kind in these days of stock and consols, that one don't much mind where it comes fwom. Now look at Wimer there, weclining back, with half-closed eyes. Hanged if I don't envy him.

St. Leger.—Yes, your poets, or rather your individuals of poetic temperament—for there are many such who revel in glorious thoughts and never let them see the world of paper—are, indeed, an enviable race.

Nettle.—Envious, you mean. I never knew a rhymester in my life, if he saw a fellow scribbler getting up upon the Parnassian carriages—for poets and poverty are not synonyms now—but would cry out, "whip behind."

Major.—Rimer—in the language of the old game, what are your thoughts like?

Rimer.—I was thinking of a little morsel from an effort of a friend of mine, which struck me as possessing some fidelity.

Major.—Let us have it.

Rimer.—It is supposed to be a student's description of his sensations in a wood at eventime.

Nettle.—How Della Cruscan!

Rimer.—

Thus had I rambled on in dreamy mood,
Brain-revelling within the silent wood,
Yet, not all silent—for the voiceful trees
Trembled in leafy melody—the breeze
In whispering undulation swept among
Nature's own glorious harps with branches strung,
Like the far off attenuated roar
Of ocean *sheeming* on a pebbly shore—
Steeping the soul in dreamy stupor deep,
And yet all conscious, like an angel's sleep.

Nettle.—"Attenuated roar" is good; puts one in mind of Bully Bottom's "Aggravated Voice." Rimer, your friend must have been indulging in chloroform to an injurious extent.

Frolic.—Or reading Dickens' "Haunted Man."

Fitzsnob.—Wegulah wubbish!

Nettle.—A metaphysical abortion.

St. Leger.—Such is the penalty of genius! The ungrateful public, forgetful of the many incomparable bouquets he has set before them, turns up its delicate nose; because this little repast is not of *quite* so excellent a quality, the lavish hospitality, the cordial welcome and the wholesome tendency are not given a thought. Had I the time, I could quote some passages from this work so caviled at, which shed additional lustre even upon his name; perhaps they may not be so numerous as in most of his creations—but who would not dig through heaps of clay, being sure to find a gem at last?

Major.—In my opinion, "Jane Eyre" is the best book of its class that has been written since ——

Nettle.—Since "The Mysteries of Udolpho." It's only Mrs. Ratcliffe in a modern dress, without her fertility of invention. Brigands have given place to romantic old love-sick noodles, and sceptres to maniac wives.

Fitzsnob.—I wead a page or two of the thing, and it was

vewy uncomfortable. I never wead anything that makes me wetched.

St. Leger.—I was much interested in the work. It is decidedly the production of a vigorous thinker; but one evidently inclined to look upon the shadowy side of human life. The characters are all boldly marked, and have a palpable individuality. They live and move before you; truthful, but exaggerated. It is a kind of Daguerreotype, which always strengthens the dark lines of the original and brings its defects into prominence; but still there is no mistaking the reality of the picture.

Major.—Where are you going, Fitz?

Fitzsnob.—To the Opewa.

Major.—It's too late, is it not?

Fitzsnob.—Not for us. We never go until it's nearly all over.

Major.—I thought you visited that place of amusement for the sake of hearing good music.

Fitzsnob.—How excessively widiculous! Not at all, my dear fellow. It's only to show ourselves amongst our own set and look the interlopers out of countenance, or have a quiet chat with an Italian accompaniment. It's wemarkably wich, I assure you—until some bwute cwies out, "Silence!"

Major.—What do you do then?

Fitzsnob.—Look indignant and talk louder. Au wevoir.

[*Exit Fitzsnob.*

EVENING SECOND.

Present:

St. Leger, The Major,
Frank Frolic, Nettle,
Fitzsnob.

Major.—Well, what do the outside barbarians say of our association?

Frolic.—Not much, that I have heard; some few, whose opinions are valuable, seem inclined to like us, if they can.

Nettle.—Now, what does it signify whether they do or not?

St. Leger.—Everything. I grant you that the good opinion of the indiscriminate mass is not worth the slightest effort to obtain, inasmuch as it is bestowed generally without the exercise of thought or judgment, but the approval of a cultivated intellect, the acknowledged sympathy which connects those who think in common; they are the payments made in the business world of intelligence—the receipt of which is proof that you are deemed worthy to be associated with the capitalists of Mind.

Major.—Very good indeed, St. Leger. A common sense, mercantile view of the subject.

Nettle.—Very! Apollo in a dry-goods store, measuring out muslin to the Muses.

St. Leger.—Nettle, your style of conducting a discussion is unfair, although by no means unexampled. I know many arguers who, like you, depending upon a quickness of repartee, fence with words instead of ideas.

Nettle.—And usually get the best of the argument.

St. Leger.—And why? Because the ear of the listener is tickled by the authentic phrases of the word-monger, and the latter receives the extent of his ambition, a laugh—the ignoble victory of a buffoon.

Nettle.—If mere phrase-making *were* so productive of risibility, what an amusing dog you would be, St. Leger.

Major.—Let the old porcupine alone, St. Leger. His quills are decidedly in projection to-day. Wake up, Fitzsnob, and acquaint us with what is going on in fashionable life.

Fitzsnob.—Cwuel old wuffian; I was wapped in wosey slumbah when you dug your Patagonian paw into my wibs. How do I know what's going on, with the mercuwy making such wushes to the top of the what's-its-name—gasometah, I believe they call it; it's a wetchedly laboh-ious effo'ht to bweathe the wegulated quantity of bweath. Fwolic, theah, knows moah about what's pwogwessing wound than I do.

Frolic.—Well, then, to tell the honest truth, upon my life, there is not much of interest stirring just at present. As to the City amusements, considering the stagnant state of society, they are astonishingly well patronized.

Nettle.—Of course; there will always be found sufficient fools to grin away their hours unprofitably.

Fitzsnob.—Nobody, that's anybody, evah goes anywhear but to the Italian Opewah. That's the only awthodox yawning-place pwescribed by the advisahs of society.

Nettle.—They're all alike. Nests of vice, emissaries of licentiousness, and schools of infamy.

St. Leger.—The choice phraseology in which bigotry and fanaticism have assailed the Dramatic Institution, from the days of Æschylus to the present time, and it does honor to the intelligence as well as the temper of the professors of the mimic art, that to such continuous abuse they have opposed the dignity of silence; although, in their own defence, they might have exhibited a black list of their immediate maligners upon the tables of vice, yet they refrained, and what is the result? The strong arm of intellect has rent the veil which superstition and ignorance had hung between the stage people and the outer world. Association gave the lie to the calumnies of the fanatic, and the Player, hitherto pictured as the social demon, the very bugbear of society, is beginning to be acknowledged as not altogether a contagious companion.

Frolic.—Then, it appears, St. Leger, that you don't believe in the decadence of the Drama.

St. Leger.—No.

Nettle.—Pooh! Nonsense! It's gone; the Legitimate Drama, as it is called. The old school. I remember when I was stupid enough to visit the theatre.

Frolic.—I know what you are going to say. Every bald-headed old gentleman says the same. You are going to dilate upon the excellence of some forgotten "Smith," or some antediluvian "Jones." Every fragment of the last century sneers at the incompetency of the present. One never speaks of the talent of some living actor, but he tells you that he's nothing to be compared with the celebrated Snooks or the eminent Snobbs—and the old school. Such confounded cant is unendurable. The old school—with Macbeth in a cauliflower wig and Othello in red-heeled shoes and a Quaker-cut coat. I go for the new school. I want to see the stage what it should be—the "abstract and brief chronicle of the time"—the present time. What have we to do with the vices and the follies that our grandfathers sucked their gold-headed canes and took rappee over? Haven't we plenty of material growing up and around us? To catch *living* follies as they fly, is the business of the dramatist—not to keep continually embalming dead ones. The mental appetite as well as the physical should be appeased with subjects fresh cooked. No one would like to dine upon a stuffed duck, taken from the shelves of a museum, when the sight of a juicy canvas-back irrigates his dentistry.

Major.—It appears to me that the *name* of a place of amusement is the principal desideratum now. Museums and Gardens are safer, in the way of patronage, than theatres, although the same entertainment be given in either case. Why is that?

St. Leger.—Because this is the age of superficial morality and skin-deep decorum. Who could discover the infamies of dramatic representation amongst a multitude of dried bones and repulsive malformations, or scent out the hidden enormities of a theatre amidst the bouquets of a fashionable garden? Oh! your gardens and museums are a splendid specimen of religious striped-pigism—a most comfortably pharisaical method to "*whip the devil round the stump.*"

Nettle.—Come, now, Mr. St. Leger, since you set yourself up as an apologist for the drama——

St. Leger.—Apologist, sir, for what? The circumstance of apology argues an acknowledgment of wrong-doing. The friends of the drama make no such concession.

Nettle.—If it were a good thing, the taste would not decline as it has done.

St. Leger.—An ex-parte assertion again, sir. The taste does not decline—never will decline, so long as the human heart holds sympathy with the True and Beautiful. Fools may look askant and fanatics calumniate, but the undying drama soars as far above its assailers as the towering eagle does above the "mousing owl," for it is upborne upon the wings of genius, and must share its immortality.

Nettle.—The genuine afflatus. Wonderful eruption of—gas!

Fitzsnob.—What wenders me wetched is, that I can't discovah what that stwange thing they call the dwama weally is. Is it any thing like Cwisty's Minstwels?

Nettle.—Certainly; since modern legitimacy consists in success!

Major.—I wish you would find some other subject to speak about.

Frolic.—Start one yourself. They are not numerous just now.

Nettle.—How about the Cholera!

Frolic.—Pleasant companion, Nettle. If there's one thing more disagreeable than another, he's sure to hit upon it.

Nettle.—Disagreeable. Not at all; the wittiest book that ever was written owed its existence to the plague of Marseilles.

St. Leger.—The Decameron of Boccacio and the plague of London formed the ground-work of one of our best novels—the Rothelan of John Galt, an excellent though but little read author. I look upon him to be scarcely inferior to Scott in felicity of invention and in choice of language.

Frolic.—Come, Major, that subject.

Major.—I can think of nothing more interesting than the living characters upon the present page of the world's history.

Fitzsnob.—Speaking of Histowy; have the Fwench fellows taken Wome yet?

St. Leger.—Yes, the war of Vandalism has ceased with the capitulation of the city. The great Republic of France, ruled by its kite's-egg President, has destroyed the lesser Republic of Rome; though for what purpose it is impossible for simple reason to divine. The judgment halts between two possibilities; either they mean to restore the despotic power of the Pope, or, under the cloak of such a design, to establish that very Republic which they have been threatening to annihilate. Diplomacy is ever tortuous, and the latter course is not altogether improbable.

Nettle.—Pooh! you're as far from the real intention as usual. The invasion was determined upon to please those boy savages of the grande nation, who, if they had not amusement at a distance, would probably take it into their heads to have a game of a similar nature nearer home. As long as that old rapscallion, Louis Philippe, kept them tilting at the Moors, he slept easily enough; but as soon as they had finished roasting the Bedouins, they went back and burnt the old knave's throne in the open street. Old Boney knew what he was about, and the material he had to deal with; he always cut out plenty of bloody work for his dear people; so that, while the thunder of that sanguinary pastime men call battle, and angels wholesale murder, reverberated through every other portion of the Continent, his home was as tranquil as an Arcadian Grove.

Major.—What an extraordinary paradox it is, that the relation of a single case of violent death seems to move the sensibility of the hearer in a much greater degree than the recital of the terrible deaths of thousands on a battle field!

St. Leger.—It is easily accounted for. In the one case it has a sudden and individual interest—in the other, it is coupled with a partisanship with either the one side or the other, together with those small accumulations of personal feeling which result in producing a loyality to a certain person or enthusiasm in a certain cause. Added to which, there must be a fierce, though terrible enjoyment in the madness of a battle which communicates itself from the actor to the reader or hearer, and what in the first case is entire and individual sympathy for suffering is in the latter a mixture of contending emotions, tossed and flung about upon the billows of excitement.

Fitzsnob.—The neawest appwoach to a battle I evah saw, was at the Astah Place, where—what's his name—Macweady, weceiving his congee from the wed wepublicans of the Bowewy, after having wendah'd himself obnoxious to the cwachahs of peanuts.

Frolic.—How did you like it?

Fitzsnob.—Well, I thought it was capital fun as long as they wemained outside. I'm a gweat advocate foh fweedom of opinion, but, paving-stones give the stwenth of the awgument all to one side. I heahd the wiot act wead and then I wan.

Major.—Let all that matter rest; the nine days' wonder comes under the sober cognizance of history now, which will not lie.

Fitzsnob.—Majah, might I twouble you to look at the clock?

Major.—Bless me! is it so late? We must separate; it grieves me to think how unprofitably we have passed the time on this occasion.

St. Leger.—That cannot be helped, my dear Major; though we are a little cloudy now, the sun may visit us bye-and-bye. The miner meets with bad as well as good veins during the progress of his operations.

Nettle.—But if he should find a bad one, he wouldn't keep digging at it.

St. Leger.—You're right, Nettle; let us take your advice and drop our shovels, perhaps the next vein we come to may be a little more brilliant.

Nettle.—"A consummation devoutly to be wished."

EVENING THIRD.

Present:

NETTLE,	FRANK FROLIC,
VISION,	FITZSNOB,
RIMER,	ST. LEGER.

Major Hilary enters with a newspaper; he is evidently excited, and takes his seat without passing the usual compliments to his companions.

Frolic—(Aside to St. Leger).—Look out for an eruption.

St. Leger.—What has put you out, Major?

Frolic.—You mean, what has fired him up?

Nettle.—That's right, Frolic, don't lose an opportunity, be it ever so ill-timed; but peck at each sentence like a pigeon-witted punster, as you are. If there be one thing more thoroughly detestable than another, it is to feel that we cannot send forth our ideas decently clad, but some social mountebank will insist upon arraying them in the garb of a sack-pudding. Confound it, Sir, why don't you say something worthy of remark yourself, and not twist and torture other people's ideas with the hope of exciting unwholesome and indecorous mirth at the dislocation.

Frolic.—You are exempt from that annoyance, Nettle. The miracle would be to straighten out the corkscrew emanations of your tortuous mind.

Nettle.—That's a mere personality.

St. Leger.—And is consequently objectionable. An argument should be carried on according to the strictest laws of the duello, *i. e.*, with equal weapons. Neither ridicule nor personality should be made use of; the one is a proof of folly, the other of brutality—independently of which the fine flashing rapier of intellect, diamond pointed and strong in its very delicacy, is more than a match for the lath sword of the Buffoon, or the clumsy bludgeon of the Bully. But, Major, may we not be made acquainted with the matter which seems to give you such concern.

Major.—It will pass away; indeed, I can't afford, at my time of life, to suffer the canker of annoyance to eat into the wheels of my vitality, for it is an undeniable result, that the more oil there is distributed through our machinery, the smoother, if not the longer, we shall continue to run our "mortal engines."

Vision.—Ah! my good friend, if the world-people could but be shaken up from the criminal apathy which pervades them, and avoiding the thousand and one devious paths which lead but to the blackness of darkness, pursue the one road, whose terminus is the universal Brotherhood of Love, then all would be happiness.

St. Leger.—My enthusiastic Vision, how many different roads have we all tending to a sublimer end, the happiness beyond our mortal bounds? We each follow that particular path which early precept pointed out in childhood, and which the associates of riper years have confirmed within the mind until it has become a thing of faith. Sir, in my opinion, the wild, uncultivated savage, who breaks no mortal tie the crude unfounded rites of his religion render sacred, may look beyond this life with hope as full as any.

Nettle.—I should like to know the means by which you would rejuvenate this grey-headed world, Vision.

Vision.—Grey-headed from the effects of premature vice; even as the over-gorged and surfeited, the wine and turtle filled voluptuary, when the unpitying gout has fastened on his plump extremities, and he writhes in agony within his easy chair, back reluctantly he flies to roots and water, nature's healthy diet—so must this self-diseased, this gouty world return to its original simplicity.

St. Leger.—How is this to be accomplished?

Vision.—Level her cities—hives of fat, lazy drones where once dwelt bees; prostrate those proud palaces where luxury is pampered; let no man be a builder; leave rocks and stones where nature planted them to consummate their tardy vegetation; let clay feed roots and not be tortured into bricks; let forests be your towns, the bush your villages; let no man wear upon his back the cost of acres, and let that accursed metal for which men barter country, kindred, bodies, *souls*, be seen no more, bury it all where mortal hand can never reach it; let your food be roots, your drink the running stream, and then the world's lethargy will pass away.

Frolic.—But surely, in this enlightened age, such stupidity cannot be encouraged.

St. Leger.—My dear Frolic, this enlightened age is one of the very darkest credulity; the superstitions of the earliest times can hardly parallel the many absurdities which have recently appeared upon the world's stage; there are no creeds so monstrous, no doctrines so opposed to common sense, no rites so repulsive, but some, nay, numbers may be found eager to join in their abominations. Ah! what must be the solitary moments of the knaves and hypocrites who willfully promulgate error and knowingly practice upon the silly-headed and weak-hearted dupes who listen to them.

Frolic.—Come, Major, we are all anxiety to hear your explanation. "Is it the mulligrubs affects my love?"

Major.—No, but egad I will tell you; I feel a little calmer now. You know that nothing but the purest Phœnician blood flows in my veins.

Frolic.—Just to the back bone.

Major.—By descent and feeling.

Nettle.—Half a dozen kings hanging (I mean nothing in the Ketch line) on your genealogical timber. I never knew an Irish gentleman who had not.

Major. Although in individual instances we may suffer annoyance from some prejudiced person or another, yet it is matter of satisfaction to observe how gradually, but effectually the violent animosities between different nations are dispersing.

Rimer.—And they must disperse, for there is a giant in progress—Knowledge, that mighty instrument through which unerring wisdom issues again the heavenly fiat, "LET THERE BE LIGHT." It is a glorious thought to let imagination wander back and see the new-born world fling off its vest of darkness to greet the first rising of the sun, while myriad flowers, warmed into existence by its genial beams, send up their mingled odors to the skies, their meed of thankfulness, the sweet gratitude of Nature. Vast, mighty and sublime as was that boon, it fell upon a world inanimate; but the God-kindled ray of intelligence breaking upon the soul of man, scatters the dense clouds of ignorance and clothes the hitherto benighted mind in an atmosphere of light.

Major.—And in no instance is the unworthy prejudice against a particular people more rapidly disappearing than that hitherto indulged in with regard to the Irish—a prejudice easily traceable, through clouds of misrepresentation, back to the cruel policy of Ireland's neighborly invader.

Nettle.—Pooh! The Irish are a pack of savages and slaves—only fit to fight and make railroads.

Major.—Savages and slaves! You take up the parrot cry of ignorance. Read, sir, read Ireland's history; there you'll find that when the Saxon despoiler first placed his iron foot upon her free valleys, her sons were famed for learning and valor. Slaves! When the alternative was offered that the Irish people should adopt the Saxon religion, language and dress, or have the hatred of a powerful enemy, the free souls, all honor to their memory, rejected the offer with disdain. "Tell the Saxon robber," said the great-hearted Malachi O'More, "he has my castles, my lands, my cattle and my coffers; let him at least leave me my faith and my liberty; they are all I am now possessed of; from God I have received them, and to God alone will I yield them up." Were these the thoughts of a savage—was that the language of a slave? Neither persuasion nor persecution had the power to force them into such a fusion; the fine old Milesian blood disdained to mix itself with that of a jumble of nations, and although half a thousand years have passed since the attempt was made, the two people are still and ever will remain distinct in almost every characteristic.

Nettle.—How do you account for the very apparent animosity which has always existed between the inhabitants of the neighboring islands?

St. Leger.—Very easily. When the conquerors found that they could not bend the proud souls down to thorough subjugation, they became savage in their unrelenting cruelties; the very blood and name of an Irishman were doomed to extermination; they were hunted like wild beasts, and to plumb the depth of degradation, placed without the protection of the law. It was then no crime to shoot a *mere* Irishman. Civilization could not shelter them. The holy precincts of the altar was to them no sanctuary; so were they maligned and stigmatized, that the credulous English masses heard the name of the "wild Irish" with a thrill of horror and disgust, to varnish over the lawlessness of their actions. Those who returned reported the wretched Islanders as something worse than brutes.

Frolic.—Just as the early Crusaders, to enhance the glory of their actions, made every Saracen a kind of demi-devil.

Major.—Give me your hand, my boy. Thank you—thank you. From you, an American, such language is warmth to my half-Irish heart.

Rimer.—As her own gifted son hath said, Ireland is still young. You remember the passage, St. Leger.

St. Leger.—I do. May his prophecy be as true as his poetry is beautiful:—

> Erin, oh Erin, though long in the shade,
> Thy star *shall* shine out when the proudest shall fade.

EVENING FOURTH.

Present:

THE MAJOR,	NETTLE,
VISION,	FRANK.

[*Enter Rimer with armful of Manuscript.*]

Nettle.—Heyday! Rimer; where are you moving your small stock of brainware to; has there been a fire on Parnassus, that you have thus desperately rushed in to save your valuables?

Frank.—Be quiet, Nettle, if you can; Mr. Rimer has obligingly promised to read me a few of his recent productions.

Nettle.—Has he? I wish you joy; where's my hat?

[*Exit Nettle in a hurry.*

Vision.—What a hedge-hog it is; never mind him, Rimer.

Rimer—(*quietly arranging his papers*).—I don't. Mr. Hilary asked me to bring a few of my disjointed effusions.

Major—(*startled at the apparent face*).—Oh!

Rimer—(*innocently*).—What's the matter.

Major.—Excuse me; thought you meant to make a joke "*few* ef *few* sions."

Rimer.—God bless me, no! Is that a joke? I didn't know, upon my life. I beg your pardon, most humbly.

Frank.—Silence! pray. Now, Rimer, we are all attention; what are you about to favor us with first.

Rimer.—Hem! I don't know whether to call the thing an imitation or not. Halleck and Byron have written in somewhat similar metre. Mind, I only say metre, for the rest, it is only a fragment, a sort of rambling run of thought, unconsciously stumbling into rhyme; but I'll read it.

Rimer reads:

INCIPIENT THROES OF A FLEDGLING POET.

I.

I feel a strange upheaving of the chest,
  To me, at least, a singular sensation,
A pent-up something; truly, at the best,
  A most unpleasant kind of perturbation.
The difficulty is to solve the question,
If, inspiration 'tis, or indigestion.

II.

At times, I fancy that I'm big with thought,
  And labor hugely in the parturition,
But for the life of me can bring forth naught,
  In any way presentable condition.
I'd like to know of what it is symbolic,
The true afflatus, or the windy colic.

III.

Just now a flock of small ideas flew
  Across my brain, but I'm afraid I've missed 'em.
It puzzles me to know what I shall do
  In this severe derangement of the system.

Take up my pen, all consequences scorning,
Or take a pill, and Seidlitz in the morning.

IV.

"Throw physic to the dogs," quoth "gentle Will,"
And so say I, my rule is dietetic.
'Tis fixed; I'll scribble; so come, friendly quill,
(It's a steel pen, but that's not so poetic),
Shall we invoke the Muses' aid, or flout them?
We'll independent be, and do without them.

V.

Such antique dames, I'm not inclined to woo,
As those old dowagers, besides, the *fact* is,
Courting nine women would be *entre nous*;
Infringing rather, on the Mormon practice,
The delectation of so many Madams,
Would task a Brigham Young, or Elder Adams.

VI.

They've jilted too, so many a poor wight,
Who, hapless mortals, thought that they had won 'em;
Oft at the very altar taking flight—
There's no dependence to be placed upon 'em.
To tell the honest truth, *I'm* not so smitten,
As thus incautiously to risk the mitten.

VII.

But if the least of all the nine should chance—
For women now and then have strange caprices—
To cast on me the slightest friendly glance,
Or even introduce me to her nieces;
I must confess that I'd have no objection
To cultivate the family connection.

VIII.

As such a prize I dare not hope to win,
For me, alas, there's no such "sweet communion."

'Tis pretty nearly time I should begin
  To consummate a less unequal union,
I'm at the age when love is not potential,
But soberly subdued by the prudential.

IX.

It just occurs to me there is a dame,
  The world, and justly, I believe, accuses
Of kindling in a million hearts a flame
  For each one lighted by the modest Muses.
A flaunting Jezebel, old, bold and wrinkled,
Though her false tresses are with gold-dust sprinkled.

X.

Her name is Impudence, and sooth to tell,
  No place so sacred, that her footsteps falter.
Even where Genius worships, she as well
  Kneels side by side, before Fame's (glorious) altar.
Not to assist his adoration, but to mock it,
For while he's lapsed in thought, she picks his pocket.

XI.

With dextrous fingers filching the great thought,
  To which he haply gave a life's endeavor,
Deeming perfection thereby cheaply bought,
  For on Time's scroll will he not live for ever?
Delusive hope, she claims the new invention,
Like —— or —— the names I'm loath to mention.

ROMANCE AND REALITY.

CHAPTER I.

It was morning in the neighborhood of Belgrave square—that is to say, fashionable morning, very considerably past mid-day, when calls are orthodox, and belles and beaux emerge from their respective beautifying retreats. Untenanted carriages dash along in one general round of unsubstantial etiquette; visits are paid by proxy; an inch or two of enamelled pasteboard representing frequently, Dukes, Earls, or Marquises, perhaps, fully as well as they represent their individual constituency. West End morning is a period of factitious politeness and unreal industry; everybody is supposed to be out, but everybody is known to be at home.

Sir Henry Templeton, of Templeton, one of the wealthiest Baronets of England, the deeds of whose ancestors, are they not registered in that sublimest of works, Burke's Peerage? sat within his splendid library, so called from the fact of its containing an unlimited number of books. But what they themselves contained was matter of profoundest mystery, both to him and to his household. A *moiety* of the diurnals, the Times, the Morning Post, and hebdomadally, the Bull, comprised the staples of this "fine old English gentleman's" literary labors. Be it observed, that he was too good a Tory to cast a glance over the pages of any paper emanating from the opposition; being one of those who like some one else to do their thinking, he confined his opinions to those of the leader of his own party.

He had just got to the "*hear! hear!*" and "*great cheering*" with which the imaginative reporters had introduced an unpretending speech of his own, which, until this moment, he has been under the disagreeable impression had been a lamentable failure. Imagine his surprise when he finds his half-dozen scarcely intelligible phrases, swollen into a goodly column of well-rounded, nicely perioded, polysyllabic English, garnished with a Miltonic quotation, and classically tailed up with a line and a half of Homer.

"Well," said the Baronet, and not without a pardonable glow of vanity at the contemplation of his eloquence, "those reporters certainly have long ears. I had no idea in the world that I made or could make so sensible a speech; but I suppose I did. In point of fact, I must have been rather luminous—Latin, too, by Jove! I didn't know that I could recollect so much."

In the full bloom of his *amour propre*, a footman entered and announced "Lord Sedleigh."

"At home."

In the interval between the announcement and the appearance of his lordship, as he is a stranger, perhaps I had better give you the benefit of a descriptive introduction. The Lord Sedleigh, but newly arrived from All Souls College, Oxford, is a tolerably fair specimen of the reputable portion of England's young nobility. Rich, without ostentation, generous, without extravagance, prudent, without parsimony, and learned, without pedantry; his title lent him no lustre that his virtues did not pay back with interest.

Hoping, dear reader, that you will not repent of the acquaintanceship, behold him—he enters—do you not agree with me in saying that he looks the very impersonage of that oft desecrated phrase, a *noble*-man?

The greeting between Sedleigh and Sir Harry is hearty and sincere. The last new singer having been discussed, and the last *liaison* deplored, with some slight embarrassment Sedleigh broke the primary object of his call.

"Sir Harry," said he, with almost startling abruptness—"you have a ward?"

"E'gad, Sedleigh, you're right there," replied Sir Harry, with a good-natured chuckle, "nor would you have erred had you said two."

"Yes, yes, I know," rejoined the Viscount. "But—ah!—I—the fact is, there's no use in mincing the matter, I have taken a most insurmountable interest in one."

"Lucy?"

"No. Arabella—pardon me—I mean Miss Myddleton."

"I'm sorry for that, Sedleigh," replied the baronet, "very sorry, for I like you."

"Why? why?" eagerly interposed the other. "Is she engaged?"

"No, not exactly that; but" ——

"But what? do, for pity's sake relieve my suspense."

"Upon my soul, Sedleigh, instead of being a neophyte in love, one would suppose you an amorado of some years' experience. Ah! in my day, people never married head over heels—but you don't want to hear anything about that—seriously, I should like to give you encouragement if I could, but you don't know the wild, wayward gipsy Arabella. Would you believe it, she's a perfect little Chartist, an absolute leveller, sneers at a title, and declares that if she ever does marry, it will be with some son of toil, some honest yeoman. By Jove, I don't know whether it's that fellow Bulwer, with his cursed empty love-in-a-cottage balderdash who has turned her little brain topsy-turvy or not, but she absolutely and positively restrains me from presenting anybody of the suitor order, who is tainted with, as she rather Carlyleishly calls it, the adventitious possession of hereditary worthlessness. I'm very sorry, by George, I am—but now, there's Lucy, couldn't you transfer your cart-load of affection to her?"

Sedleigh, who fortunately had not heard the last morsel of mercantile philosophy, suddenly exclaimed, "she objects to a title?"

"In toto."

"Full of romance?"

"Brim."

"Do *you* object to my trying to influence her?"

"Not in the least. But, by Jove, I can't introduce you."

"I don't ask you, if I have your consent. I'll manage the best myself."

"That you have, Sed, my boy, and my best wishes for your success. But what do you mean to do? By Jupiter, I don't think you'll ever get her consent."

"Nous verrons."

CHAPTER II.

Lucy and Arabella Myddleton were orphans, with good, though not great fortunes—both left to the strict guardianship of their uncle, Sir Henry, the deed expressly premising, that, in case either married without his consent, her fortune was to revert to the other.

There was but one year's difference in their age. Arabella was the older, but being a blonde, with exceedingly beautiful, young-looking hair—glossy hair—looked many years her junior. Lucy, on the contrary, was a beauty of a severer nature; a magnificent brunette, with large, lustrous eyes of the darkest hazle, and hair like a raven's wing. Their dispositions were as opposite as were their complexions. Lucy was a proud, high-souled creature, with a step as stately as a pet fawn, and a sort of regnant look, that plainly kept familiarity aloof, while Arabella was all life, spirit, elasticity and wildness. The very soul of joy beamed from her sparkling eyes, and mirth itself dwelt within the ringing echo of her laugh. So that, although Lucy attracted every eye by the majesty of her appearance, and the fawn-like gracefulness of her deportment, yet Arabella won every heart by the yielding sweetness of her temper, and the gladsome smile that played for ever on her lips.

Two or three mornings subsequently to that on which the conversation mentioned in the last chapter took place, as Arabella was leisurely strolling through the conservatory, which opened with glass doors on to the drawing-room, she perceived a young man, plainly, but elegantly dressed, with his collar thrown back à la Byron, displaying a throat of womanly whiteness, clime up the trellis-work, and jump at once through the open window. Her first impulse was to scream; but perceiving that the stranger was remarkably handsome, and moreover, as she was in the act of reading Zanoni, her susceptible heart was predisposed for any romantic incident. Seeing that his attention was directed towards a bust of Byron, which ornamented the conservatory, and that she was as yet, unperceived, she quietly waited the denouement.

Sedleigh, for 'twas he, approached the bust with rever-

11*

ence. Giving his hair the conventional thrust back from his forehead, and flinging himself into a theatrical attitude, he exclaimed, elocutionally—

"Oh, thou undying one, upon whose ample brow high intellect doth sit enthroned, from whose expressive eye the lightning of the soul, the fire of genius, seems incessantly to flash, upon whose every lineament the mighty hand of nature hath irrevocably stamped the evidence of an immortal mind—spirit of poesy, my soul doth kneel to thee!"

What an exceedingly nice young man! thought Arabella, as he, with increasing fervor, proceeded—

"And thou wert of that tinsel throng men bow, and cringe, and fawn on, and call *lord*. *I* cannot call thee so; thy genius lifts thee higher than the highest pinnacle of rank could e'er attain. I'll call thee what thou wert, a *man*, spurning the gauds of title—an inspired, an independent, but ah, most persecuted MAN!"

These sentiments so entirely coincided with those of the romantic Arabella, that forgetting the time, place, her ignorance of the individual she addressed, everything except the glow of enthusiasm which his words had kindled, she flung Zanoni aside, and rushed forward, exclaiming—

"He was! he was. You're right, sir, he was a persecuted man."

Sedleigh started with well-simulated astonishment, exclaiming in a faltering tone, "Miss Middleton, here—I—pray your pardon. I" ——

"Don't apologize, I pray," said the rapt girl, "sweet poet—but" ——. Suddenly recollecting herself, and blushing deeply, she continued, "I beg your pardon. You are a stranger—at least, I do not remember having had the pleasure of an introduction."

"Alas, never!" exclaimed Sedleigh, sighing profoundly.

"But that I *have* seen you before, I am certain."

"Many a time, and in many a guise hast thou observed me—nor didst thou know, that all those varied forms contained but one devoted heart.

"Indeed! what mean you?

"As at the balmy twilight hour the other eve you walked, a mendicant sailor you did encounter, with leg of wood, a pitiable patch across his face—'twas I. I asked for charity. You gave me sixpence, but the coin was naught compared with the sweet sigh of sympathy which hallowed the donation. In menial garb for months I've waited on thee, paid by a look, enchanted by a smile. At Beulah-Spa, a gipsy I did personate, and as I gazed upon thy beauteous palm, I promised thee what from my soul I wished, and still do wish, a long, a joyous, cloudless, sunny life."

"I don't recollect the sailor or the gipsy," said Arabella, feeling, as he spoke, in a strange, incomprehensible flutter, for his voice was sweet, and his manner peculiarly impressive.

"Sweet lady," he continued, "will you deign to pardon the presumption of one, who, although a simple unit from the presumptious herd, yet dares to utter his aspiring thoughts within thy hearing?"

"How like Claude Melnotte he speaks," thought Arabella, rather flatteringly, it must be confessed; it was sufficient to show that Bulwer was a piece of golden-colored glass, within the windows of her soul. "Would it be too much, sir," said she, in that matter-of-fact way which romancists frequently fall into, as the exception, "would it be too much to inquire who and what you are?"

The question was almost too abrupt for Sedleigh, too earthly, now that his imagination was abroad upon the wings of fancy. However, with a still more extensive respiration, he replied:

"Madam, to be frank with you, I'm a gentleman; but alas, the spirit and plaything of hard destiny, which, had it emptied all its store of woes upon my head, makes ample recompense by now permitting me to speak to thee. Oh! let the soft music of thy voice, steeping my soul in melody, bid me not despair. 'Tis strength of love alone that lends me boldness, for I feel, I know that I am unworthy of you. The possessor only of a poor cottage-home, where love might make its rosy dwelling, but where worldly riches enter not."

Arabella felt strangely excited. Here was the realization of her every wish, untitled, wealthy only in abundant love. She hesitated, and in accordance with the veracious proverb, in that moment's unguardedness, Cupid, the vigilant, abstracted her heart for ever.

Sedleigh was crafty enough not to prolong this introductory visit, which was meant but to show Arabella that she had a devoted adorer. Affecting to hear an approaching footstep, he cried in an agitated voice—

"Some one comes! Oh, do not send me away without a ray of hope to light existence."

"What can I say?" replied the really agitated Arabella.

"That you do not hate me?"

"No."

"You'll let me see you again?"

"No."

"I must, I must. Oh, say but yes. Remember the happiness or misery of a life depends upon your answer."

Arabella was most imprudently silent; for Sedleigh construing it advantageously, exclaimed—

"Oh, thanks, ten thousand thanks for that voiceless eloquence. And now, for a time, farewell, my first, my only, everlasting love, farewell." And hastily opening the window, he withdrew, the same uncomfortable way that he had entered, leaving Arabella in a fearful maze, but whether of joy or apprehension she hardly knew herself. But the chord of sympathy had been touched, and still vibrated to her very heart—for she acknowledged that of all men living, he was the only one for whom she had ever felt the slightest approach to a sentiment of love.

Now would she laugh at the absurdity of being so taken with a mere stranger, and suddenly find her recollection dwelling on his features—thus struggling like a bird in the net of the fowler. Slowly and silently she returned to the drawing-room, hearing, as she went, the loud, hearty laugh of her uncle in the library, little thinking that she had furnished him with matter for such uproarious mirth; for Sedleigh was at that moment relating to Sir Harry the success of his first interview, and the tears rolled down the old gentleman's crimsoned cheek as he listened.

Next day Arabella was very busy at her toilette, and Lucy, curious to know what could so occupy her attention, crept stealthily across, and peeping over her sister's shoulder, beheld the half-finished likeness of a remarkably nice-looking young man, with beautiful dark hair, and brilliant eyes. Pulling down the corners of her mouth with a good-gracious-me sort of expression, she quietly returned to her chair and said nothing—sensible girl!

CHAPTER III.

For several weeks had those secret interviews—so secret that they were known to the whole household—transpired, and Arabella, who tolerated them at first, from the mere caprice of a romantic disposition, soon began to look forward to their coming with what one might call a heart-hunger. The truth was, she loved Sedleigh, the—as she imagined—poor, unfriended youth, with an affection the most ardent and overwhelming, and now, for the first time, a shade of gloom dimmed the radiance of her brow as the thought incessantly arose before her that Sir Henry could never, by any possibility, be induced to countenance a match so unworthy. Many a time did she determine to throw herself on her knees before her uncle, and try the unequal contest of woman's tears against a man's will, but as often did her heart fail her, at the full certainty of refusal, and the consequent dismissal of Sedleigh.

Poor Arabella's perturbation of mind and uneasy demeanor, as one might suppose, were matter of pleasant observation to Sir Henry and Lucy, who, in full possession of every item that occurred, could construe every look and action of her who thought herself the very focus of mystery, the very incarnation of romance.

It was now near the time on which her lover usually made his stolen visits, and Arabella, making some trivial excuse, rose, and with a beating heart, sought the conservatory, Sir Henry and Lucy stealing quietly after, and ensconcing themselves within a seeable, though not a hearable distance—treasonable encroachment upon the precincts of Eros, King of Hearts.

Not long had Arabella to wait. With a mysterious glance around, and with a noiseless, stealthy step, Sedleigh approached.

"Dearest love," whispered he, most tenderly, "again am I in the presence of my soul's ray, again the cheering influence of those beaming eyes imbue my seared and withered heart," for as he was making love medicinally, he was no homœopathist. "Oh!" he continued, with a glance of unspeakable affection, "how have I languished for this blissful hour; a blank, a void, a dull, cheerless nullity has been the intervening time since last we parted, and were it not that thy bright image ever dwelling here within my heart of hearts shot through my breast a ray of joy, and kindled hope within my soul, despair and death had, ere now, claimed their victim."

Now Sedleigh thought, at first, that by enacting these scenes of high-wrought and overcharged romance, he would disabuse the mind of Arabella, and thereby induce her to listen to him in his real character; but he was much mistaken, and but little knew the page he had to study; for as the purest, deepest love had taken possession of her enthusiastic young heart, she looked on all he said or did as the perfection of their kind. Oh, bounteous dispensation of the heart's disposer, that so inclines and tempers each to each, that to its own choice the enraptured soul can find no parallel! What a short time since, even in the midst of her romance, she would have deemed absurd, now in the very soberness of her reflective moments, her partial heart found full excuse for, and why? because his was the expression of a true and sacred love, although in an exaggerated mask.

"The sun will warm, tho' it do not shine."

This interview lengthened out to an unprecedented extent—outstaying even curiosity, for Sir Henry and Lucy were tired off in about half an hour—brought a definite issue, which may be inferred from the following conversation which took place in the library a short time after:

"Well, Sed, my boy—my gay deceiver, how do you get on, eh?"

"Famously!"

"Does she surrender at discretion?"

"No. Most indiscreetly."

"How so?"

"Be in the drawing-room, but not in view, at twelve o'clock to-night, and you shall see."

"Why, zounds! You don't mean that you are going to" ——

"Gretna Green, by the Lord Harry."

"Ha! ha! ha!" roared the Baronet. "Give me your hand; by Jove, that's capital. An Elopement Extraordinary, a young lady running off with a Viscount and ten thousand a year, and thinking that she's throwing away a good fifteen thousand to unite her fate with a cottage-keeper's grow-your-own-vegetables sort of a fellow—ha! ha! ha! try that port it's too good, by George, it is." Whether the Baronet meant the wine or the joke, was doubtful and immaterial.

The evening wore on, and all around bore an aspect of abstraction. A sort of mysterious atmosphere seemed to envelop the place; never were the girls so silent, and never did the Baronet go off into so many unaccountable explosions of laughter without condescending to explain the various witticisms. At last Arabella rose, and, as was her custom, before retiring for the night, embraced her sister and her uncle. There were tears in her eyes as she gave Lucy a long, long kiss, but when she approached Sir Harry, something again appeared to tickle him amazingly, for it was full five minutes before he subsided sufficiently to receive his ward's affectionate salute.

"Good night, you little—pooh! hoo! ha! ha!" and off he went again.

"What *can* be the matter, uncle?" gravely inquired Lucy, with the slightest possible smile resting on her proud lip.

"Nothing, child, nothing; a good joke I heard to-day, that's all; a capital joke; but come, 'tis foolish to laugh so much," and with an altered, and now serious countenance, the good, kind-hearted old gentleman kissed Arabella affectionately, saying, "God for ever bless you, my pet; good night," and she retired.

Some two hours after, the lights being all out in the drawing-room, save one small lamp, and Lucy and Sir Harry, with a cambric handkerchief stuffed into his mouth, snugly concealed behind the ample window-curtains, a soft step was heard gently approaching, and the little fluttering run-away crept into the apartment. It was as much as the Baronet and Lucy could do to restrain their emotion as they saw the seeming giddy child fling herself upon her knees, and burying her face in her hands, burst into an agony of tears.

A few moments after, a signal was heard. Hastily wiping away the pearly drops from her eyes, Arabella started to her feet, threw a note on the table, and snatching up from thence two miniatures, one of her uncle and the other of her sister, kissed them fervently, and then placed them in her bosom.

Sedleigh joined her, and it was with much and earnest persuasion that he at length induced her to accompany him. They went out, and as they crossed the garden, Arabella thought she heard either a smothered laugh or a sob, or both.

Crack went the postillion's whip, and off they dashed, northward, at the rate of twelve miles an hour. They need not have been in so great a hurry—nobody followed them.

CHAPTER IV.

Gentle reader, oblige me by filling up the hiatus as your imagination may point out, and skip with me three weeks.

Having done so, now let me show you the interior of a small, but for the life of me I cannot say comfortable, cottage in Devonshire, the humble residence of Mr. and Mrs. Sedleigh. He is sitting on a chair, dressed in a gamekeeper's sort of fustian jacket, cord continuations, and high leather gaiters. A gun rests on his arm, and a magnificent pair of thorough-blooded pointers recline at his feet, with mouths all agape, and tongues quivering in proof of recent exercise. Seated opposite to him is his sister, the Lady Emma Sedleigh, her noble contour but ill-concealed beneath a maid of-all-work's coarse habiliments. You may hear Arabella in the adjacent small garden, singing like a very bird, and as happy as one. Now for our story.

"Well, brother mine," rather pettishly exclaims the Lady Emma, "this notable scheme of yours don't promise much success. Just listen to that extraordinary wife of yours, warbling away as though this were a palace, and not an odious, unendurable hovel."

"Patience, Emma love," replies Sedleigh, "all will yet be as I wish. I have noticed already, *moments* of discomfort; they'll soon swell to *hours*, hours to *days*, and then for my lesson; depend upon it, we shall soon contrive to make her feel uncomfortable."

"Do, do, for gracious sake," replied the petted child of fortune, who undertook this matter as much from the excitement of novelty as for brotherly love; and now the former had passed away, the latter scarcely sufficed to keep her to her promise.

"I have commenced already," replied Sedleigh, "by placing a brick across the chimney, and see the result," as a puff of smoke clouded into the room.

"Oh! delicious," exclaimed his sister, clapping her hands, "she'll never be able to endure that; hark! she's coming; I must return to my *place* in the hope of soon changing it;" and the Lady Emma, or rather, as she is now called, by the familiar term *Mary*, vacated the parlor for the poor kitchen, heartily sick and tired of her *situation.*

In bounded Arabella, radiant with happiness, and all aglow with health. "My own, own husband," she exclaimed, "never did I in my wildest dreams anticipate the fullness of joy that now inhabits my soul."

"My beautiful, my wife," ardently responded Sedleigh, "happiness is but a fleeting shadow, and its opposite may obtrude itself even among these rosy bowers."

"How! you look sorrowful, my Sedleigh; dear husband, has anything happened to vex? any light word of mine? Oh, I would not bring the slightest shadow of a cloud upon thy brow for millions of worlds," tenderly exclaimed Arabella, the mere alteration in his tone chasing her smile away upon the instant.

Sedleigh, with difficulty obliging himself to go through with his design, said—

"The fact is, dearest, I am rather close pressed in the pecuniary way, just at present. I owe a trifle; my creditor has been here, and" —

"Pay him! pay him, certainly. I will, myself," energetically cried Arabella, but suddenly checked by the thought, for the first time in her life, of being without the means.

"But no matter," rejoined Sedleigh, "that I can put off, but present wants must be supplied; dinner is imperative. I must away and try and shoot some game if his lordship's well-stocked grounds be not too closely watched."

"Are you obliged to leave me, Sedleigh?" said she, with a small pout.

"Else we have no dinner," he replied. Giving her an affectionate embrace, he left her to digest this, her first practical lesson, in the comforts of "Love in a Cottage," and, to say the truth, poor Arabella felt at this moment very far from happy; the leaves began to drop from the roses, and the concealed thorns to make themselves seen and felt.

It was in this mood, that on sitting down to reflect, a puff of smoke descended the chimney, covering her in a black cloud of soot. Putting her hands over her eyes, she screamed for Mary several times, stamping her pretty little foot in positive anger. At last, with the characteristic listlessness of her *rôle*, the Lady Emma crawled into the room. Wiping her hands in her apron, she drawled out, "Did you call mum?"

"Call mum," replied Arabella, with a rather dangerous expression of eye—"I did *call* enough to waken the dead."

"If they wern't too far gone, I s'pose, mum," provokingly rejoined the maid-servant.

"No impertinence!"

"What do you please to want, mum?"

"Why, don't you see?" said Arabella, pettishly.

"See what, mum?"

"The chimney."

"Yes, mum."

"It smokes."

"Law, *do* it mum? Well, so it *do*, a little, I declare," said she, as another volume of sooty vapor swept into the place, "but don't take on, mum," she continued, "it always do smoke when the wind is in one direction, and it generally almost always is, so that you'll soon get used to it."

"Good Heaven," said Arabella, "I cannot endure this; I must go out into the air. Come here, put my collar straight."

"Can't, mum."

"Why not?"

"Cos my hands is all black-leaded," said the lady-servant,

going out of the room with an internal conciousness that matters were progressing to a climax.

And now poor Arabella began seriously to deplore the dark prospect which rose before her imagination. Her little feet went pat pat upon the uncarpeted floor, and if she had been asked at that moment how she felt, she would have replied, decidedly miserable; but her true woman's heart soon conquered every discomfort, and she said within herself, 'tis my Sedleigh's fate; if he can endure it, so shall *I*, without a murmur: so that when he returned, instead of finding her as he supposed he should, in sorrow, her beautiful face greeted him with smiles more gladsome than ever.

It was some days before Sedleigh could make up his mind to bring matters to a crisis. He was becoming himself, rather fatigued with his rustic life, and so with a view to investigate the state of Arabella's feelings, he one morning seated her beside him, saying:

"Now, dearest love, since you have had some experience in this our homely country-life, tell me frankly how you like it? Does it come up to, or exceed your expectation?"

"Sedleigh," she replied in a tone of earnest seriousness, "I married *you*, and not your station, swearing at the holy altar to be yours, in health or in sickness, in joy or in sorrow. If I can shed one ray of happiness upon your onward path, though ne'er so humble, 'twill be my glory and my pride."

"But now," continued he, "were I to find myself within a somewhat better sphere, were fortune to bless me with increase of means—say, now that by some strange freak a title were to fall to me."

"Sedleigh, husband," replied Arabella, with enthusiasm, "I *would* not love you *less* were you a beggar, I *could* not love more were you a king."

"I'd like the former chance before the latter," smilingly

rejoined Sedleigh. "Heaven reward your sweet, disinterested love. I *have* a somewhat larger and more commodious house; it has just been put in order at some little cost; we shall remove there, dearest, after dinner. 'Tis but a short walk from this. Now for our meal. Mary!"

In vain they called; Mary had incontinently vanished, and with her, all hope of dinner.

"Never mind," said Sedleigh, "we *may* find something at the other house."

"I hope so," gaily responded Arabella, "for I am furiously hungry."

Delighted at the anticipation of being anywhere out of the atmosphere of smoky chimneys, Arabella put on her little plain straw bonnet, and taking the arm of her husband, sallied forth. In a few minutes they came in view of a splendid castellated mansion, situated in the centre of a spacious park, with herds of deer browsing here and there, upon the velvety grass.

"Goodness me, what a lovely place!" said Arabella, as they entered; "may we go through here?"

"As often as you please, dearest," replied Sedleigh, "the owner, I think I may venture to say, will not interdict you."

"Indeed, then I shall take many a walk beneath the shade of those fine old elms," replied Arabella.

"I hope so, most sincerely," replied Sedleigh, "and I too: and then we *might* fancy this delightful place our own, and stroll about as though we had a right."

They now neared the entrance to the castle, and Arabella perceiving that the marble steps were lined with servants in rich liveries, shrunk timidly back. But what was her surprise to find her husband walk directly towards the group!

"You are not going in there, Sedleigh," she cried, in a voice of alarm, a sensation akin to fear creeping over her.

"Yes, dearest," he replied, "I know some persons connected

with the household. Indeed, I believe you have met them occasionally; so come, fear nothing."

In a sort of wondering maze, Arabella entered, and leaning heavily on the arm of her husband, traversed the statued hall and noble picture-gallery. As she neared an inner apartment, a sound proceeded from it that made her thrill with vague indefinite anticipation. It was a peculiar laugh. She could have sworn that she knew it, and she was right. A pair of large folding doors flew violently open, and in a rich, but elegantly appointed room, mellowed by the soft light of a glorious tinted window, Arabella almost fainted with overpowering excitement as she beheld, rushing forward to embrace her, Sir Henry Templeton and her sister Lucy. Scarcely had she recovered the shock of pleasurable surprise, when the quondam Mary, splendidly attired, flung her arms round her neck, exclaiming—

"Dear sister, let me be the first to welcome the Viscountess Sedleigh to the domain of her husband. His, by right of heritage, hers, by right of conquest."

Arabella gave one glance of unutterable love at her *lord*, through eyes made brighter by tears

> That came not from a soul-cloud charged with grief,
> But were from very over-brightness shed,
> Like heart-drops falling from a sun-lit sky.

JASPER LEECH.

THE MAN WHO NEVER HAD ENOUGH.

The hero of my sketch, Jasper Leech, was, to use the stereotyped expression, born of poor, but honest parents; his infancy exhibited no remarkable diagnostics by which to illustrate or establish any peculiarity of character, saving, perhaps, the simple fact, that with him, the process of weaning was protracted to a curious extent, any attempt to cut off or diminish the maternal supply being met with obstinate resistance, in spite of all the ingenious artifices usually resorted to on such occasions to induce a distaste; still he sucked and sucked, until the female visitors, one and all, voted it shameful in a great fellow like that.

At school, young Jasper was famous for the steady snail-pace at which he crawled through the rudiments, and also for the extraordinary *penchant* he evinced for anything in his proximity which was, or appeared to be unattainable at the moment; say one of his school-mates was in possession of a new toy, Jasper would first envy him, then covet it, cunningly waiting the moment when the novelty being past, the boy was open to negotiate, then would he chaffer and diplomatize, almost invariably gaining his desired end. Thus he went on steadily accumulating, until what with a natural appetite for trading, and a calculating eye to the profitable side of a bargain, he managed to shut up the market altogether by exhaustion. The very spring-time of life, which generally passes by in gleesome sport, was to him a period of anxiety and care; for while his mates were rioting in boisterous play, he would sit apart, his whole brain wrapped in the maze of speculation—a *swop* is in progression, and he must have the advantage.

Thus passed his boyhood; his schooling over with his strong common sense undulled by too much book-lore, he was duly inducted into the mystery of shoe-craft. He served out his time with exemplary diligence, working leisurely of days that he might keep reserve of strength to spend the nights for his own profit, thereby saving a considerable sum from the employment of his over-hours.

Once his own master, he deliberated long what road he should travel in pursuit of the blind goddess, invisible as well as blind—that intangible phantasma which men wear out life and energy in seeking, only when found to confess with tears of bitterness how misspent was time in the attainment.

At last our ambitious friend ventured humbly into trade on his own account, declaring that should anything approaching to success crown his efforts, and that at the end of five or six years he could command a thousand dollars, he would be the most contented, the happiest fellow on earth.

He was lucky, curiously lucky; it seemed as though, Midas-like, all he touched turned to gold; money swept in, so that before he had been three years in business, instead of the limited one thousand, he was master of *five*. "Now," said he to himself, "if I could but make that five, *ten*, I might not only be enabled to enlarge my stock, and thereby increase my returns, but I think I might even venture to look about for a helpmate with an equal sum;" for Jasper would just as soon have thought of investing the best part of his capital in the establishment of a lunatic asylum as of marrying a portionless woman.

The sun shone on—in less time than he could possibly have anticipated—ten thousand was at his command. Very good, thought he; this, with ten or fifteen thousand more, as a premium for encumbering myself with a comforter of the snarling sex—for the ungallant Jasper had a thoroughly mercantile business man's opinion of the angelic species—will be sufficient. I must investigate.

So he set out on a tour of the watering-places, and such like wife-markets, where Cupid, the most wide-awake of auctioneers—it's a libel to say he's blind—knocks the little darlings down to the highest bidder. Of course, Jasper stopped at the first-class hotels, where he scrutinized the *habitués* of the ladies' ordinary with uncommon interest. There's no use in disguising the fact, he sought not a wife, but a fortune; in extenuation, allow me to say, he was not at all singular, there are plenty of those individuals extent, young, tolerably good-looking fellows *bien gantés*, and redolent of whisker, who linger about the ladies' drawing-room, in the faint hope of fascinating something available (prudent maternity avoids this class with pious horror), middle-aged beaux, who dress seduously, and toady *chaperons*, carry fans, are always *so* attentive and *so* obliging, dine regularly, and affect a Burgundy decanter, which looks easy circumstanced, but which the poor waiter is tired of carrying backward and forward, ticketed some hundred and something.

Jasper, though indefatigable, as you may well suppose, met with strange adventures during his wife-hunt. Pretty women, after short experience, he avoided utterly, for he found that they were usually too extravagant in their expectations with regard to *personnel*, and as Jasper could not, by any stretch of his imagination, fancy that he ranked in the category of Fredericks and Augustuses, he endeavored to make up the deficiency by a liberal display of wealth-prefiguring ornament, a kind of strong-box index, which he shrewdly suspected might tempt some ambitious innocent to investigate the contents thereof.

Perhaps it would be well at this period, as our hero is gotten up at no small expense, to give a rough pen-and-ink outline of his appearance. In the first place, he was twenty-eight years old, by his own account; as he could scarcely be expected to know exactly himself, it's not to be wondered at that he and the parish register differed a few years; but that was of little consequence, for he had an accommodating curious-colored complexion, which, as it made him look at least forty, will no doubt return the compliment by making him look no more at sixty; his hair was about as indefinite, being a factitious auburn, a dry, wiry red, something like the end of a fox's brush in hot weather, crisp and tangible, like fine, copper-shavings; one could not help fancying that if he shook his head each individual hair would jar audibly against the other. The whole arrangement gave one an idea of intense heat, and an involuntary hope that the poor fellow had but a sprinkle of hydrocephalus; he was of undecided height also, varying from five feet four-and-half to five feet four-and-three-quarters, at the option of his boot-maker; but the most remarkable features, if we may use the expression, in his conformation, were his hands, which were gaunt and bony, of a tanned-leathery consistence, and of a streaky, mottled, castile-soap color, covered with a straggling crop of light, sandy hair, and ornamented with several *wedding*-rings—evidences of broken hearts, which some men are fond of displaying as certificates of gallantry. Dressed in irreproachable black, and capped and jewelled in the most orthodox style, it may be imagined that Jasper was the *object* of no small solicitude to the "anxious mothers of slenderly-portioned daughters; he certainly had an an air *bien riche*, if not *distingué*—and that's the marketable *materiel* after all.

Months were unprofitably spent, and Jasper was beginning to think the time irretrievably lost, when an occurence of some little interest varied the eateraceous-drinkability of hotel monotony. The Blodgerses arrived, *en route* to the fashionable ruralities.

Now the Blodgerses were extensive people in their way. They were originated somewhere in Pennsylvania, and affected the tone of the far south; travelled with huge trunks, two lap-dogs, a parrot and a liveried African. The head of the family was a pursy, important chairman-of-an-election-committee-looking man, with a superabundance of excessively white shirt-frill, and a great deal too much watch-chain; the latter appendage he invariably swung round as he conversed, its momentum indicating the state of his temper during an argument; let him speak upon uninteresting topics—literature, for instance, or any of the useless arts—you notice but a gentle apathetic oscillation, but let him get upon the tariff, let him hurl denunciations against his political enemies, or eulogize his particular Presidential candidate, and round it goes with astonishing velocity.

Blodgers had been a grocer, or something of the kind, and having, during a life of assiduous saving and scraping, accumulated a very large sum, now flung himself with extraordinary *abandon* upon the full stream of gentility—and, to say the truth, most uncomfortably he found it; for many a time would he acknowledge to his wife that "this flying about from steam-car to steamboat, was far more fatiguing, and not quite so profitable as quietly serving out lump sugar. Then would Mrs. B. indignantly check such compromising thoughts, for she was a person of great pretension, had had a slight acquaintance with Mrs. Judge Pinning, and once visited, by accident, Mrs. General Jollikins, so felt herself bound to talk of "society." "They don't do this in our set;" or, "it's not the etiquette in *society;*" and such like sidewinded hints of her position, formed the staple of her conversations. As for the heiress to the wealthy grocer's store, there was an indescribable something in her air and manner which plainly indicated, "I am worth looking after!" She talked loudly, stared rudely through a magnificent Parisian double glass, and in fact broke through all the recognized rules of good-breeding with that insolent familiarity which but poorly imitates the *nonchalant* ease of the really *distingué.*

No description of deportment could have made so great an impression on Jasper. She looked ingots, she spoke specie, and her *prestige* was altogether redolent of *rouleaux.* He was struck, but the stricken deer took the precaution to investigate realities before he advanced a step toward acquaintanceship. Now, thought he, if she but happen to have some ten or fifteen thousand, she'd be just the wife for me. The result was satisfactory. He discovered that a larger sum was settled to be her marriage portion—and so laid vigorous siege instanter.

Now Araminta Blodgers, although decidedly not qualified to grace the pages of the book of beauty, had a strange predilection for "nice young men;" so that at first Jasper met with decided, and not over-delicately expressed, opposition. But he was not a man to retire from the first repulse; he persevered, and finally so deceived the sympathetic Araminta into the belief of his ardent affection, that, one fine summer evening she sighed forth an avowal that she and her expectations were at his disposal.

Fresh from this successful attack upon the heiress' susceptibilities, with a feathery heart Jasper snapped his fingers at love, and danced down the corridor of the hotel to the infinite wonderment of the waiters. Either from force of habit, or as a means of tempering the exuberance of his spirits, he plunged into the mysteries of the guest-book, where, alas! for Araminta Blodgers, and for true love! the first name he saw was that of Mrs. Skinnington, the rich widow from his own immediate neighborhood; she whom he had sedulously church-ogled from the opposite pew every Sunday, astonished at the vastness of his presumption; she, the *bonâ fide* and sole possessor of nearly half his native town. Here was the shadow of the shade of opportunity. She was alone. Jasper hesitated. Araminta's fortune was ample, but when there was a chance of more, it wasn't *enough!* Finally he determined to wait the first intereviw with the widow, and be regulated by her manner.

They met at dinner, and she was singularly gracious. The fact is, those eye-assaults had told a little; and I'm sorry to say, for the character of the sex, that the widow, in case the siege should be renewed, had predetermined on capitulation.

The result may be anticipated. The endurable Araminta was thrown over for the intolerable widow and her superior wealth. They were married in a curiously short space of time; and when Jasper found himself master of the widow's hoard, "Now," thought he with a glowing heart, "a few thousand dollars more, and I shall be content. One hundred thousand is the acme of my desire; let me but achieve that, and I shall then retire and spend the remainder of my days in quiet comfort.

In process of time he did realize the coveted amount; but did he keep his word and retire? no! he had enough of that. Home was to him the worst of all miseries, a sort of domestic tartarus; the presiding fury, his elderly wife, who, incapable of inspiring a sentiment of affection herself, yet assumed all the caprice of a girl. Jealous to very lunacy, she gave vent to the agonizing sensations of her soul by scribbling heart-rending sonnets for the Fiddle-Faddle Magazine. Thin, withered, romantic and exacting, you may suppose that to the unfortunately lucky Jasper, home was no *dulce domum.*

The consequence was, that he, dreading the *tête-à-tête* domestic, confined his attention to his monetary affairs. Retirement with an unlovable and moreover intolerably suspicious companion as Mrs. L., or, as she signed herself, Sappho, was out of the question; so he determined to stick to the counting-house. And now a great idea filled his brain almost to monomania, which was to make his one hundred thousand, *two.* Once conceived, every thought and action was merged in that one absorbing idea. Heedless of the domestic tornadoes that ever and anon swept over his devoted head, he slaved, fretted, lied, I think I may venture to say, cheated, but honorably, and in the way of business, until after a few years of health-destroying worry, he beheld himself within sight of the desired haven. But five thousand more, and the sum would be accomplished; one stroke of luck—one piece of indifferent fortune, and he would then be really content.

Worn out by constant exertion, he fell dangerously ill. During his sickness, news arrived which brought him within a few hundred of his maximum. Notwithstanding his bad health, and in opposition to all remonstrance, he called for his books, and with weak hand, and weaker brain, attempted to calculate. After many hours labor, altogether unaware that he was thus unprofitably expending his last flickering of life, he gave a long, sorrowful sigh, and gasping forth, "Not enough! not enough!" expired.

Not many days after, a few feet of earth were sufficient for THE MAN WHO NEVER HAD ENOUGH.

NIGHTMARES.

I.

THE LAMP FIEND.

A QUIET, peace-loving, good tempered, domestic martyr was Mr. Theophilus Puddiwag—going through the duties of his allotted station in life with a praiseworthy doggedness, and exercising his small amount of virtuous requirements with a regularity quite satisfactory and Christian-like.

Puddiwag's hours of relaxation were few, for he was an exemplary man of business, sacrificing, with Spartan severity, all those delicate traits of character which are comprised in what are termed the amenities of life. Acknowledging but few duties, he consequently discharged them with extreme punctuality; he adored traffic, because that was the staple of his ideas; he loved his home, because it was his physical resting-place; he endured his wife, forasmuch as she kept its locks and hinges in excellent order; paid his debts, because if he didn't he wouldn't get credit; delighted hugely to make tight bargains when there was no fear of discovery—and, in a word, was highly respectable in the eyes of all the money-loving community.

Thus Puddiwag's life of perpetual usefulness—to himself—would, no doubt, have calmly glided away, but that he had one great inquietude, which would ever and anon darken the sky of his mercantile properity. There is no man without his share of annoyance, and his was *the temper* of *Mrs. Puddiwag.*

It is a wonderful psychologic study, the temper of womankind generally; but that of Mrs. Puddiwag was perfectly inexplicable, like a sudden cold in the head, you never knew how it was produced. You think of a thousand reasons, changing your under-garments, sitting in a draught, having your hair cut, going out in the rain—but not one of them may be right.

It is just as probable it may have resulted from some homœopathic accident, such as a breath of summer air through a key-hole, cutting your finger nails imprudently short, or eating your food with a damp fork.

Therefore it was that the least agreeable portion of Mr. Puddiwag's existence was passed beneath his domestic roof; and it was, indeed, a red letter day in his calendar when even that small period was passed harmoniously.

Upon the eventful occasion which we are about to chronicle, Mr. Puddiwag, who had that day succeeded in consummating a highly profitable piece of allowable chicanery, as morally wrong as it could well be, and yet, as no legal statute was infringed upon, he only considered it a remarkably smart "business" transaction—the sagacious and self-satisfied man of respectability wended his way homeward to his little retreat among "the avenues," wondering, as was his wont, what sort of a temper Mrs. Puddiwag would be in, not that he ever confided to her the details of his daily operations, but if she should happen to be in one of her crooked moods it would interfere most materially with the delightful after-contemplation which generally results from a successful stroke of sagacity. But this time it was Mr. Puddiwag who was out of temper.

It will be necessary to reveal the secret history of the Puddiwag Family at this moment.

There had been a slight disagreement on the previous night.

Mrs. Puddiwag was ambitious, and wanted gas in her house.

Mr. Puddiwag was economical, and insisted upon burning oil.

Somebody suggested a compromise in the shape of camphene, but Mrs. P. thought it vulgar, and Mr. P. had a very proper and terrible apprehension of the murderous liquid, which he took care to express, as it happened, with unskillful and injudicious vehemence.

Whereupon Mrs. P. became suddenly sulky and silent, and Mr. P. rejoiced inwardly at the apparent victory.

Short-sighted Puddiwag!

It was, therefore, with a vague presentiment that Mrs. Puddiwag's temper was on the shady side of amiability, that Mr. Puddiwag turned the corner of his street; the evening had rushed down in a hurry, for even time has no time to take its time in this "push along" country—and astonishment took possession of his every sense, he rubbed his eyes and doubted their evidence—his house was one blaze of light. The usual sober blinds were heightened into positive illuminations, the place looked like a newly-established tippling-shop or the head-quarters of a political club.

"God bless my soul!" gasped Puddiwag; "can that tremendous female have put the gas in, in spite of my opposition!"

Puddiwag grew extremely red in the face, but nobody saw it, for it was dark. He made sudden rush up the stone steps, and pulled a sharp, authoritative, irritable pull, that must have thrilled through the nerves of his better half like an electric shock.

Puddiwag had a latch key, but he wouldn't condescend to use it, for *Puddiwag* was *angry*.

But, if his anger was great on the door-step, what was it in the parlor when he beheld half a dozen great glass bellied camphene lamps blazing away from all corners of the apartment, and Mrs. Puddiwag seated in the centre, rigid and inflexible, like a concentration of the Parcæ.

Had he been obliged to smoke a cigar to the stump, sitting up to his elbows in a powder magazine, walk the streets of New York after dark, or travel up the Hudson in a racing steamboat—he could not have been more fearfully agitated by consternation and alarm.

For a few moments he gazed in mute despair upon the flaming scene, while never a word said Mrs. Puddiwag, nor did the stern expression of her iron countenance relax in the remotest perceptible degree. At last he mustered up sufficient courage to say, in a spirit-quenched, deprecatory tone of voice, "What is all this?"

With her full, round, light grey eyes still fixed unwinkingly upon him, and her attenuated arms still rigidly entwined, Mrs. Puddiwag slowly opened her mouth, and ejaculated, "CAMPHENE!"

"The devil!" cried Puddiwag, jumping up as though each syllable had been fired at him through a double-barrelled gun. "Bloodthirsty and remorseless woman!" he cried, "are you ignorant of the frightfully destructive agent you have introduced into the house? Is there a week, a day, which has not its tale to tell of death or disfigurement resulting from that atrocious and diabolical invention?"

"*Gas!*" quietly responded Mrs. Puddiwag.

"I cannot exist amongst these latent infernal machines," said Mr. P.

"*Gas!*" reiterated Mrs. P.

Now, everybody knows that when a woman of Mrs. Puddiwag's force of character makes up her mind she sticks to it, and the consequence was, a compromise was finally entered into, to the effect that if the obnoxious lamps were extinguished, Puddiwag would "*see about*" the gas in the morning.

In accordance with this solemn domestic treaty the lights were in due time put out of danger, and ——

We must allow Mr. P. to tell the rest in his own way:

Rendered extremely nervous and agitated by the great danger I had been in, for I did not breathe freely while one of the cursed things was in operation, and considerably annoyed by the obstinacy of Mrs. P. in insisting upon the extravagance of gas, when we had been burning oil all our lives; I retired early to bed in the hope of tranquilizing my nerves, having previously taken a narcotic in the shape of my usual rum toddy, which, in consequence of the shaking of my hand in pouring out the spirits, was, I believe, a little stronger than usual, it was some time before I could get to sleep, for at every attempt I made to close my eyes two great round globes of fire came in their stead, and blazed in upon my very brain.

At last I slept—not long, however, for I was suddenly awakened by a most unpleasant and peculiar sensation, as though a hot blast of air were running through my ear.

I started, and rubbed my eyes. There *was* a hot blast, and a voice piercing through my sense.

"Get up, Puddiwag, instantly," it said.

I turned round to look at the speaker, when, never shall I forget the sight which met my startled gaze—a figure, having the appearance of an enormous animated camphene lamp, stood by my bedside. Its face was a large crystal globe, but ductile and capable of distention and contraction; the eyes were two flames, which shot luminously forth; and when the mouth opened it displayed a burning chasm, from which the forked tongue darted like a lightning flash.

What the rest of its dreadful anatomy was I could not say, for it was dressed in the extreme of fashion, in a short-tailed dress coat with pantaloon sleeves, terminating in the tops of white kid fingers, which had the angular shape of glass-drops. Its greatest peculiarity, however, was that it had but one leg, rigid and inflexible, and apparently fluted like the shaft of a Corinthian column, which was clothed in an exceedingly tight pantaloon, and displayed a large, flat, square foot in a patent-leather boot.

"Get up, Puddiwag," it repeated, laying its stiff-pointed fingers on my shoulder.

Trembling with horror, and perspiring at every pore, I did as I was told. With fear would I have cried out, but at each effort the sound died within my heart.

"Dress yourself," cried the form.

I proceeded to do so, feeling at the same time a frightful sensation as though my head were swelling out to a prodigious size, and also a singular dread of its coming in contact with any hard substance, it was so slight and brittle. But what was my consternation to discover that, after I had gotten one of my legs into my pantaloons, I *couldn't find the other*—it was gone.

On looking closer, I saw that my foot was a plain piece of marble. Almost fainting with terrible apprehension, I cast a glance into the toilet glass which was opposite to me, and horror of horrors! I perceived that my head was a counterpart of that of my spectral visitor, in short, that *I was a gigantic camphene lamp.*

I could feel the devilish element of destruction rolling and surging within me, as it yearned to fling itself through the contracted spaces at my eyes and mouth. Every sense, save one, was intensified to agony. I tried to speak, collected al. my energies to shout out, but the intention failed away into few spluttering hisses.

At last the chamber door opened, and in came Mrs. Puddiwag, but exaggerated to five times her original size.

"Good gracious," she exclaimed, in a voice like distant thunder, "who left the lamp on the floor?"

Oh! the tremendous efforts I made to tell her who I was, and for Heaven's sake to be careful; but it was all in vain, not a syllable could I utter, not a muscle could I move in resistance, as she took me up in her hands and placed me on a table, which stood in the centre of the room, most dangerously near the edge.

The horrible fear of falling off, and the thought of the terrible consequences which would ensue, made me feel faint and giddy. My spirit sunk within me, and my eyes burned dim and uncertain.

"Why, the lamp is going out," I heard Mrs. Puddiwag cry; "I wonder where the fluid is."

With a sensation of dread utterly indescribable I saw her search for and find the vessel which contained the camphene. I saw her approach. I felt her take off my head, and lay it quietly upon the table.

Slowly she raised the fatal instrument!

"Good Heavens," thought I, "*she won't fill me while I'm burning.*"

SHE DID!

"Well, and what followed?" said Puddiwag's companion, to whom he made the relation.

"What followed—why what should follow? I BURST——into a most uncontrollable fit of joyous laughter as I found myself lying on my back, quietly contemplating the top of the musquito net."

II.

POLITICAL AMBITION.

If there is anything in the world that worries me more than another it is the hubbub, confusion, and personal annoyance consequent upon election time.

What an extraordinary excitable, drum-and-fife people we are to be sure? My next door neighbor is candidate for some small office; he's the grocery man at the corner, and, I presume, reckons upon his insolvent customers giving him their "sweet voices," in lieu of other payment, in his ambitious aspirations.

The consequence is, that, with the mass meetings, preceded by drum and fife, and propitiatory serenades, including all the available force of somebody's brass band, scarcely a day or a night passes without ear-piercings and brazen bellowings sufficient to fright all Manhattan from her propriety.

The effect of these uproarious demonstrations upon a naturally nervous temperament, which I confess mine to be, may be imagined; but the climax was reached the day before yesterday, when the numerous friends and admirers of the opposing candidates, with banners, bands, platforms, and iron-throated public speakers took up their station in the vicinity.

The uproar that ensued was perfectly indescribable. The antagonistic bands tore "Hail Columbia" into shreds, in their frantic endeavors to outblast each other. The infuriated drums rattled continuous thunder; the embattled fifes squealed like insane steam pipes on an unearthly burst; mad rockets went it with an incessant rush; while the intervals were agreeably filled up by the roaring, itinerant politicians blackguarding each other, after the approved fashion of the genus generally.

I had a dinner party that day, consisting of three or four particular friends, and one new acquaintance from Europe, whom I was especially anxious to impress with a favorable notion of our cis-Atlantic manners and customs, according to the prevalent and commendable wish dictated by a combined feeling of patriotism and hospitality, of the majority of my countrymen.

Conceive, if you can, placid reader, the purgatory I endured from the commencement to the conclusion of the independent, no-way-to-be-averted political charivari that raved and roared, thundered, fizzed, shrieked, battered, besieged and rent

"Great Nature's universal tympanum."

In vain did my friends alternately apologize, and try to make jokes about the hideous din. In vain did my new acquaintance, one of the politest of Englishmen, whose very quintessence of suavity have somehow, to me, a spice of sarcasm. I could see behind the specious mask of ill-assumed ease that he was not prepared for such a tumult. His "Oh, my dear sir, don't mention it," when the occurrence was seriously deplored, and his "Oh, ah, very good indeed," when it was made the subject of a jest, were both delivered with the same imperturbable gravity of face, and the same rigidly polite inflection of voice.

As a matter of course, the elective franchise ballot-box, and all the intricacies of political elections, formed the staple of our conversation, for whenever induced by a lull in the contending elements without, literature, the fine arts, or some other interesting topic crept into the arena, "Three cheers for Wiggs or Griggs" dashed us back upon the sterile promontory of politics. Then would our Saxon guest enlighten us upon the subject of ten pound freeholders, the parliament, the brilliant court, the imposing aristocracy, and all the couleur de rose accessories which radiate from England's brightest side; but of its gloomy and terrible shadow, the darkness of whose blackness rests upon its prostrate sister, Ireland, he said not a word. Neither did he, I must do him the credit to say, indulge in Cockney impertinences towards our country, for, although slightly imbued with the patronizing manner which Mr. Bull assumes towards all other nations, whatsoever, he was a gentleman, and, therefore, half concealed his conscious superiority behind the veil of good breeding.

Every now and then, some not very complimentary allusion to either candidate belched forth with superior energy would reach our ears, little piquant episodes of family history, stripped of all delicate clothing, would be given to the gaping crowd. Then I *did* blush for my countrymen, and only wonder what a terrible goad ambition must be to urge a man through such filthy ditches.

It was during one of these infelicitous moments that my most intimate friend inquired why I, who (he flattered me by saying) had considerable influence, and some aptitude for public duties, did not aspire to make my debut on the great political stage?

"What," said I in disgust, "to undergo the tortures of this evening in my own proper person—to listen to Heaven knows what, raked from the slime of malevolence, and hurled against me—to have those whom I love and respect assailed—nay, perhaps, the honored tombstones of my dead relations blackened with defilement? No, no!"

However, the evening waned at last; my guests departed, and I began to breathe more freely. Flinging myself upon a sofa, I gave my mind up to quiet meditation, for the noise without was hushed, and the neighborhood had resumed its usual quietude.

Alas! how various and contradictory are the impulses and intentions of man? I had scarcely reclined upon that comfortble lounge for more than a dozen minutes, when I presented in myself a most astounding instance—I, who had hitherto shrunk like a sensitive plant from the remotest association which could present even a chance of my being mixed up in political matters, now formed a sudden and absorbing determination to seize upon the standard of ambition, and, having inscribed my name thereon, dash through every obstacle until I could behold it floating from the highest pinnacle of public fame.

In the height of my glorious promptings, I started to the floor, and, in floods of impassioned eloquence, astonished and delighted imaginary Senates. Strange that so mighty and overwhelming a gift should have been so long hidden, even from myself; but what a change a few short moments had produced! The Promethean fire had touched the clay—the soul-spark of noble emulation thrilled through my nerves as though with an electric shock. Yesterday, I trembled at the sound of my own voice, stammered and blushed, and lost myself in an inextricable maze of bashfulness, at a vestry meeting, to regulate the price of pews—now, with calm pulse and full unquailing glance, I could address assembled millions and not falter.

"My avocation is distinctly pointed out at last," cried I, in a spasm of rapturous delight. "What a singularly fortunate country is ours! no sooner does an emergency arise than with it comes the man to meet it. I *am* he!"

It was perfectly wonderful with what supreme contempt I then looked back upon my past life, wasted in the useless drudgery of mercantile pursuits, foolishly laboring, to fill up a banker's book the world will never know one syllable about, when, if I had but devoted the same attention to the honorable emulation of political life, my countenance might now be familiarized by countless daguerreotypes, or cut an extraordinary figure in the pages of *The Atlas.*

"But the past cannot be recalled," thought I, "so now, to make up for the time lost." So absorbed was I in contemplating with my mind's eye the splendid vista which extended itself before my imagination—breakfast time, and breakfast too, arrived without my knowledge. I could eat but little.

Very soon after, one of my friends called—at least, I suppose so, for I didn't hear him ring to enter the room, but, on looking up from one of my reflective moods, there he was laughing before me.

Singular to say, he knew exactly what I was thinking about. It was my friend Boblett, he who spoke to me last night about entering the political arena.

"Ha! ha!" he shouted, "I knew you'd change your mind."

"My dear friend," said I, "it is not so much from any particular inclination of my own, but because I am firmly persuaded that the safety of our glorious country and the permanence of its unequalled institutions, depends upon my individual exertions."

A tolerably fair commencement that, you must acknowledge, for a fledgling politician—insincerity, blarney, and egotism, mixed in equal parts and bolted whole.

"My dear Mudshank," replied Boblett, rather seriously, "I am perfectly alive to the appalling state of our beloved country, and the terrors of the approaching crisis. You are, doubtless, aware that Cuba and the Sandwich Islands have sent members of strong *antiphlogistic* tendency?"

"Have they, indeed," said I, rather vaguely I admit; the fact is I did not know that either of the places named had been recognized as States—to tell the truth, I was not aware they had ever been annexed—neither did I know what political party the epithet he had named alluded to. However, I had not yet read the morning papers, which accounted for my ignorance.

"Now, Mudshank," he resumed, "in your position, as the mouthpiece and popular exponent of public opinion"——

"What, I the mouthpiece"—

"Certainly," he continued, "it would be false diffidence in you to deny it. As a distinguished member of the illustrious Senate, representing, as you do, a constituency of the most enlightened"—

It was not until that moment that the rapidly following events of the past two or three seasons suddenly occurred to me. I don't know how it was, but I had nearly forgotten the fact of my having gone through the regular gradations of Assembly and the House, while indulging in my reverie. Now, however, it all flashed upon me at once, and the importance of my station enveloped me in a haze of self-satisfied hauteur. Of course, I could not now be so familiar with Boblett, so I accordingly proceeded to freeze him with my civility.

"My good Boblett," said I, with a supercilious glance, laying one finger patronizingly on his arm, "those matters are not for you to interfere with, leave them to us, if you please, good Boblett. When I go to Washington"—

"Go *to* Washington?" said Boblett, "why, you *are* at Washington."

On looking around me, I found we *were* there, in one of Willard's most elegant parlors, and yet, so much had I to think of, and so absorbing is the nature of public business, that I had really forgotten it.

Boblett, nothing daunted by my frigidity of manner, continued to give me what he called sound constitutional advice, interspersed with hints at a certain Government appointment which, he asserted, I had promised him on the occasion of my recent election, but which I don't believe I ever said a word about.

At last, tired of his importunity, and moreover expecting a visit from some of the foreign ambassadors, I gave him a flat denial. Upon which I found that the real venomous and malevolent nature of his disposition developed itself.

He was furious with rage and disappointment. Striking his clenched fist upon the table, he cried—

"Beware how you make me your enemy; I know the villainous means by which you mounted into power, and can expose it. I am acquainted with your family history since the time the original Mudshank, the peddler, sold powder and ball to the Tories, that they might shoot his own mother."

"Merciful Heaven!" said I, "I never heard that."

"But it's true," cried Boblett, and there are people living who can swear to it—didn't your uncle's grandfather's first cousin's aunt whop her own daughter to death for stealing plums out of a Christmas pudding?"

"Poor child!" cried I. "Did the old woman act so cruelly?"

"And wasn't that child sister to your own great grandfather?" Boblett went on with a fiend-like expression of countenance.

The relationship, I must confess, confused me, and I was silent. He saw his advantage.

"You know it," he cried, "and yet, forsooth, you are the independent candidate for the next Presidency. You, who never did a thing for your country beyond swelling her revenue, by guzzling French brandy."

I *do* take a glass of wine at dinner, and now and then plead guilty to a quiet liking for a moderate "horn," but to be stigmatized as a habitual drunkard would give me infinite concern.

When, therefore, Boblett declared he would parade my

drunken orgies before the world, I condescended to tamper with the fellow, and absolutely went to purchase his silence by a lucrative consulship, which I just remembered was in my gift.

The result was magical—no sooner was the official seal appended, which I did at once, he launched out into the most fulsome adulation of my disinterestedness and patriotism and declared that nothing could now prevent my attaining the summit of my desire—the Presidency.

Finally, he took his departure, to my infinite relief, and, being alone, I began to ponder upon the conversation which had taken place. I could scarcely believe my senses—arrived at eminence and honor in so short a space of time; nay, a candidate, as Boblett said, for the supremest position in the civilized world.

It must have been at the solicitation of partial friends, for, to my knowledge, I had never put myself forward, although, in my own mind fully qualified for the high office.

I took up the paper which was lying before me, and there, sure enough, at the head of the leading article, I saw, in large letters:

For President:

MELCHIZEDECH MUDSHANK.

For Vice-President:

JEROME BONAPARTE.

My heart gave one prodigious throb, and, although it puzzles me to find my name linked with one of the Napoleon Family, I soon remembered that it was the great influence of the Harper Brothers, assisted by the Rev. Mr. Abbot, which had implanted a deep admiration for the virtues of the Bonaparte Family deep in the American heart.

My breast swelled with joyous emotions. Self-love, pride, ambition, love of glory, all were satisfied.

But now for the awful contrast.

I took up another newspaper—strange names were at the head of the column. With a dreadful presentiment of ill, I looked through the pages, when, frightful to relate, my eyes fell upon a paragraph, interspersed with all the etceteras of italics, stars, capitals, and pointed digits.

It was called THE FAMILY HISTORY OF MUDSHANK.

Hastily I ran through it. Every crime in the calendar was not only imputed to me and mine, but some substantiated.

In the midst of my shame and terror, a stranger unceremoniously entered the room—a beetle-browed, stern, unsatisfactory looking individual. He held a suspicious looking paper in his hand, while the handle of a large revolver protruded from his coat pocket.

"Is your name Melchizedech Mudshank?" cried he.

"Yes, sir," I faintly gasped, forced into civility by fear of what was coming.

"You must come with me. I have a warrant for your apprehension," and he flourished the document before my eyes.

"What for?" I stammered.

"Murder only!" replied the stolid official.

Like a flash of light the recollection just blazed upon my mind and vanished, that I had killed somebody somewhere. The instinct of self-preservation, however, gave me instantaneous energy, and I grappled with the intruder.

"Oh! that's your game, is it?" said he, flinging me off as though I were a child, and presenting the revolver full at me. "Will you surrender?" thundered he.

"Never," cried I, "to be made the gaze of mankind in a public court; far better die at once."

"Then your blood be upon your own head," he savagely exclaimed, firing all the barrels at once.

The shot startled me into the consciousness that I was lying full length upon the carpet.

On looking at the table, I saw the contents of a champagne bottle, from which the cork had just popped, fizzling out in a white froth, while the clanging echoes of a drum, row-de-dow-dowing, in the distance, admonished me that my recent political glory was nothing but a dyspeptic dream.

III.

MURDER!

No less strange is it than true, that adventures as thrilling as have ever been told in the pages of fiction—nay, tragedies as appalling as ever entered into the imagination of the playwright—are transpiring within and around us, nearly every day. It is only when an immediate interest is given to the circumstance, by the public character of one or more of the actors, that it obtains a limited notoriety, to be wiped out of the general mind by the advent of the next celebrated singer, or the expectation of the next Military parade.

I was led to the foregoing remarks by witnessing, accidentally, a day or two ago, a terrible murder committed in the open street, and at mid-day.

I happened to be walking with a friend, to whom I had that day lent a large sum of money, through one of the busiest portions of the city, when suddenly I saw a man rush towards another, and deliberately plunge a knife into his heart. The act was so quickly accomplished, so entirely unexpected, that there was no time for the expression of such horror as it is natural to suppose would be exhibited by the surrounding populace upon so terrible an occasion. My friend and I rushed forward, instinctively, to the support of the wounded man, who lay upon the sidewalk, his life-blood fast welling from the hideous gash in his breast.

There was a Doctor's store nigh, and with the assistance of some of the crowd, ever gentle and considerate in such calamities, we carried him there. Stretched along the floor, with an inverted chair under his head, whereupon was placed a soft white pillow, brought by a tender-hearted woman in the house, he lay dying. But few words could he articulate: the man's name who had stabbed him, and the cause—jealousy—unfounded, as he declared; and, indeed, I firmly believe so from his manner. Even if not true, however, it was chivalrous, and pardonable to screen the erring female as he did. It seemed to be his only thought.

"*She* is innocent," he faintly gasped: "the man is madly jealous—he had no cause!"

A great crowd now blocked up the doors, and glued themselves to the windows; for the public loves the horrible, and from the dangerous feats of the daring gymnast, to the enforced gyrations of a tortured criminal, gazes upon everything that promises a horrible termination with a most ferocious appetite; and much did I regret to observe many females were there, looking with curious avidity upon the bloody scene.

There was an outcry of many voices, shouting—

"He's caught! stand out of the way there!"

"Oh! the villain!"

A lane was made, and in an instant more, the murderer stood in the presence of his victim. The latter merely opened his eyes with difficulty, and slightly nodded; for the world was going from him fast.

As for the ruffian himself, he absolutely glowered upon the people who were assembled around him; almost as white as him whose life he had taken, he stood with arms folded, his bloodshot eyes ranging round fiercely upon all, save the dying; he dared not look there.

In a short time came the Coroner, and in the most business like manner, proceeded to take the deposition of the wounded man.

"Who saw *this* murder committed?" asked the functionary, as coolly and properly so, I suppose, as though he were pricing a piece of goods.

"I," said my friend.

"And I," "and I," came from the lips of many.

There were witnesses enough.

"Can you speak?" said the Coroner, addressing the dying man, who answered not.

"Can you hear me?" continued the other.

A slight nod of the head was the only indication.

"Very good," said the Coroner, "that's important. But we must lose no time. Can you see this man in custody."

The poor fellow tried to open his eyes.

"Bring him closer," said the Coroner. The officers did so.

With a great effort, the poor victim half opened his eyes, and nodded again.

"Very good."

"Did this man strike the blow?"

There was a momentary pause, after which the wounded man slowly and distinctly whispered—

"Yes."

A thrill of terror, like an electric shock, passed through the assemblage, as sundry voices uttered simultaneously, in an under-tone—

"*He* is dead!"

No sooner was that word spoken, than the murderer fixed one malicious look upon the lifeless body, and scowled at it with a kind of contemptuous defiance.

A few minutes after, the villain was handcuffed, and on his road to prison. The crowd dispersed to seek for other sources of amusement. And with oppressed feelings, my friend and I wended our way homeward.

Now my friend, whom I shall call "Sterling"—for I believe him to be most sincerely attached to me and my interests—was, and I am happy to say is, a man of the most exemplary conduct and character, in every relation of life, hospitable, generous, truthful and unselfish. I mention this now, and will vouch for its correctness, notwithstandingw hatsoever contradictions may appear in my short narrative.

Sterling dined with me that day—meaning with us, my wife and I; for I have had the good fortune to achieve a capital prize in the lottery of wedlock, an earthly blessing which cannot be over-estimated.

As a matter of course, our conversation after dinner turned upon the frightful occurrence we had witnessed in the morning.

"Did you ever see a more ferocious countenance," said I, to Sterling, "than that fellow possessed who did the foul murder?"

"It was a most determined one," replied Sterling; "but to tell the truth, I examined his features most attentively, and they struck me as being rather intellectual."

"A murderer intellectual? Impossible!" said my wife, in the easy style in which women usually jump to conclusions.

"It may be," continued Sterling, "that poor wretch is more deserving of pity than reproach. Who knows what continuous pressure of circumstance may have urged him to the commission of this terrible crime? You know the dying man declared that it was jealousy."

"Jealousy?" exclaimed my wife, with a sudden interest; "Do tell me all about it!"

"My dear," said I, "you know as much as we do. The dying man simply said that jealousy was the cause of his being murdered."

"I wish I could make you jealous of me; but you are too fond of your books and your business people," said my wife, thoughtlessly, to my great annoyance.

Whereat Sterling smiled, as I thought, very peculiarly, which annoyed me more.

"No circumstance," said I, in resuming the conversation, "can, by any possibility, excuse the commission of so frightful a deed. Surely, man has sufficient self-will to control so horrible a passion."

"I don't know that," replied Sterling. "I have known many noble and kindly dispositions which have been strangely warped by the irresistible force of untoward circumstance: how many a man, instigated by sudden temper"——

"Oh! there I grant you," said I; "a quarrel may arouse the fury of a bad temper, even to the most fatal result; but this murder was evidently preconcerted, planned beforehand."

"It may have been so, and yet the murderer be not unworthy of our pity," continued Sterling.

"Oh! Mr. Sterling, how *can* you say so?" said my wife.

"Is there a more insane and heart-crushing passion than jealousy?" said Sterling.

"Especially when it's unfounded," my wife went on, with a queer look at me, which I remembered afterwards.

"It distorts—nay, destroys—the very truth, and sets at naught the evidence of one's very sense," continued Sterling.

"And makes a home exceedingly uncomfortable," said my wife.

"On a badly constructed mind, perhaps, ruined by an intemporate and ill regulated state of life, I grant you, this wild passion might lead to such a fearful catastrophe; but surely not on one who is held in check by religious obligations, and duty to society in general. For instance, not to be too confident in my own rectitude, do you suppose that any amount of jealousy could urge me to the commission of such a deed?"

"That it wouldn't; I wish to goodness it would!" said my wife, in a half laughing tone.

"Don't say that, even in jest, my dear," replied Sterling, solemnly.

I must confess, I *was* a little surprised at my wife's sudden seriousness, at Sterling's remark. She wouldn't have ceased laughing so quick for me, thought I. One look, however, in her clear, honest eyes, and a blessing on her true and loyal heart, sunk deep within my own.

As for Sterling, our argument continued all the evening, and I felt somewhat chagrined at the pertinacity with which he adhered to the overpowering influence of circumstances upon man's destiny, until it became, as I thought, an inferential doubt as to my own ability to withstand temptation; and for the first time in the course of our acquaintance, there was a manifest diminution of cordiality in our parting for the night.

My wife's quick eye observed it, and it evidently clouded her brow also; therefore, it was not in the best humor with myself or the world, that I retired for the night—satisfied, however, on one point, circumstance could never shake my determination to act uprightly to all, notwithstanding. Poor, weak, unstable mortals as we are, how little we know of ourselves! A terrible blow awaited me, and I sought my bed, happy in the affection of a beloved wife, rich in the sympathy of a tried and honored friend, sufficient and to spare of the world's necessary store, and in so brief a time to be despoiled of all! But let me not anticipate.

I had scarcely lain my head upon my pillow, on that eventful night, when an alarm of fire startled me from the slumber I was gradually sinking into. The number of strokes of the bell indicated the district in which my store was situated, and, unfortunately, my policy of insurance had run out but the day before, and had not been renewed. Hurriedly I tumbled into my clothes, ran towards the vicinity, and there, even as I had dreaded, the building was irremediably in a blaze! Mournfully I gazed upon the work of destruction. The smoke was so intense, that I could not enter to save even my books. Meantime, the engines, with awful din and confusion, congregated around, uselessly; for there was not a drop of water; it had frozen so intensely during the night, that the water was a solid block within the hydrants.

Seeing that it was impossible to save anything, and, moreover famishing with cold, I suddenly turned my footsteps homewards, a horrible sensation of approaching calamity hanging around me like a pall. I had lost everything that I had possessed in the world, except the sum of money which I had lent Sterling the day before.

As I neared my house, however, the natural buoyancy of the national character came to my relief. I began to consider that while my wife and my friends were left, all was not lost. Hope, health, and perseverance were mine, and with the money which Sterling had, I should begin again.

I rang at the bell. There was no response—a strange misgiving took possession of me. I pushed the door, it opened, and I went in. All was dark and desolate!

It was now early morning. With a vague presentiment of dread, I rushed up stairs, calling loudly for my wife! Heavens! there was no answer!

Through every room I searched, but she was gone—the servants were gone—there wasn't a soul in the house but myself. Petrified by this accumulation of events, I flung myself into a chair in my own room, when a letter, lying open, on the table, caught my eye. I clutched at it madly, and my very sight was blasted by the following words in the well-known handwriting of the atrocious scoundrel, Sterling:

"Forgive and pity me, Henry. The force of circumstance was too powerful even for my ardent friendship. Devoured by an unquenchable love for your wife, who returns my affection with still greater ardor, I have considered it more benevolent to make two people happy amongst three, than that these two should be doomed to everlasting misery."

"A malediction on his arithmetical villainy," groaned I.

"The money I borrowed from you is intended to defray our expenses in a foreign country, where we shall be shortly beyond all possibility of discovery. So, my good friend, look philosophically upon the matter, and be practically convinced that circumstance will triumph over the most virtuous intention."

I dashed the perfidous scrawl upon the ground. I stamped, raved, and tore my hair in mad fury.

"This explains the motive of his devilish argument," I cried; "this accounts for those peculiar looks I observed yesterday. Oh! vile, vile, heartless, abandoned woman; and you, false, demon-hearted friend; but I'll pursue them, even to the uttermost corner of the earth. Nothing but his blood shall wash out the shame and the injury!"

I know not how the morning passed, but early the next day I found myself pushing through the crowded streets, unmindful of acquaintances, all regardless of the wondrous looks that followed me.

I reached the wharves. There was a foreign steamer just about to embark. I looked upon the upper deck, and there, filling my brain with madness, I saw the wretch Sterling with my faithless wife leaning on his arm. He pointed me out to her; she looked towards me full in the face, and laughed, waving her kerchief at the same time, while he politely raised his hat.

Rooted to the spot with unspeakable horror, I could move neither hand, nor foot, nor tongue! I saw the gang-plank taken on board; I heard the captain give the word to cast off; beheld the first revolutions of the paddle-wheel. Slowly and majestically the noble vessel floated into the channel, and, in a few moments, sped rapidly on her way!

Yet, not a muscle could I move, to run or cry out; but tongue-tied and motionless I remained while she was in sight. A few moments more, and a line of black smoke near the horizon was all that told me of the ship of the destruction of my life's hope.

To my infinite surprise, as I turned away from the spot, careless of what might now occur, I saw a figure that I knew disguised in a large cloak, and evidently trying to elude me. Had I not seen Sterling on board the steamer, I could have sworn it was he.

I followed the figure closely, however, and unnoticed. A gust of wind now blew the cap from his head, and I caught sight of his features, and a demon-like joy seized me.

It *was* he!

I was mistaken before. I could have rushed out and clutched him by the throat as he stood, but I preferred to dally with my revenge.

Upon a butcher's stall, close beside me, was a large knife. I took it and concealed it up my sleeve, and crept after Sterling.

"Confusion!" I heard him say to a bystander; "the vessel is gone, and *she* is in it."

Now I was convinced—my heart became steel—nevertheless, I was collected and wary. I drew my hat over my eyes, altered my dress, and succeeded in thoroughly disguising my identity, so strangely and effectually that even he couldn't recognize me. I passed before him to make sure of it, and, to my infinite delight, he looked vacantly upon me, as though I were a stranger.

Ha! ha! I was sure of my vengeance.

"Could it be possible," said he, "to reach that vessel in a boat—she moves but slowly?"

A thought instantly struck me. I pushed forward, and gruffly replied, "I'll row you there, sir."

"Will you, my man?" replied he; "come, let's on at once then, and I will pay you well if you accomplish it."

At the risk of discovery, I could not help saying, "I mean that you shall."

He paid no attention to it, however, and we both entered the boat.

With a few quick, nervous pulls, I reached the middle of the river, and then rested!

"Why do you not go on?" said he.

"I'm going no further," I replied solemnly.

"What do you mean?" said Sterling.

"Revenge!" I shouted in a voice of thunder. "Behold!" and I flung off my hat, and stood up in the boat, brandishing the butcher's knife.

"Is it you? oh horror!" cried Sterling, covering his eyes with his hands. "What do you mean to do?" he tremblingly continued.

"Kill you, false friend, as you are!" I replied, with desperate calmness, at the same time flinging myself upon the atrocious scoundrel, and burying the knife up to the handle in his heart.

In the death struggle the boat was upset, and we both tum

bled into the water. The weight of his lifeless body carried me down, down like a plummet, while the roaring of myriad thunders reverberated through my brain. I dragged myself from the dead man, and succeeded in gaining the top of the water, but in an exhausted state. I have an indistinct recollection of being picked up when I was going down for the last time, and of being brought home and placed in bed.

The thunder was still in my ears, however, only the claps were at more regular intervals—a dreamy sense began to break through the black night of insensibility.

"What is that dreadful noise?" I asked faintly.

"Nothing, love, but the guns firing for somebody's nomination," replied a soft, gentle, and most musical voice, which made me shudder at first, but afterwards send a prayer of thankfulness up to Heaven as I turned and saw:

MY WIFE!

The Bunsby Papers.

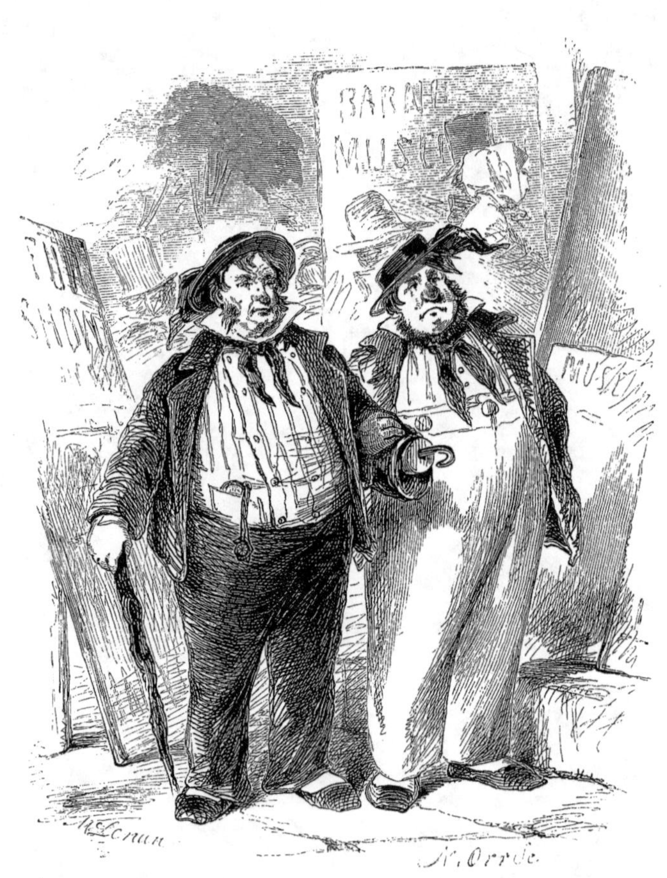
SHOW

THE OPINIONS AND OBSERVATIONS OF

JACK BUNSBY, SKIPPER,

AND OF

ED'ARD CUTTLE, MARINER.

I.

"Opinions as is opinions."

My name's Jack Bunsby!

Now according to the hobserwation of my old messmet, Cap'n Ed'ard Cuttle, mariner, of England, I was christened John; but as the aforesaid respectable authority likewise remarks, I might be called anything else—it wouldn't a hinjured the craft, carryin', as it did, sich a ballust o' mind. I haint much of a man o' larnin'—a marlin spike or a harpoon 'ud fit better in my fist nor a pen; howsomedever, I've had some schoolin' and kin make my mark.

It is really astonishin' to a man of retirin' natur', like the indiwidual as now launches his little cockleshell of hobserwations, to remark how impossible it is for a fellow as has made hisself somebody on the other side of the big ferry to go for to think that he can sneak through this here land of liberty as if he was nobody. There's no use in inwestigatin' the reason, but there *is* certain people all over the world as insists upon it that knowledge is getting too cheap, and that them ar' newspapers is at the bottom of every sort o' mischief.

When I think of it myself, I haint so sure but they are too; look at the willinous ideas they puts into people's heads, as they reads about foreign states gettin' walloped by the pop'lace—it stands to reason that if they was kep' in that ar' "blissful hignorance" the poets writes about, they wouldn't be able to read, and consequently they couldn't take no bad examples from other people.

My name's Jack Bunsby! Skipper! man and boy, nigh hand forty year, and I never know'd any good arisin' from the sailors knowin' more of the ropes nor the cap'n. Why, bless your soul, if there warn't every now and then a hactual mutiny there 'ud be the etarnal fear of it, which is worser; more betoken, what is it as keeps a lot o' chaps under proper subjection? nothin' but the superior strength of your own knowledgibility. How could a skipper quiet his conscience, after givin' a ordinary hand a dozen or two, if he know'd that he was a floggin' one equal to hisself. And who's agoin'—now I axes this here question skyentifically and for the benefit of polyticians in general—who's a goin' to put a cargo of sticks into the hands of the vox pop'ly to break the backs of them as *is* in authority?—and echo answers:

"We ain't such darned fools."

Well, as I was a sayin' afore, them newspapers is the cause of all the rev'lutions, res'lutions and hyfolutions as is now a hagitatin' this here earthly planet; and moreover, the pint of my hobserwations goes peticklarly to American newspapers. What has them hincendiarys bin a doin' for the last fifty years? I'll tell you; they've been a lightin' a big paper fire —you must take the meanin' of my remarks in the happlication thereof, as my friend Ed'ard beautifully remarks—which has gone on a burnin' and a burnin' until the light from it has crossed the Atlantic itself. What light is that ere from the west? they began to inquire. They soon found out it was the light of knowledge; a light as penetrates into the dark corners of oppression and exposes things as ought never to be seen—no where—no how. Well, the poor deluded wretched as wouldn't a knowd o' their miseries if they were kept where they were—in the dark, must keep trying to kindle the same kind of a light for themselves, and singeing their wings in it like a lot of foolish moths.

Therefore, if so be as the poet says, that

"*Hignorance is bliss,*"

Why then, in course it follows, nateral enough, that

"*It's folly to be otherwise.*"

But, as I said before, it's unpossible for a man as is known elsewhere to flatter hisself that he *kin* remain unknown here. *I* couldn't, although it was my intention to come in a hunhostentashus way, just like Father Mathew, and do my little bit o' good under the rose, as a body might say. But where's the use; the minute it was known that Jack Bunsby had arrove, the whole city was alive, from Union Square to the Five Points, and although they didn't ezackly carry the joke so far as to get long-winded horations by heart to pelt me with at the landin' place, or show me to the curiosity hunters at so much a head, yet I'm creditably hinformed that the President hisself, with his cabinet-makers, is coming north for the sole purpose of hofferin' me a situation in the Custom House; but hinasmuch as there is a sort o' shippin' for a four years' cruize, and not on the permanent sarvice, I ain't agoin' to take it nohow.

Talkin' of cabinet-makers, I have an obserwation to make

about them. I can't speak of my own account, 'cause I don't know nothin' about the trade; but they do tell me that it is carried on in a werry singular sort of a way here, seeing that they only uses one peticklar kind o' wood in the manifactur'; and I says to that ere—why not? For who ever wants to see three legs of a table mahogany and the fourth pine—it ain't natural, nohow; and moreover, it's a werry strange philosophical fact that if the pine leg lets itself be stained so as to look like the mahogany, the chance is that it will be allowed to remain where it is, but if it don't, off it has to come; but thems pollyticks—and after all, if the table is well-covered, what *does* it signafy what the legs is made of.

Therefore, the bearin's of my obserwations is this—that, if so be as I can't enjoy my dignified retirement to myself, and moreover, as I rather likes to be a hobject of public hinterest, I intends to *print my opinions*, inasmuch as it will at least leave me my sleepin' hours unmolested by the pleasin' trouble of national hadmiration.

Werry well, then, if so be as hany thing comes across my wision as is worthy of remark, you may expect to hear from me agin; but if so be, on the contrary, as I don't meet with nothin' hinterestin', why then, you needn't expect nothin' of the sort; howsomedever, it won't be necessary, in either case, for you or any body else to put yourselves at all out of the way; the blessed sun will continue shinin', and the univarsal earth rewolwin', jist for all the world as if none of us never saw the one, or was whirlin' about with the other.

II.

Jack, not finding anything more interesting to begin his letter with, moralizes upon authorship in general and his own feelings in particular—He contemplates a cruise up Broadway, and meets his friend, Captain Cuttle—Profound reflections thereon—He describes the present houseless condition of the street—Occupying the time with many irrelevant matters until he reaches Barnum's, which he and the Captain enter—The imposing array of subjects furnish themes for discussion, which they incontinently lay hold of as drowning authors will catch at straws.

WELL! there's no use in anybody's tellin' me that a man *kin* hold the rudder of his hinclinations hisself. The skience o' navigation may teach him how to handle a wessel, and a knowledge o' the chart may keep him clear o' quicksands and sunk rocks, but the humane bark upon the hocean o' life is guided by a some'at as we don't know nothin' about—a some'at aloft, so far above our wision that we can't get near it nohow—and that ar' little bit o' sea froth we calls brains, haint got the *nous* to take in; and though speklatin' dealers in all sorts o' humbug has bein' a manufacturin' telescopes upon telescopes to bring it nearer to the heye o' man, it's jest as far off as ever.

Now this here is my opinion. When a seaman wants to make a certain port, why, in course, he knows where that ar' port is sitivated, clears out fair and square and makes for the aforesaid port according *to* the course as is laid down in the chart; but if so be as a man wants to bring up in the harbor o' happiness in the world to come, he'd most likely be puzzled by the wast number o' charts that's laid down for him. To be sure he would; and werry often, trustin' to chance, shut his eyes and drift about upon the sea of uncertainty.

Moreover, I has my own notions on that ar' subject and them's this. That, if so be as there's warious courses by which the same port can be made, and though some of 'em may cross the others' tracks a trifle, yet, purwidin' the craft's a good craft, and the heads and hands aboard are all right and proper, it don't much si'nafy which on 'em a man takes passage in. That's my opinion, and I don't care who knows it.

My name's Jack, and the bearin's of those few obserwations has reference to myself in particklar, as regards the unpossibility of a man's markin' out his own course, even for an hour, upon the hocean of hexistence. This werry blessed mornin' I says to myself as I was a shavin', Jack, says I, old tar—for I was in a werry good humor with myself. Jack! says I, you must take a cruise about this here city by yourself, and take some obserwations for that ar' Paper as does you the honor to think them worth puttin' into prent. Talkin o' prentin', what a curos sensation it is when a chap sees his thoughts made public for the first time. My heye, what a hurry I was in to git the copy what contained my few remarks last week. You should a seen the way I scudded to my caboose, and when I got there, I read every thing else all over first—my stupid ould heart beatin' faster an' faster as I got nearer to my own stuff; but when I did come chock a block on it, lor' how my heyes danced. A sort o' second edition of a sea-sickness—as near as I can recollect—came over me; at last I took courage and a quid, and dove into it.

Jingo! how I liked it at the first. Well, that ar' feelin' wore off mighty quick; but when I came to a hobserwation as I had intended for a chunk o' wisdom, and found it turned, by them ar' compos' they tell me,—into some'at as much like it as the leg of a stool, it pulled me right down—and by the same token it did me good, for instead o' fancyin' myself a hangel o' hintellect a flyin' through skies of sense, I dropped down into the werry hinsignificant lump of mortality as I is.

Well, as I was sayin' afore, I determines to surwey the

queerosities, nateral and otherways as I should meet, makin' the cruise all by myself; but jest as I swung round the corner o' the street, I heerd a woice, sich a woice—one of them woices as wibrates upon the hear like a pleasant breeze a playin' among the riggin'. That ar' woice belonged to Cap'n Ed'ard Cuttle.

"Awast?" says he.

"Aye, aye," says I.

And in a minute more he drops alongside, and so we rode in convoy for the rest of the day, by which you may perceive the drift of them few remarks I made at the beginnin' of this here paper; and there haint nobody, not if he was as wise as a cargo of Solomons, as *kin* say to hisself, I know what I'm a goin' to do to-morrow. Therefore, what *is* the hodds! So it is—and so let it be.

Very well, then. Cuttle and me goes along steady enough, until we kem to a sort of dilapidated, choked-up thoroughfare, as looked as though it might a be'n one of them ar' Mexican streets as the sojers walked into, makin' a road through the houses for variety's sake; this, we diskivered upon axin' the question, was called Broadway.

And to tell the truth, I think it will be a werry convenient place, both for business and pleasure, when it is opened to the People—and the great press of Public Business doesn't prevent the hauthorities of the City from makin up their minds whether it is to be paved or not. After havin' made what headway we could across piles of brick and barricades and hexcawations—them at Pompeyseye was a fool to some of 'em —we brought up at last, all standing', opposite to a great sprawlin' Noah's Ark of a consarn, covered all over with picters of creeters with crackjaw names, Giants as high as the mast-head, a sort of prize-fed female, as looked like as she had a ship's waist under her stays, a hexibitin' one of her timbers in a way as brought the red flag in Cap'n Ed'ard's countenance. Mine haint so easily mounted. And what I thought was a correct view of the hinterior of a colored mad-house, but what I diskivered was a lot of singing negers. Then there was a band of musicianers outside, most elegant to listen to except the trombone, which I'm sure had a werry bad cold in its head, and a little trumpeter, that bellowsed away jest as if he or his hinstrument, or maybe both on 'em, was cracked.

At that moment o' time Cap'n Ed'ard Cuttle, as was a gazin' in hadmiration upon the himposin' sight, says to me, says he:

"Jack," says he.

"Aye, aye," says I.

"That ar's Barnum's. Let's overhaul our nateral curiosity, and inwest a quarter," says he.

"Agreed," says I.

So there bein' a pritty tolerable clear passage across, we got over safe, and havin' left our quarters at the door, tumbled up stairs and got into the Museium; but, my heye, how we were sold—the things as looked so bright and lively on the houtside, was nothing but dust and dry bones, and the canvass giant had a werry great advantage in the regard of size over the real one.

Bym bye we takes and we goes up another hatchway, and may I never chaw if it wasn't a sort of reg'lar built ship-shape play-house, with real play-actor looking chaps a showin' away.

I'd a jest a soon a thought o' seein' a meetin'-house full blast in Bartlemy Fair—there it was stowed aloft, and it took the wind right out of the cap'n's sails, too.

"Hillo! mesmet," says he, "this is a kind o' privateerin' business as I don't like; right's right all the world over, but this here ain't the cheese no how; live and let live is a werry good toast and sentiment. I goes for givin' every body a chance, but I hates to see some indiwiduals a holdin' on to somebody else's as well as his own. S'posin' now—I makes the remark by way of an hillustration—s'posin' the butcher as you buys your jints of, was to jine on to it the trade of a hatter, wouldn't all the hat fellows be down on him? in course they would, and sarve him right, too. Now here's a curosity maker as haint content with his halligators and hover-grown pigs, but he must take a slice out of the playing-purfession as well. I has a regard for players as is players, and I'd like to see 'em come right out agin it."

"Bless your soul, Cap'n," says I, "my opinion is that there don't nobody come here but them as shuts the eyes of their senses for the comfort of their conscience; if this here cock-loft was called a play-house they'd no more venture near it than if it were the mouth of the pit itself; but it aint, you see, and that makes the difference; the beauty of it is, its exactly the same thing, only werry hindifferently hexecuted."

"Werry well, then," says the Cap'n, "it 'ud be a thousand pities to deprive the poor souls of this thin ghost of an amusement, since it's their scrupleosity as keeps 'em away from any other. I honors *them* as has a real feelin' of religion in their hearts, but I'd have all those hypocritical teachers up to the gratings werry soon as makes world capital out o' frightenin' weak-minded folks."

"Well, Cap'n," says I, "I haint much of a hargufyer in them 'ar matters, but it strikes me that things is gettin' better nor they used to be that way, too. People is beginnin' to run their wessels on their own hook, and not be towed by the ould mud-scow of superstition. Why, there was a time, they tell me, when folks paid for their passage into the other world by puttin' all they were worth into big buildin's for the comfort of the lazy boatmen as said they owned the ferry, and all the bloodshed and villainy they had done through their lives was blowed away by the breath of just as big a sinner as themselves. Them dark days is gone; but there's a werry dusky twilight left yet as wants a ray or two of sunshine let into it afore a hordinary human creatur' can find out his way ahead."

"That ere's sense, Jack," says the Cap'n, with one of his beautiful looks. "That's what I call sense—uncommon sense, and therefore not fit to be talked about in this here place, no how; so let us overhaul our travelin' tickets, and when found weigh anchor."

So, wery much edificated by the performances, we took our departure accordingly.

III.

The Captain and Jack having left the Museum, the former indulges in sage reflections, and ventures an opinion upon the intellectual capacity of the present age generally—He indulges in simile, and bases his argument on straws—He goes back to his juvenile days—comparing the educational systems, then and now—Jack coincides with him—They fall in with a bird-seller, who raises the Captain's indignation and is rebuked—The Captain thereupon moralizes, taking "Birds" for his theme.

If so be as how as you've kept the run of this ar' log, there won't be no use in my tellin' you that Cap'n Ed'ard Cuttle and me, Jack Bunsby, had just left that ar' himposin' hedifice, Barnum's Managery o' dead hanimals and lively show-actors, when my little coil of hobservation was payed out, and consiquently I kem to the ind o' my rope.

But no sooner'd we navigated our way back agin into the street, when Cap'n Cuttle began a shakin' his head werry sagacious to look at, then solemnly elewating' of his hook, he says to me—

"Jack,"

"Aye aye," says I.

"Old mesmate, they say that straws 'll show which way the wind blows."

"I've hard tell o' that ar' remark," says I.

Then the Cap'n, looking at me werry significant and pointin' of his hook towards the Museium, let out one o' them chunks o' wisdom as has made him a hobject of respect all over the humane globe.

"Jack," says he, "I looks upon that ar' house in the light o' one of them werry hidentical straws: A straw," says he, a shuttin' of his eyes and lookin' like a wenerable patriarch as the sentiments kem out of his mouth, "as shows which way the wind o' hintellect is blowin' in this here centary."

"'Taint much of a gale, nether," says I.

"Not a catspaw," says he. "To be sure, some of the manufacturers of the harticle tries to persuade theirselves that they are kickin' up a jolly breeze—for wanity is considerable of a magnifyer—but after all it's only a puff."

"But how does the bearins' of that ar' remark apply to the hobserwation regardin' of straws?" says I.

"Werry natural," says he. "Where's yer head? What's become of yer sense, Jack? Overhaul yer wisdom wigorous, and when found, keep her *so!* Straws *is* straws—haint they?"

"In coorse they is," says I.

"*Werry* well, then, they haint ginerally stuffed with lead —are they?" says he.

"Not as I knows on," says I.

Werry *well*, then; it doesn't usually take the tail ind of a hurricane to lift 'em up."

"Not all out," says I.

"Werry well, *then;* whenever you sees a huncommon light straw a lyin' on the ground, stationary like, doesn't it hargify that there can't be much of a breeze a blowin'?" says he, in such a conwincin' manner that there was no sayin' nothin' agin' it, and so I held my tongue.

"Why, Jack," says he, "when I was a youngster, hinstruction was mixed up with hamusement, in werry unequal parts as regarded the last hingredient. We didn't have no picter books to seductivate us into larnin'. Not a bit of it. Nor not no hillustrationed halphabets to lay hould of the letters and tow 'em into yer mind. Nothin' of the sort. We had to lug along the heavy, awkward lookin' A B C without any help whatsomedever. Now, while a child's eyes is hoccupied with the purty hembellishments the letters flies into his mind of their own accord; but in my time, the poor fellow had to stick 'em in hisself, and werry hard scratchin' it was too. Then, the pathway to hedication was up-hill, stony, and full o' ruts—now, it's levelled, gravelled, and bordered with flowers."

"That ar's a fact," says I. "I knows it in my hown hexperience; but has the himprovin' of the road himproved them as travels it?"

"On the contrary—not a bit of it," says he. "The werry heasiness of it has made 'em careless; it's that self-same coverin' over the ladder o' larnin' with roses and posies, that makes many of 'em as is a climbin' miss the solid rung. The smell o' the flowers keeps 'em a lingerin' about, and they seldom or ever gets werry high up."

"That's deep," says I. "Unkimmin deep; and 'taint every body as kin fish the meanin' of it up to the sarface."

"Right, Jack," says he. "And haint it hevident to the small slightedest indiwidual, the heffects of such a hot-house system of hinstructin'. School-boys is men afore the down comes on their chins. It stands to reason that they must be shallow lakes as gets so soon filled; gentle breezes may make 'em ripple elegant, but come a cap-full o' wind it blows the water right out."

Jest then we run foul of a crowd o' people, and the conwersation, which was gettin' awful hinterestin to me, was turned out of its channel in the followin' manner accordingly.

"There's some'at the matter," says the Cap'n. But there warn't. It was only a chap as was a gettin' a livin' by sellin' birds, and the folks was a hadmirin' the tricks as he had taught 'em. Some of the little wabblers was a standin' on their heads, and some of 'em a balancin' of theirselves on bits o' wire; but the remarkablest thing was, that the poor creeturs had to haul up their food and drink to the bars, every time they wanted to feed. There was a sort o' savage hexpression kem over the Cap'n's face, and he gev his hook a bite as showed he warn't pleased at the sight, though the fellers round was a grinnin' like so many tickled baboons. I seed there was a small wolcano a blazin' in the Cap'n's breast, as *would* have went somehow—and it did.

"Mesmet," says he, softenin' of his woice wonderful, considerin' the head o' steam as he had on; but the Cap'n never does lose sight of the safety valve of discreetness. "Mesmet," says he, "is them your birds?"

"They aint nobody else's," says the trainer.

"You needn't tell me that—I know it; but they were Heaven's birds once," says the Cap'n, a raisin' up his tarpaulin. "It's bad enough to imprison them in those six-inch jails, lettin' them look out upon the broad univarsal hair that they can't get at, but to make 'em pull up every grain o' seed and drop o' water, is hintroducin' slavery into natur' itself. What do you do it for?"

"What should I do it for, but to sell 'em," says the fellow.

Then the crowd, as had got werry great, set up a laugh at the Cap'n; but he never took no notice of them, only shrugged up his shoulders and says to me, as he pushed through them,

"That ere's the way of the world. A man mustn't take no heed of the abuses as he sees around him. The poor deluded hignorant pop'lace, as has got so used to wiciousness and willainy that wholesale man-killing is now called glory, and him as fills the most bloody graves is rated as a hero, won't stand bein' talked to about their smaller wices."

"In coorse not," says I. "The large crimes swallows up the little ones. A man as is jest condemned for murder, wouldn't be likely to be tried for picking a pocket."

Then the Cap'n he went along, glumpy-like, and never said nothin' for a long spell. I know'd he was put out, and so I kep' never mindin', for in my own opinion there haint anythin' as is so onpleasin' as to keep chattin' to a man when he's a thinkin' hard. Howsoever, werry soon he busted out.

"Jack," says he.

"Mesmet," says me.

"Them ar' bird prisons got me a thinkin' wicious, and I've kem to the kinclusion, that when the pop'lar voice calls a man—as it wulgarly does at times—'*a bird,*' they haint so far wrong; for we arn't none of us nothing else, no how. Overhaul the similytude and when found make the happlication. Is there hany of us as isn't caged in by some'at or another? You haint a goin' to tell me, but what many a lovin' couple sees the bars right afore their mental wision, as plain as if they was made o' werry strong wire. There's some on us as is surrounded with goolden net work, and then agin there's some on us as has to put up with iron; but whatsomedever the metal may be, they're all on 'em cages. Some on us has the meat and drink purwided in elegant conweniences of chayny and glass, right under our noses; others again has to tug unkimmon hard to lift it up—werry often to see it slip away just as it gets near their beaks. Jack, when I hears a chap a callin' another 'a bird,' I haint a goin' to laugh no more."

The rest of the hobserwations that he made, 'taint my hintention to reweal, for several reasons.

In the first place I haint got no room; and in the second—stop, I b'lieve the first'll have to do.

IV.

Jack and the Captain continue their cruise up Broadway, and before they are aware of it get entangled amongst a fleet of fashionables, being unfortunately on the silver side—The Captain thereupon institutes a comparison between nature and fashion, very much to the disadvantage of the latter—They get clear of the crowd, and in crossing the street encounter the usual omnibus peril, in consequence of which much profound reflection is elicited from both, touching omnibus drivers, street regulations, and municipal government generally.

It's a beautiful sight, I tell you, is that ar' Broadway, if you takes it jist at the time we did, when the folks as has got nothin' to do but show themselves, goes and does that same accordin'ly. Why, it comes slap upon the Cap'n and me as suddent as a Halifax fog, though with a werry different heffect.

We was a workin' gently up stream, droppin' alongside o' the shops every now and then jist to take a hobserwation of the helegancies therein, when all at once a fleet o' first-raters bore down upon us—sich a cloud o' canvass!—when I says canvass, in coorse I means silks and welwets; but every stitch was spread in re'lar holiday rig: there warn't no getting out o' the way, no how.

"Hillo, Jack," says the Cap'n, "meetin's out, aint it?"

"Some show place is broke up, sure," says me.

But we soon diskivered that it was the quality time to take a little hair an' hexercise, likewise to tumble over piles of dry-goods and try the patience of dandy shop-tenders, for rich folks always goes in a flock like wild geese, and one on 'em would jist as lief be without a hopera box, or a fashionable complaint, as to take a healthy walk at a hunfashionable hour.

The Cap'n and me tried hard to push our way ahead, but we were hobligated to give in soon, for with all our navigation, we couldn't help touching some on 'em, and you'd a thought as how as we was fire-boats with the fuze a-light, to see the signals o' distress they hoisted. At last the Cap'n hove to, in a state o' desperation!

"Jack," says he, a moppin' of his venerable head, for he was out of his latitude among sich craft, "heave to and let go; I'm blessed if they shan't navigate round *us* for a spell."

And so there we lay for as good as a quarter of an hour, a wishing that we could cut our way through, but nether of us havin' the pluck to do it, some of the dainty passers by turnin' up their noses at us as if we warn't sweet—and others a laughin'—'specially them as had good teeth, which we didn't mind no how.

Howsomedever, werry soon the Cap'n, as haint got far to go for sense when he's at a nonplush, whispered in my ear, werry mysteriously, indeed—

"Mesmet," says he, "we're on the wrong course here, sartain—this here's forbidden water for such vessels as us. We haven't the papers for it, no how."

"How do you know that?" says me.

"Overhaul your hocular wision, and when found, look over on 'tother side," says he.

Accordingly I did look, and sure enough, though the offin' that we were in was chock full of all kinds o' dandy rig, there warn't nothin' in the other but a few stragglers a scuddin' along in a werry business-like manner.

"Dangerous navigation there, p'raps," says me, seein' the Cap'n's eyes a fixed inquirin' like on mine.

"'Taint that, Jack," says he, "'taint that, old shipmet," a closin' of his eyes from the weight o' wisdom as was pressin' on him; I saw that he was fishin' in a hocean of sense, and I knew he'd pull up a chunk in no time, which he did.

"Jack," says he, "the navigation haint worser, not a bit of it, but—here's the chunk—'taint the fashion. Natur's natur', and Fashion's fashion; but there arn't two things in the world more hopposite nor them two is. Natur' invites you to walk in the sweet smellin' fields, with the beautiful breezes a blowin' health into you from all sides; but Fashion swears you must preambulate along a bilin' hot street. Natur' tells you to henjoy your hexercise where you have plenty o' room to swing your limbs about, but Fashion hobligates you to jam yourself into a crowd. Natur' gives a woman as is a woman, space enough for disgestable purposes; but Fashion squeezes her abdominables into the shape of a hour-glass, where, it stands to reason, the sands o' life must find it unkimmin difficult to force a passage, werry often bringin' them to a full stop altogether. Natur' perwides us with clean bills o' health, but Fashion only aggrawates *them* as is hinterestin' to the doctors. Overhaul your bills of mortality, and when found make the happlication. That ere's logic, Jack, and moreover there haint no contradictin' it, as I knows on."

"I haint a goin' to try, Cap'n," says me.

"Werry well, then," says he, "s'posin' we tack."

"Tack it is," says me.

With that we filled and ran across without no haccident to

speak of, 'ceptin terrible near bin run into by a lumberin' craft of a homnibus as was makin' wiolent headway, by reason of the horses havin' run off with the consarn—by the same token, such catastrophes must be in no ways unkimmon, for the people didn't seem to mind it a bit. I didn't so much wonder at the quality side of the street bein' hundisturbed, for the Cap'n tells me that it haint fashionable to be hagitated about nothin'; but them as was supposed to carry some sense aboard not takin' no notice of it, proved werry conclusive that such dangerous conduct on the part of the horses—or the drivers, I haint sure which—warn't no novelty in Broadway.

Howsomedever, when I called the Cap'n's attention to it, he made me feel quite down in the mouth, he gev me sich a rebuke.

"'Taint possible, Jack, no how," says he; "haint they got a Mayor and a Co'poration and policemen, for to keep the city in order. Doesn't them ar' luxuries walk into the city treasury above a trifle, and do you think them as is so werry well paid for so small a duty, would neglect it so shameful as to let horses carry on, as them ar' runaway fellows did jest now, riskin' the lives of the citizens, if it warn't a haccident? in coorse not. Jack," he went on, "it warn't the driver's fault—hooman natur' forbids me to think that. It warn't the fault of the hauthorities—my respect for the city gov'ment won't allow me to imagine that; but I'll tell you what it was, old mesmet," and he looked like the werry picture o' heloquence as he spoke—"it was the flies!"

"Me'be it was," says me, "and then again me'be it warn't. Anyway, them flies must be unkimmon thick about here, for there's a couple o' homnibusses a bearin' down now, just about as mad fast as scud before the moon."

And sure enough, on they came, thunderin' down the

street, the drivers a cuttin' at their horses in sich a savage manner as made the Cap'n bite his hook wicious—the tip top of their hambition seemin' to be, to find out which on 'em could pass the other so close as to tear the most skin off o' the horses' flanks with the wheel of his wehicle. In a minute they dashed by us, cursin' and hollerin', and slashin' their hanimals, and there warn't nobody as cried *shame*, 'ceptin' the Cap'n; he roared out—"Shame! *shame!* SHAME!" as if he were a roarin' through a speakin' trumpet, right in the teeth of a nor'wester, but it didn't have no heffect; the noises that they made war only more hungenteel, and when I looked at the Cap'n, there he was a tremblin' just as if every cut them poor horses endured had left a welt in his own skin, which caused him to smart.

"Jack," says he—right out loud—it's my opinion jest at that instant he wouldn't a cared if all creation could a heard his woice, he was in sich a state of *bile;* "Jack, I'm werry doubtful as regards them flies. Moreover," he went on, lookin' up and down the street, with a whole dictionary o' meanin' in his heye, "it strikes me forcible that when I spoke about the gov'ment of the city, I might as well a left out the police."

"Cap'n," says me, "its a nateral curiosity as has puzzled the larned for a long time, to know for sartain whatever does become of policemen and pins. There *is* policemen, we know, jest as we know that there *is* pins, bein' a kind of knowledge as is acquired under difficulties—indeed, I saw one once myself, with a sort of nothing-to-do look, a contemplatin' emptyness at the corner of a street. The poor fellow seemed to me as if he'd a took it as a werry great favor if some kind-hearted hindividual 'ud a pitched him into the middle of the road, that he might be quite conwinced that he warn't a fixture. Howsomedever, I hear that they do talk o' puttin' down a great many unregularities as has been winked at up to now."

"It's werry heasy to *talk*, Jack," says the Cap'n; "but I wants 'em to *do*, not that it's any business o' mine, only jest as a true seaman likes to see a craft he loves, shipshape from stem to stern."

"Mayhap they will some day.* Who knows, eh, shipmet?"

V.

The Captain and Jack continue their conversation, and somehow stumble against Pythagoras and The Transmigration of Souls, with especial reference to omnibus horses and their drivers—Exhausting that subject, they run up against the Broadway Theatre, which they enter, expecting to see the play, and are amazingly "sold;" they find themselves in "high" society, and make the most of their position.

THERE haint no man in this here world, I don't care who he may be, but has a bit o' bad temper layin' somewhere about him. Some on 'em has it werry near the sarface—others, at various degrees of depth; but there aint nobody—I repeats the hobserwation solemnly—as has it stowed away so deep that the "lead" of annoyance can't reach soundings. Now as hevery body knows when the lead *does* touch bottom the bubbles *will* rise, so in the humane creater, when a hinsult or a haggrawation drops down on the feelin's, up must come the hanger.

By the same rule o' hargeyment, them as is deepest laden in the regard o' sense is the hardest to rouse up into a rage,

* The reader need not be reminded that the Captain alluded to the lax state of the police establishment a few years back. Thanks to the vigorous and energetic rule of our present Mayor, the hope expressed above has been effectually realized.

for this here reason, because the bad thoughts bein' the lowest in the heart, or wherever it is the're sitivated, in course the greater the weight o' wisdom as is a top of them the more they'll have to work agin in the comin' up.

But on the other tack: if so be as it *is* hard to rize their passions, it takes a mighty long time for them to get back into their or'nary coorse.

This here bit o' philosophy kem into my mind as I was a watchin' the Cap'n, while the storm of passion about the homnibus drivers was a lashin' his face into wrinkles; I never did see sich a pictur of a gale in the humane countenance. It was hawful to watch the black cloud upon his for'head, expectin' to behold the helectrical fluid hissue from his heye every moment, while the red pimples rode on the waves o' hexcitement like fire-boats in a small hurricane; and then his nose, it seemed as if it was a shakin' itself to pieces with the fear of bein' washed away.

Howsomedever it warn't of long duration, so after lettin' out two or three reefs in his conwersation he purceeded along steady.

I thought I might wenture a remark, and so

"Cap'n," says I.

"Aye, aye, Jack," says he, turnin' his jolly old figure-head full on me as smooth as a lake once more.

"Them homnibus drivers haint much troubled with hearts," says I.

The Cap'n turned right round, like a seafaring Solomon, as he is, and

"Jack," says he, "'taint the drivers—'taint the horses—'taint the police—'taint the city authorities—'taint nobody, nor nothin' but Fate, Fortin', or, as the book-makers calls it, Destiny. I knows it is; I'm conwinced of it. Why mesmet', when I sees bein's as *looks* like men—hanimals standin' hupright on two legs as should naturally have at least four—indiwiduals with heads what has the happearance of heads—and trunks where the doctors tells us their hearts ought to be, I say when I sees them a hactin' as if they had neither one nor the other, I begins to b'leeve in that ere stuff one of the Haythins preached about in the ould time. I aint able to lay howld of the name, but the thing itself was called the transmogrification o' sowls—meanin', when we die our spirits goes hinto dogs and cows and sharks and halligators, and sich like warmints; so that purwided a man commits any crime or wickedness, he has to take a lifetime of the hexperience of whatsomedever hanimal his doin's was most like while he was in a two-legged state o' hexistence—Do you see?"

"Werry clear," says I. "'Sposin that a chap cheats and bamboozles during his life, he has the chance of findin' himself fillin' out the skin of the fox that he has been a himitatin'."

"That's it, Jack, percisely," says the Cap'n; "and a rapacious litigatious devourin' pettifoger, would most probably diskiver himself floundering about the Gulf Stream in the likeness of a shark, or basking in the mud of the Mississippi or the Ganges in the form of a halligator—You take the meanin'?"

"Distinct," says I.

"Werry well, then," says he. "Them ere homnibus horses is inhabited by the sowls of wagabond post-boys, jockeys, huntsmen, and all them breed o' brute-killers as keeps continually a slaughterin' indiwidual hanimals, hendeavorin', at the same time, to persuade the houtsiders that it's all to improve the breed, which is nothin' but gammon of the richest description, an' honly said to disguise the cruelty of their doins'."

"If so be," says I, "as the horses is hanimated with the sowls o' sich like, what sort must the drivers have?"

"Second-hand ones, Jack—second-hand ones," says he; "sowls as has become werry hinsignificant after havin' passed through the whole of Nateral History and come back for a second turn.

"Mind now and don't misunderstand me. There's some on 'em as is as marciful as they can be hunder the circumstances, but it's only the brute-minded ones as I has reference to, willains as 'ud kill their fellow-men if they had a safe chance; but not havin' such a chance, content themselves with killin superior hanimals—the horses."

It was jist at that hinstant o' time we kem close upon a beautiful buildin', the windows all over picters a painted on the werry glass hitself; the front all bedizened with great shiney bubbles, which I took to be hallegorical representations of all the wonderful stars as shined within, done in gas! For we found upon consultin' the sheet of paper as was hexhibited houtside, that it was a theatre—and, moreover, the Metropolitan Theatre. The meanin o' which the Cap'n hexpounded to me. The same bein' this here:

"That it belonged to the Metropilis, which is the City."

"Werry good," says the Cap'n. "If so be as there's hanything hinterestin' to the people in the playhactin' way, this ere must be the place to run in sight of the same. Let us shorten sail, steer in and see what's a goin' on."

"With all my heart," says I.

So in we went, with a hextensive crowd, through an elegant marble floored gangway, up to the kind of port-hole where the money was a slidin' in like smoke. It was some time afore it kem to the Cap'n's turn, but when it did—

"What part?" says the man hinside.

"Pit," says the Cap'n. "Eh, Jack?"

"In coorse," says I. "Never mind the hexpense for oncet.'

"There ain't no Pit," says the money-taker.

"What!" says the Cap'n, "not no Pit?" a melancholy hexpression playin' about his heye, at the hignorance o' the harchitect.

"There's a Paraqueet," says the man.

"A what?" says the Cap'n.

"A Paraqueet," he says.

"Who's a Parqueet?" says the Cap'n, a waxin' warm at the hinsult as he supposed it to be, and hindeed so did me, until a gent as was a himpatiently waitin' to get his ticket, wolunteered a hexplanation, by tellin' us that a Parqueet was the fashionable name for the Pit, for bein' called after that, in my opinion, werry noisy and disagreeable bird, the quality goes there in droves, whereas, if it retained its horiginal wulgar name, they wouldn't never be seen near it, no how.

You never see sich a look as kem over the Cap'n's face when he heard the hexplanation, it jist as plainly si'nified "pickles" as if the syllables kem right out of his mouth.

"You've got a gallery, haint you?" says he.

"There's a Family Circle," says the man.

"A Family Circle?" says the Cap'n. "Why, hany body kin have that at his own home, purwided he's got a home, likewise a family."

"Aint you got no other place?"

"Certainly," says the haccommodating hindiwidual, "there's third circle."

"Is that too genteel for us?" says the Cap'n.

"I should say not," says the fellow.

So the Cap'n and me paid our money and got aloft, ever so high up, sky-ways.

"Hello," says he, as he saw some werry nice lookin' females all in first-rate rig, and quite fashionable in the regard of not havin' their busteses too much hencumbered with drapery.

"We've got among the top-sawyers after all."

Well, we didn't know how to better it, and so hexpectin' hevery minute that some dandy fellow 'ud come and horder us hout, down we sot—and, if you'll b'leeve me, some o' the real ladies kem alongside and hentered hinto conwersation with us in the most good-natur'd and condescendin' way possible. Indeed, two or three on 'em gev the Cap'n an' me a werry kind and pressin' hinvitation to call and see 'em, and it was honly for fear of offendin' any on 'em that we declined the honor.

After a little time the fiddlers struck up; there was a unkimmon lot o' scrapin' and tearin', but neither on us could make out any tune that we know'd, although the Cap'n said he thought that he could distinguish the flavor o' "Black Eyed Susan."

Well, it stopped at last—thank heavens—and there we war wonderin' what play there was to be—for we had never a bill—when all of a sudden crash, bang, split, fizz, up went the rag to an airthquake of unnatural noises, caused by the combined hefforts of the musicians to drowned the humane woices on the stage, while the aforesaid woices worked mighty hard to do the same for the hinstruments.

"Cap'n," says I, a hollerin' in his ear, "what blood-wessels them screamers must have."

"Reg'lar pencil-cases," says he; "but I wish they'd leave off and let us hear the play."

But they didn't, not a bit of it; at it they went—now one, now two or three, now the whole crew, for one blessed hour, 'till at last the curtain kem down upon a hurricane o' sounds from a penny whistle to a good sized clap o' thunder, mixed in with grunts and shrieks and musical gymnastys, jist as if they wur a keepin' high holiday in the lower regions.

As soon as hever the buzz of the battle left our ears, the

Cap'n axes a fellow as was standin' by what time the play was a goin' to begin.

"Why, it has begun," says he. "That's it you've bin lookin' at."

"You don't say," says the Cap'n.

"Yes," says the stranger, "it's a hopera."

Then it was a treat to see the Cap'n start up, and me too.

"A hopera," says he. "What's it about?"

"I don't know for sartain," says the man, "it's Hightalian."

"Hightalian, eh?"

"Werry well, then," says the Cap'n, "them folks down there as is making' sich a fuss, in coorse they knows hevery word—they wouldn't come here if they didn't; but I confesses my hignorance, and so I'm going to start. Come along, Jack."

As we was a makin' our way out, we heerd some one laughin' behind us, and when we looked too see where it kem from, I'm blessed if two or three of the "real ladies" warn't a takin' a hobserwation of us with a sort of humane quadrant.

"Werry remarkable behavior for ladies of the *hupper* class," says the Cap'n; "but it's the march o' hintellect, I suppose."

VI.

Captain Cuttle lets us into his ideas with regard to Italian opera and its patronizers, and describes the peculiar qualities in a singer required by the world of fashion, which he illustrates by an anecdote, familiar, probably, to the reader—He and Bunsby have a small discussion on the subject of beards, their varieties and uses, during which the Captain administers a very well-merited reproof to those bare-faced individuals, who, like the cropped fox, would fain curtail the hirsute appendages of others, taking occasion also to rap his countrymen over the knuckles for ridiculing foreign customs.

"WELL, Jack, old tar," says the Cap'n, when we had touched terra firma once more, and had got well away from the houtlandish Hitalian noises, "we've been a spendin' a werry fashionable hour among them ar' big wigs, and hastonishing hinstructiv' it was too, as far as it went."

"So we have, and so it was," says I, "any way we kin sport our larnin' now, and, moreover, kin have it to say that we wisited the hopera, and in my opinion there was a tidy lot of them haristocratical listeners as went for no other purpose."

"You're right there, mesmet," says the Cap'n, "'taint the music, Jack, it's the folks as sings it, is the principle thing as they looks at. Why, bless your soul, if them ar' wabblein's and woice twistin's was hever so well done by a chap as had nothin' foreign tacked on to his name, it 'ud be woted wulgar, and them ar' "kids" 'ud lie asleep in the lazy laps of the nobs as had 'em on hand. But let Mounseer Thingamy, or a Si'nory Whatyoucallem, wag his beard at 'em and they'd fairly crack their stitches with unthuseymuseyism."

"It's a werry true hobserwation," says I, "that no good thing kin come out of the fashionable Nazareth."

"In coorse it is, Jack," replies the Cap'n, "I confesses my hignorance with regard to sich matters, and proud am I so to do; but I was hinformed by a gent as I'm acquainted with, one as *does* pursess a knowledge o' the ins and outs of crotchets and quavers, that there was a raal stunner at the screamin' business wentured to uplift her woice at that werry Temple o' Somnis as we've bin a sufferin' in—it was a young 'ooman, Jack, and consequently had the claims of the sex upon the male odds an' ends o' creation, hindependent of her gen'us and talons—would you b'leeve it, though judges as was judges pronounced her a reg'lar progedy in the way o' singin', yet the nobs wouldn't have her no how—'cause why? 'cause she warn't born some three or four thousand miles off. The *biscuit* had a little anchovy paste about it, to be sure, but they soon diskivered that though it had a Hitalian kiverin' it was only a Boston cracker, and it warn't to be swallowed nohow by a fashionable stomach. That ere's metyforicle, Jack, so I s'pose you can't make the happlication."

"Not all out," says I.

"Werry well, then," says he, "we'll let it rest where it is. But you take my word, Jack, the fashionable world is mighty hinsignificant in respect of hinfluence, when compared with the rest o' creation—one is a duck puddle and the other a wast hocean. Let a cacklin' goose plump upon the surface o' one, and hagitation wisits its hextremities; but a whole legion o' cacklers, might drop upon the other and not be heerd of beyond the next wave."

"Let anybody try to contradict that if they kin," says I, "and if they aint hable, why, don't let them take no sich trouble."

This here conwersation took place at the corner of a street as seemed to be hinhabited by Hafricans and Hitalians; sich hairygated specimens of the hooman face diwine as some of the latter persented 'ud take the conceit out of any sweepin' broom. My heye! what capers they'd cut with their chin hornaments! Some on 'em had their mouths covered hentirely with hair. The Cap'n hinsinivated that as they lived a'most halways upon soup, and was werry doubtful about the hingredients, they kept that hairy sieve for the purpose of a strainer. If that's the use of it, I hexcuses the look of the thing for the sake of its hinginuity, but hothers o' 'em I thought had no sich apology, fellows with a couple of leeches under their noses and a furry tuft runnin' down the middle of their chins.

It appears, howsomedever, that I was wrong agin', for the Cap'n told me the use o' them, which was, that as they were all great snuffers, they filled them muskeeters, as they called them, with sich nastiness, it havin' the double heffect of ticklin' their hollowfactories and a dyin' of the hair hitself, that same bein' naturally of a werry different haspect in regard o' color. What the chin fringe was for I couldn't find out, hexcept it seems to afford them wonderful hamusement to keep luggin' at it. When I pointed that out to the Cap'n, he made the following hobserwation:

"It's natural, Jack," says he, "for a man to have somethin' to do when he's happeriently a doin' o' nothin'. A Henglishman inwestigates his pockets, a jinglin' whatever may be therein contained; an American hoccupies his time a shavin' of a stick; and a Hightalian, as you perceive, pets his muskeeters or keeps a tuggin' at his himperial."

One pompous little chap was a curiosity to look at—the hair on his head was as close as a rat's back, but below the nose it was equal a'most to the mane of a Buffulo; you'd a swore that he was turned upside down as far as the neck; but warn't he proud of it? I b'leeve he was to. There was he a sleekin' of it and a hexhibitin' of it to the passers-by as if it was a werry credible thing to look like a goat.

"Well," says I, without thinking what a stick I was cuttin' for to lay upon my own back, "there is a houtlandish lot o' monkey-bred wagabones."

When the Cap'n heerd me a makin' that ere foolish remark, he shook his head an' his hook werry sagacious at me, sayin':

"Old mesmet, you're wrong, haltogether wrong—mayhap it's the custom o' the place they kem from to keep all that stuff on, jist as it some countries the people wears bones through their noses, or necklaces o' sausage-meat for to flavor the hatmosphere. Mayhap, Jack, our bare cheeks is matter of as much hastonishment and derision to them. 'Taint the first time ne'ther as I've heerd an' seen folks—'specially Henglishmen too, I'm sorry to say, as ought to know better —a sneerin' at and abusin' customs and peculiarities, for no reason in the world but because they happen to be contrairy to what they've bin in the habit o' hindulgin' in theirselves. It stands to reason that it must be unkimmon pervokin, to be continually a snubbed for doin' this and that as has come nateral, from the fact of seein' it done all round.

"Now I puts it to you, Jack, this here way: S'posin' as you ownded a house which you'd took a halmighty deal o' pains to furnish in yer own way, hintirely for yer own comfort and conwenience, and jist as you had it all shipshape and agreeable to hinclinations, some two or three chaps was to come in—not inwited guests ne'ther—and do nothin' but find fault with your furniture; one arter the other sayin' as how yer sophia ought to be in sich a place, and yer piehanner in another, or you oughtn't to have no rockin' cheer, that yer walls warn't papered right, and you burned the wrong sort o' coal—what would you say to 'em, bo?"

"Say to 'em," says I, a fizzin' at the thought o' such himperence, "why, I'd say that I furnished it to please myself, and if they didn't like it, they might put on their hats quick."

"Werry well, then," says the Cap'n, a flourishin' his hook, "overhaul yer sensibilities, and when found, make this here happlication, whenever yer in a stranger's house or in a foreign country, don't show yer hignorance by findin' fault with things as yer not haccustomed to yerself. Remember that in either case yer only a wisitor, and haint got no right to behave hoffensive."

"All correct, Cap'n," says I, "I bows to the rod werry submissiv'. I haint a goin' to find fault with no man's beard agin, nor no country's customs ne'ther. John Cheneyman may suck his opinion, and henjoy his rat-pie an' bird-nest soup, 'taint nothin' to me. Mounseer may swallow his frogs by the bushel, I won't heven helevate my nose. The man-seller may trade in humane flesh, and have his receipt wrote in blood an' signed by the Devil, for what I care. The himpatient New Zelander in his hungerin' for knowledge may swaller hinstruction and the schoolmaster at the same time, but I'd take no more notice of it nor if it was a mutton chop he was a munchin'."

I don't believe the Cap'n was hover an' above pleased with my hobserwations, for he didn't say nothin', but gev me a duberos kind of a look, as if he warn't quite sartain whether I was a jokin' or not.

Howsomedever I was tickled with it unkimmon; and when a man's satisfied hisself, my opinion is that it don't signafy much who aint.

Therefore, if so be as this here epissle isn't werry sea-sarpinty in the regard of length, it'll take some'at of a divin' bell to reach the bottom of the meanin' thereof in the matter of depth.

VII.

Jack begins to work unwillingly, after having made several futile calls upon his imagination; he however weighs anchor, and drifts down the stream of Circumstance. The Captain and he converse on various subjects, becoming illustrative, analytical, and almost metaphysical, until their thoughts and theories are broken into by bits of fact. They visit the Model Artists, and are astonished at the perfection of machinery, &c., &c.

Did you ever knock at the door of your brains just to see if there war any highdeas at home, and diskiver the hinterior of your sense lodgin' as hempty as a sucked hegg?

If you have, you'll know the percise feelin' with which I'm now a tryin' to coax the words one by one from the end o' my goose quill. I spose they'll come if I sticks at it long enough. What a pity it is that there haint no kind of mental spur to wake up a lazy himagination. Mine, sich as it is, lies curled up in some dark corner of my freeknowledge box, and I can't get it to budge an inch.

Moreover, I've promised to scribble this 'ere harticle, and have been so amazin' hoccupied by the duties of my seafarin' purfession, that ould Time, takin' a mean adwantage o' my habstraction, jumped over my back, days and all, knockin' me werry near into the middle o' the week, afore I knew what I was about.

Howsomedever, some'at must be done, and so here goes—ah—I'm blowed if I can. This here writin' agin time, when the ould fellow has twenty-four hours start o' your pen, is unkimmon hard scratchin,' 'specially when you has to stop every now and then to pick up a highdea, jest as the chaps pick up stones in that 'ere singular kind of a runnin' match you reads in the sportin' papers.

Stand by! now it's comin'. I feel as I'm a goin' to open a wein o' wisdom as rich as California gold, that is to say purwided you jest break through the coatin' of clay as will naterally stick to the lumps.

I read a lesson to-day as was writ upon the page o' sarcumstances, that made a wonderful himpression upon me, and likewise upon the Cap'n.

We was a spyin' in at one o' the pictur' shops when a poor woman kem up close alongside, a lookin' out of her heyes as plain as her tongue could speak it, "I'm hungry." Now you needn't tell me that hevery body as she passed by couldn't jest read that same; in coorse they did, but not one of the sleek-lookin', well-dressed people, with their noses poked up to the sky, took the trouble to succor, in the smallest way, the distress as was starin' them in the face; she warn't a beggin'. I can't say as I likes them sort o' cattle—they are generally lazy or worthless, but this poor sowl dragged her weak limbs along, silent, but oh! how full of sorrow. She made no sound, no more nor a printed book could, but you might read her story jest as easy.

"Jack," says the Cap'n, his blessed woice a tremblin' with hemotion, "there's a large wolume of sufferin' writ on that once beautiful face. That there poor, degraded, unnoticed creeter was a child once, with bright, sunny eyes, and a heart full o' hope and joy—look at her now. What years of misery must have torn those deep furrows in her cheek—what floods of sorrow's tears must have quenched the light of that once flashing eye. Aint it a disgrace, Jack, to think that while the newspapers is overflowin' with the speechmakin's of skin-pious spec'lators, a cajolin' money out of the pockets of scared ould women o' both sex, for the purpose o' affordin' hinstruction to the man-eaters and wagabones of far distant countries, them snufflin' schemers should be so short-sighted, in the regard of sich destitution as is under their werry noses. It's a good and a proper thing to look arter the health of people's souls, but a little concarn for the comfort o' their bodies might be slipped in by the way."

"That's true, Cap'n," says I, "it is a disgrace at this time of the world's age, that there should be any poor people at all, except them as desarves to feel poverty from their misbehavior. There's a wast multitude of ladies and gentlemen as busies themselves—werry commendable—in the distribution o' tracks. Now, in my mind, if they'd play that air with the wariation of a loaf o' bread jest now and then, the moral hinstruction wouldn't be the less useful because the happetite was satisfied."

Then the Cap'n said, "I feels strongly hinclined to have a talk with that 'ere poor 'ooman, I will, too," and so he did, first puttin' half a dollar in her hand, which triflin' sarcumstance brought a flash o' fire into her heye, and then a big tear that put it out again, quick.

We found her story was the old one of an early marriage and a bad husband, the sad but common relation of patient, passive endurance, linked with brutality, drink and violence.

Just at that time, a magnificent carriage, with a conceited-looking nigger afore it and behind, decked out in the nearest approach to a haristocratic livery as republican simplicity can hindulge in, dashed up to the hentrance of a fashionable store. Down kem the wigorous footman, bang kem the door open, and out jumped a daughter o' Heve, with the price of a baker's shop, stock and all, a kiverin' her skilleton, and the cost of a halms-ouse a hangin' gracefully on her shoulders. As this perfusely hillestrated hedition o' nater swept by us like a seventy-four a passin' a mudscow, the Cap'n looked at me and the two women werry significant. I knew what he was thinkin' of jest as well as if I war hinside o' his west, and nodded accordingly. There was pride in the heye of the pampered piece of humanity as she condescended to touch the wulgar earth, and envy in the poor wretch's countenance as she turned to look at her more fortunate sister.

"There's what I would like to see altered," said the Cap'n; "that fearful jump from the top of the humane tree to the bottom. People as has compassion for the destitution of their fellows ought to find some way of elevatin' them that's below, or if they don't, the world some day will set itself right by bringing them down as is aloft."

"It's a werry remarkable fact, that 'ere," says I, in answer to that obserwation o' the Cap'n's, "that, generally, the world will right itself at the proper time jest like the icebergs, that wicey warseys themselves, when the haction o' the water makes their lower ends lighter nor the hupper."

"Werry right agin, Jack," says the Cap'n. "But how

often do we see hot-headed, self-deluded indiwiddials as thinks they knows better nor the great Bein' as regilates the world's machinery,—fuss and fidget, and declare this here wheel is out of order, or that 'ere jint wants hoilin', a thrustin' his little grain o' sense among the wast and incomprehensible works as goes on a rewolwin' jest as if there warn't nothin' o' the sort near it, no how. Take my word for it, shipmet, men as tries to guide sarcumstances, had much better 'bout ship and let sarcumstances guide them. It's jest for all the world like a sailor's a bustin' of his cheeks to get a wind, instead of takin' advantage of whatever's blowin'. There haint no storm without a cloud, Jack, no more is there any change in the hoccurrences o' the world, without a hindication as can be laid hold on by them as has wisdom enough to make the happlication.

"But come, Jack, we've had enough of this dry stuff. Let's go somewhere where there's a fiddle."

"Werry good," says I.

Jest then the Cap'n's heye caught sight of a henticin' sort of a pictur' bill, as represented a group o' dancin' statuary, or some'at of the sort.

"That ar's machinery," says the Cap'n, "we're close to the place (it was called Wallhello, I think, as near as I kin recollect), so we'll go and see it."

No sooner said than done. We found out the place, paid our quarters, and went in.

There we seed a sort o' himitation o' natur', only terrible ondecent for machinery; there war a lot o' hunproportionated figgers, wax, I spose, or some werry hindifferent composition, a stuck on a kind o' round table, in the most disgraceful warieties o' hattitude. The place was chock full o' disrespectable-lookin' people, and they laughed and hollered, but what they could see in the hexibition except a miserable libel on hoomanity, was a puzzle to me. Whoever moddled them ought to be ashamed to show sich perductions to the public heye.

"Well," says the Cap'n, as he gazed upon the tabloo, "the hingenuity o' man is wonderful. I never did see such mechanism as is displayed here. If it warn't that no human creetur *could* so degrade his species, nor none o' the species would consent to be so desperately hinfamous, I do declare I should a'most say they war alive."

You should a heard a grey-headed ould reprobate roar out when the Cap'n made the hobserwation.

"You're right, sir," says he, when he'd had his fun out, and likewise distributed the joke, whatever it was, all round him. "They certainly have brought machinery to werry great perfection." Then they all laughed agin.

"The machinery's well enough," says the Cap'n, "but the dressmakers must be terrible bad off for stuff to kiver them with. Why, no! Jack! I'm blowed but there's a heffigy hain't got hardly a blessed rag on. I don't like that, let's go!"

"Don't be foolish," says the ould boy, "It's only machinery, you know," whereat they all laughed louder nor ever.

The Cap'n and me war a tryin' to make our way out, when our ould friend overpersuaded us to take our seats agin.

"You'll be glad if you do," says he; "the great triumph of mechanical hart comes next. Stay a minute or two longer, and you'll see the Helephant."

"Oh! there's a Helephant, is there?" says the Cap'n, "I don't mind stoppin' to see that!"

Then the curtain drew up, but there warn't no hanimal o' the sort, only the same lot o' figures a standin' on the floor o' the place: the fiddlers struck up, and the wax work began a dancin' a quadreel, jist as natural as if they was hanimated folks. That 'ere dance finished the hexebition, which, I must say, was most hungenteel and disreputable, even for stuffed himitations. As we were leaving the place, the Cap'n tapped me on the harm, and with a look as spoke wolumes in the way of hexpression, says to me, says he:

"Jack."

"Ned," says I.

"There's a doubt on my mind respectin' o' them heffigies."

"What's that?" says I.

"May I never see salt water agin," says he, "if I don't feel half inclined to b'leeve that they wor alive."

"Alive?" says I. "What, real men and women, with hearts and feelin's? Not a bit of it. There's laws in the city —there must be—old mesmet, as 'ud soon put a stop to sich damnable houtrage as that 'ere would amount to."

"In coorse they would," says the Cap'n, "and it stands to reason that they haint nothin' but himages.

We didn't see no helephant though, arter all.

VIII.

Jack describes his first Sunday's experience in New-York, the difference of the church-calling bells here and at home, and the sensations in his mind produced by each—From the bells, by a natural transition, he approaches the belles, touching dangerous ground, but getting off safely, it only being an opinion—He and the Captain visit Trinity Church, and record their impressions, &c. &c.

Last Sunday the Cap'n and me spent the time a lookin' round to see what was to be seed, an' how the folks here passes the day generally; I've seed the way in which people hoccupies their time at home an' abroad, for a chap, even when he don't know that he's a doin' it, sucks in hobserwation with the werry wital hair as he's a breathin'.

It's a beautiful sight, in some of the fine old willages at home, to see the whole pop'lation a steerin' churchways, while the solemn bell prepares the mind to remember some'at more nor the noise an' tumult o' life. I must confess that I misses that ar' bell, but then I s'pose it's because it's what I was used to in the times gone bye; and if it's hard to wean a hinfant, what must it be to wean a full-grow'd man from familiar things? I have seed the French fellows a spreein' and dancin' after the hour of devotion is passed, an' I must do 'em the credit to say that whether it's a prayin' or playin', they henters into both on 'em with a hearnestness o' spirit, as is perfectly hunaccountable to us cold-blooded Hangle-Sextants.

It stands to reason that I was shocked at the hunreverend way that they behaved themselves, bein' onused to that same line o' conduct myself, but then agin, it warn't for me to say that they were to blame, for merely doin' as was "their custom on a arternoon," specially o' Sundays. Where there's no wrong *meant*, there's no wrong *did*; that's my opinion, and I don't care who knows it.

But to go back. The Cap'n and me put on our Sunday goin' togs, an' out we started. It seemed as if the day had got its best coat and trowsers on too, for it was one of the brightest an' softest an' beautifulest as ever basked in the lazy warmth of a September sun, when that ar' ginerally hobstropelous month condescends to look pleasant. The church bells was a-goin', not like ours, with some'at o' joy in their tones, mixed up with solemnity, hinspirin' the heart with a feelin' o' delighted gratefulness for the Sabbath rest, and the blessed privilege of breathin' the musical air, as the sweet chime wibrates through it, like some'at alive; but slow and hard and sudden on the nerves, like a helectric shock, to the Cap'n and me, as warn't haccustomed to the sound, it driv away the sense o' thankfulness for benefits received, as ought to accompany one to church, and left nothing but the dread of punishment for the herrors we had committed. No doubt it has a different heffect on them as has heard it all their lives; at all ewents I should be werry much grieved if they were to halter it on my account.

The streets war crowded with people, and what struck the Cap'n and me uncommon forcible, was the habsence of all look o' poverty or distress. Heverybody was well-dressed, and had a hair o' comfort about 'em, that *I've* never seen in any other part o' the globe as I has bin through. Sich a city full of black coats an' shiny hats, I'll defy you to perduce; and as for the ladies, why there hain't nothin' as walks as can beat the young ones—bless yer sowl, they're so airy-like and delicately light, they look as though they might skip along the foam of a sea-wave, and not damp their hancles—a sort o' connectin' link between men an' hangels; the whole animated creation can't come anyways a nigh 'em when they are in the bud; but our women goes ahead a them in the regard o' blossom. Whether it's in the breed or the cultiwation I don't know, but it's a remarkable fact, at least it's my opinion, and, moreover, the Cap'n's too. But mayhap we may be hinfluenced by hearly himpressions with regard to belles as well as bells, and it haint hardly fair to make sich a hobserwation. Howsomedever it's out now and can't be recalled, and I hope nobody won't take no offence, none bein' hintentioned.

Together with the crowds of sober-lookin' and steady goin' people as was pushing along nice and quiet, every now an' then would rush by some wehicles a travelin' unkimmon fast. When the Cap'n seed them, he says:

"Jack," says he, "them chaps is in a hurry for first sarvice, no doubt," but they didn't stop at no church doors as we could see. Mayhap they worships out o' town somewhere.

Well, we kem to a fine, noble buildin', of helegant proportions exceptin' the hentrance, which, in comparison with the height of the steeple, looked ezactly like the little hole as is cut for the conwenience o' hens, in a barn-door, but the lots of fine folks as rolled up in their carriages, and kep' a streamin' in. "My blessed wig!" says the Cap'n, a givin' of his hook the highest point of his "hastonishment" helewation. "Old mesmet, jest look at the welwets and the satins. Ain't it a sight! what with the bright colors an' the stiff gale o' perfumery, don't it put you in mind of a movin' pannarummy o' livin' flowers?"

So we edged in on the tail end o' the flood, and the fust thing that made itself hevident, was the onpossibility o' seein' any thing comfortable, by reason of there bein' not no light.

"A blessed inwention of the harchitect," says the Cap'n, reverentially. "He knew that a church warn't ezactly the place to study the fashions in. When there's too much light, bonnets hinterferes with Bibles in a remarkable degree."

We didn't stay long there, not out of no disrespect to the place nor the occasion, but there was a hatmosphere of restraint about us, as didn't agree with a feelin' of dewotion; so after we had given our hearts considerable bumpin', by reason of a kind of shamfacedness as would creep over us in spite of ourselves, we plucked up courage, and bolted, quick.

When we got fairly hinto the street, the Cap'n gazes hup at the himposin' structure, and says he solemnly, "Hif the quantity o' worship is to be hestimated by the quality o' the worshipers, there's a wast amount o' dewotion in that ar' hedefice."

"Jest so," says I, "an' if the half o' the money as was expended in the hornamentin' of that 'ere religious temple was laid out in cheerin' the hearts of the poor people as lives near about, I don't think as how it 'ud be less hacceptable to the Great Being in whose name it has been herected."

After havin' wented our opinion in that ar' way, we happened to meet with a friend of ourn, and he told us that we were quite wrong, which mayhap we war, for that we hadn't seen the "fashionable" church yet.

"The what?" says the Cap'n, with a werry natural frown o' hindignation on his benevolent heybrows. "The *Fashionable* church! I've heard tell of fashionable places of hamusement, but never knowed till now as places o' worship was hincluded therein, "but it is hastonishin' what we larns as we gets hacquainted with the ways o' the world."

"Where is the fashionable church? since there is sich a place," says I; "it must be worth seein' jest for the purpose of obserwin' how much the hupper crust condescends to do in the way o' piety."

"Oh! you'll find it as you goes along," says our friend; "its a warigated specimen o' harchitecture, that looks like a small himitation o' the great cathedrals as you sees cut out o' card-boards."

"I've seed it," says the Cap'n; "let's make sail, Jack, at oncet."

"'Taint no use," says our hinformer. "There's nobody there now, it bein' the waterin' place season. The most of the wisitors is doin' the helegant at Saireytoga an' sich places, and them as is in town wouldn't be seen there, nohow, but shuts themselves hup to make b'leeve that they're gone too."

"What a hall-powerful thing that ar' fashion is, to be sure," says the Cap'n, "sence not only our eatin' an' drinkin' an' dressin', but our werry religious feelin' must bow to its dictation."

"That ain't no affair of ourn," says I.

"Werry true," Jack, says he, "so we'll overhaul our helements o' discretion, an' say no more about it."

"Agreed," says I.

IX.

The Captain and Jack venture to touch on Nationalities, which, considering that it is rather a ticklish subject, they dispose of satisfactorily; from that they diverge into Irish matters, in which a real Emerald Islander takes a peculiar part, accounting for some apparent puzzlement in Hibernian Statistics, finishing up with a touch at Historians, Polemics, and Philosophy generally.

The Cap'n an' me had a sort o' conwersation to-day, wherein some hobserwations was made as I feels hinclined to make public, that is to say, as public as the circulation of this here "waluable wolume" *kin* make sich remarks, which, in coorse, is considerable, if not up'ards.

I don't know ezactly what it was brought it up, nuther does it sinnafy much one way or 'tother; but we'd been a talkin' with a crowd o' chaps premiscious like, Americans and English, together with a few as belonged to other countries as ain't no consequence, some'at brought up national feelins, when the Cap'n loomed out large upon the subjeck.

"I respects the man," says he, a slappin' of his hook upon the table with a bang as made the glasses cry out—for it was grog time. "I respects hany man," he continued henergetically, "of hany country, as stands up for the flag of that ar' country—no matter what sort of a rag that same may be, I repeat it, I respects him, aye, if it war a Hottentot, always purwidin' those savages possessed the blessin's of buntin'. Show me a feller as says that he kin look at the hemblem of his birth-place without a jerk inside of him, as if his blood was a tryin' to pump itself out, and I'll tell him that natur' sent him into the wide world without no heart at all. There's a great many feelins and haffections as belongs to the humane creetur, such as love and friendship, and the likes; but there haint one of 'em as is worth a pinch of snuff, unless loyalty is mixed well up among 'em. Kin you love a woman without bein' loyal to her? No! Kin you respect a friend without bein' loyal to him? No! Werry well, then, if so be as you can't help bein' loyal to your love and your friend, no more can you prewent yerself bein' loyal to the flag of your country. Why it's next akin to the love for one's mother; I don't know if it ain't afore it, for trace back your pedigree, and your mother earth is the first of all."

"And are you proud of your country?" says one of the company as happened to have the honor of bein' kittened somewhere else.

"Proud on it," says the Cap'n, "in coorse I am, as in duty bound."

"A pretty place to be proud of," he went on; "pressed down and overborne by taxes an white slavery—look at"—

"Awast, friend," the Cap'n said; "stand by one minute; I takes it for granted as you had a mother some time or another, if I haint greatly mistaken, eh?"

"You're right, old tar; go on," says the chap.

"You loved her, I suppose?"

"I did indeed, and do still, I'm glad to say," says our friend, in sich a way as made you feel he warn't gammonin'.

"Werry well, then," says the Cap'n; "I jist axes you this 'ere question; hif your own blessed mother was to be sick for a spell, or ketch some complaint, would you turn agin her for that?"

"No!" says he out loud, "not a bit on it."

"No," says the Cap'n, louder still, "nor no one as carries a man's heart under his ribs; but I'll tell you what you'd do;

you'd pity her condition, and try to ease her sufferin' in the best way you could. Well, now, it's jest the same thing with a feller's country, hif it has little diseases, hif it's troubled with a cough or a cold, never mind, so long as the constitution is hearty—a little wholesome diet will bring it all round agin comfortable."

Well, there was a big lump of a Irishman in the party, that spoke right out—sayin'—

"That's all mighty fine, Misther Capt'n, and I must say exceedin' proper of you bein' what you are. But here am I now, a Irishman, what have I to love—Ireland—I suppose you'll say. Well, that I do, better than life—God knows; but where am I to find it, there ain't no such place, it's swallowed up body and breeches. A housekeeper is only a housekeeper as long as he owns a house, and how is a chap to call hisself a Irishman, when there ain't a yard square of that 'ere lovely country he can say belongs to him or his. I can easily understand a man's takin' a interest in a house as he has had left to him, furnished and all proper for to live in; but say that a bigger or a richer chap comes along, an' between coaxin' and swindlin' turns him out by degrees; first getting him down from the drawin' rooms to the parlors, after that into the kitchen, from thence into the cellars, at last right into the street. Why it stands to reason, that though he may love the bricks and mortar, the old roof-tree and the once hospitable hearth, he can have no werry great feelin' of friendliness for the strange dwellers within his father's home."

"I must confess," says the Cap'n, "that the stream of sarcumstances has had most wariable currents in regard to that ar' unfortunate country."

"Why, my good friend," says the Irisher, "I see you are a reasonable man, and kin hear the truth spoken without puttin' up a cat-back. The history of that ar' spot o' ground is as much a secret to the general people of the world as that of Ashantee or the Abroginies of America. Ireland is not the place to look for Irishmen, not a bit of it, there ain't a dozen representatives of the real old Irish stock in the whole country,—think of that, sir. Think of a hentire nation driven from their rightful possessions, banned and persecuted, until a doubtful existence in other countries was preferred to the certainty of oppression in their own; but are those families, rich in intellect and the power of talent, extinct in consequence?" —I'm a tryin' to put down his werry words as near as I kin —"No," says he; "look at the lists of other nations, and see if the names highest on the roll of fame, have not in many instances a most familiar sound. Through the entire of Europe, and across the ocean which divides us, the names of Irishmen have travelled—there is no need to mention them for they are household words."

It was really beautiful to hear him talk, and there was a good deal of sound sense in what he said, though a little bit too flowery; but that's their fault or forte—I don't know which is right, howsomedever he said so hisself.

"There's a good time coming for Ireland," says the Cap'n.

"You allude to the great result expected from the Queen's visit," says the Irisher.

"God bless her!" says the Cap'n, lifting his hat and giving his hook a flourish of the most henthusiastic description.

"Amen!" says the Paddy. If it was only for the intention of doin' good, some of the vagabonds insinuated that she might meet with disrespect, perhaps with harm—the libellous villains! in the first place, she was safe, because she was a woman; secondly, she was respected, because she was a good one; and thirdly, there's enough of the loyalty of right left in the remnant of Irishmen; that if she was neither the one nor the other she might rest perfectly contented in their prowerbial hospitality to the stranger.

"Well, now," says a chap as was a listenin', "I think them poor stupid slaves of Irishmen ought to remain in their degradation, for having bowed down to the idol, whose influence has helped to crush them."

"A werry purty figure of speech," says the Cap'n, in his way. "Don't you know that there haint a thing as occurs in the world but is liable to be twisted into all sorts o' shapes, the werry best hintentions in sich cases bein' often made to look as if they were any thing else; why look at the gover'ment of any country as you speak of, then overhaul the newspapers, and when found jest mark the difference of opinion; haint there heaps of organs, as they calls them, and don't they all play different tunes, praisin' this, and blowin' up 'tother, and there haint any two of 'em as agrees; as it is in little things so it is in big, and the future reader of present history will receive his himpressions from the personal feelings and party prejudices of the chap as happens to be the writer."

"It's a good thing," says the Irisher, "that there is a hopposition in the politics of a country; the gover'ment couldn't no more go on without it nor a weighin' machine could work without a balance."

"Yes," says the Cap'n, "I agrees to that ar', but I don't like to see estimable characters maligned and saturized merely to serve party purposes; take for instance the chief magistrate of these ere United States,* is he exempt from the serpent's fang of party? No! The man whom the uniwersal woice of this great country elewated, in spite of all opposers to the sovereignty of the largest population in the world—

* Written when General Taylor commenced his Presidency.

honored, esteemed, almost rewered in private life, and in his public actions crowned with glory and renown. Yet scarcely is he seated within the magisterial chair, when out bark the snarlin' dogs of party, as though the fire which is to blaze in triumph for the future chief ruler, must necessarily consume the present one.

By this time we had a confused amount of grogs, and everybody knows that all the religious and political excitement in a man's composition, floats upon the top of them 'ere stimulatin' drinks, and consequently bein' near the sarface, haven't far to go; moreover, as no two people ever did or ever will think alike on sich subjecks, and in either case it only requiring a very slight difference of opinion to raise a tempest of discussion—a discussion we had accordin'ly.

I should like werry much to let you know the partic'lars thereof, but inasmuch as they were all talkin' together, and added to which, candor obliges me to say that there was more whisky than wisdom in their conwersations, I don't think you will lose much, if you should never hear a word about it.

X.

The Captain and Jack take another stroll up Broadway, and courageously venture into Palmo's—What they see there and what they do there with the train of thought produced on the occasion—A passing dissertation on womankind in general, in which the Captain describes his predilections and antipathies—Jack agrees with him, of course, and ventures also a small opinion on his own hook.

In the continuin' of our hexcursions and our hincurtions about the city, we sometimes gets into hextraor'nary places—sich places haint to be ekalled nohow as I've seed, and I have travelled a little.

It was only the other night, as the Cap'n and me was a-beatin' about, duberous-like as to where we should go or what we should do, when all at oncet we purceived a lot o' people steerin' into a half play-actin', half grog-shop lookin' place. I found they called the concarn Palmo's; it had another crackjaw name, as I disremember. Howsomedever it seemed to us a sort of henticin', and so the Cap'n says:

"Jack," says he.

"He's here, owld salt," says I.

"What say you to a turn?" says he.

"Agreed," says I. "What is it?"

"Haint got a hidea," says the Cap'n, "but there's no knowin' of nothin', unless it's inwestigated."

So in we marches, bold enough. My blessed wig, what a sight was there, surely. Sich a heap o' zoological Rooshians and Prooshians, and coorosities from all countries as there was hassembled, and sich a conglomeration and confusion o' tongues never was heerd since they suspended hoperations upon the tower o' Babel.

The Cap'n was for boltin', but jist then the corner of his heloquent heye fell upon one of the helegantest specimens of the humane form diwine as hever hoisted the flag o' woman-kind—he struck, without firin' a gun.

"Jack, old mesmet," says he, a pintin' of her out, "that's what I calls dreadful. Haint it awful that a fellow should have to hencounter sich broadsides o' fascination as is poured out from them peepers. What a blessed thing a woman is, Jack; meanin' in coorse a woman as is a woman, one as is tender to you, and leans upon you, and feels when your harms is around her, that lightnin' couldn't strike through their purtection—always soft, and sweet, and gentle, and mild-spoken. Ah! them's the ones, Jack, as sets a chap's heart afloat upon a hocean o' happiness, an' steers it about jest where they likes."

"My sentiments, Cap'n, to a charm," says I.

"I doesn't want 'em to know too much, neither," says he. "They warn't hintended for hanythin' but home and love, and where there's a wonderful chunk o' wisdom, it don't leave much room for any other feelin'. Puddin's and poetry doesn't agree, nohow, and the hands as is constantly holdin' o' pens, gets too stiff to flourish a needle."

By this time we had sot ourselves down at a fine marble-covered table, and sure enough up kem one of the beauties as kep' running in and out among the men-folks like pretty pinnaces sparklin' through a fleet o' colliers. I was in a bit of a flutter as I heerd her little woice a haxin' of us "what we'd take to drink"—the hintoxicatin' creeter a bewilderin' on us by starin' with a sort o' bashful bowldness right into our werry heyes. I stood it like a brick, but the Cap'n gave in soon.

"Jack," says he, when she'd gone for the rum, "I surrenders. That 'ere marmaid has captiwated me. I don't know —but if she could make up her mind to share Ned's hammock."

"What," says I, "give up your liberty for the sake of a minute or two's look at a purty face. Take a stick o' candy and begin a-suckin' at it, for the babby's coming back on you strong."

"You're right, Jack, I'm a stupid old stock-fish. What has a world-wanderer like me to do with sich inclinations?" says he; "ah! here's the grog. Thank you, my lass."

Well, he took a mighty pull; and after he'd wiped his chin, he leans hover to me, solidly, and says:

"I loved a woman oncet, Jack."

"Only oncet," says I.

"Only oncet," says he. "No man or woman—no, nobody don't love more nor oncet. I knows it: they may think they do, and many of 'em wears out their lives respectable enough, and never knows the differ, but it ain't in natur' for the real clingin' together of two hearts to hoccur with more nor one. Matches and marriages has been made by the thousand, for conwenience, or the mistakin' of some'at else for the truth of love. Well, mayhap they goes on smooth and easy, in the respect of the not seein' the real hobject, but put the case that they do meet. What si'nafies the bridles o' custom or the breath o' man. The sowls belong to each other, and they'll either break in silence, or come together in spite of fortune."

As soon as the Cap'n made that 'ere hobserwation, a kind of unwisible hopera started off full blast, and werry sentimental music it made; we declined ourselves back in our cheers, and what with listenin' an lookin' at the music and the lovely creeters as was perambulatin' round, a half an hour was stole out o' the glass of time in the most delightfullest sort of habstraction.

I didn't ezactly know what it was that kem ower me, whether it was the effects of the singin', the starin', or the todies. I don't know, mayhap it was the combined hinfluence of hall three on 'em, but there war a hinterval of ever so many minutes, as I couldn't remember anythin' satisfactory about. The Cap'n said I was takin' a nap. And now that I comes to think serious on it, I believe I did drop off, into the harms o' slumber.

But it was the blessedest sort of a wision, as long as it lasted.

XI.

Jack takes a stroll by himself, to see how the city looks at night—He gets into a parenthetical train of thought, and gives the highly-favored reader the benefit of the same—Jack's opinion of ancient worthies in general, and of Alexander the Great in particular—With many other matters wonderfully interesting to the general public.

IT's worth a man's while, meanin' a man as is in a contemtemplatin' sort o' humor, to take a walk by hisself, in the night time. That ar' mysterious hour, when the gay sun-ray fades out, and the smilin' flowers is asleep, and everything a'most is at rest, preparin' with wholesome insensibility for the labors of to-morrow.

Not as I means to say that nothing good is to be found awake o' nights, for hif the half o' the world has lost its laughin' sunlight, don't the smilin' stars wink down on it, as though the contented skies was agoin' off into a comfortable doze, but had to keep themselves alive for the purpose of watchin' over their slumberin' charge.

In the busy hustlin' bustlin' day-time the thoughts get jostled out of you in the confusion of contentin' hinterests, hevery body is a pushin' along with sich a hair o' business marked on the figure-head, either real or haffected, that a fellow naturally takes his place in the stream, and strikes out too—but hif he wants to do a bit of sober thought, let him wait until dark when nobody can't take no notice of his countenance, then he kin think away, like a whole ship's crew o' philosophers, and the folks as passes along won't fancy that he's a subjeck for the mad-house, or agoin' to burst up the next day.

The sarcumstances as hobligated me to get on this here coorse was jest this here

Arter we'd cut ourselves out o' that are small paradise o' Palmo's, without tastin' none o' the forbidden fruits as is there hexhibited, the Cap'n felt snoozey, and turned in suddent. Whereas, I bein' fresh, and in a hobserwin' state o' body, sallies out again a seekin' for hadwentures, jest like hany other knight-arrent, in the howlden times, Don Quixote or Halexander the Great.

Talkin' o' them antick worthies, what a hexaggerated size the distance o' time makes them appear to us pigmyites o' the present day; some'at like the sun when he's a settin', the farther he's hoff the bigger he looks, and indeed, to tell the truth, there hain't no gettin' at the real size o' neither on 'em; it a sort o' depends more upon the sharpness of a fellow's eyes, or as the medium as he looks through. Now, for hexample, I axes what that there Halexander was, and did. As far as I've bin able to make out, he was a mighty hemperor hover a tract o' ground amost ekal in pint of hextent as New Jarsey, but not comin' near it nohow in the regard o' usefulness. To be sure he did get a crowd o' wagabones together, and slaughtered his way into Hasia, but sarcumstances halters cases, and there hain't a dozen Halexanders as could do that now. The pop'lation was werry scanty then, and hafter all, they couldn't a bin no great shakes, none on 'em, for him and his whole harmy turned tail from a big sarpent. When there's no hopposition, it's heasy enough to get along; so it would be to walk through the walls of a house if it warn't for the bricks; therefore, I naterally comes to the conclusion that *bricks* was unkimmon scarce at that time.

We all knows, as knows hanything, that hif you sets hever so small a story rowlin', it 'ill grow faster nor a snowball, so each successive builder up of history sticks a slice on, until a man that in his own time ate and drank and etcetera'd jest like one of us common fellows, looms out like a three-decker alongside of a jolly-boat.

But this here piece o' hinformation is a reglar shoot off from my subjeck, so I must 'bout ship, and take up my recknin' reglar. I b'leeve I made the remark that I felt a sort o' coorosity to see how the city looked with its nightcap on, and consequently out I went.

It was a still, solemn, beautiful night. The moon was a tryin' her hardest to outshine the sun hisself, and failed hawful in the hattempt. It was werry light, to be sure, but then it was a cold, dank, unwholesome sort o' brightness, one of the heloquent things in natur' as talks as plain as printin', hif a chap has only the gumption to understand it. That 'ere moon ray spoke as loud as a skipper's trumpet in a storm, "Old boy, you ought to be in bed; this ain't for you to look at—leave my beams to the howls and the night phantoms," (for that there *is* night phantoms I b'leeves as I b'leeves my Bible, a'most).

One thing, howsomedever, she could consolate herself with, and that was, that if so be as she couldn't take the shine out of the sun, she beat him all hollow in the respect of shade—such a black line as there was all down the centre of the street, and along one side of the houses, as looked ezactly like a grim row of big monuments, except now and then a blaze of light would stream up from the liquor vaults, makin' you think of the henterance to a certain underground locality werry unfashionable to talk about.

And now jest you take the word of a owld hobserwater o' sich things. There's more henterances to that 'ere place of punishment than people thinks on. 'Tain't necessary to pint out peticklar an' indiwidual spots, and call 'em the hexclusive gates, as some o' the high-pressure parsons does. You take and mention the name of a playhouse, for hinstance, to one on 'em. Up goes the whites of his eyes as much as to say, that's the old boy's quarters, and some on 'em *does* speak it out; but I tell them that it ain't the place a man is in as leads to hiniquity, but the state of his mind. If a fellow thinks wicked, and is bent on doin' of it, what does it sinafy whether he's at home or abroad, in his own house or in a friend's, in a playhouse or in a church, aye, a church, if a man's thoughts is wicious. The werry doors as ought to lead him to happiness hereafter, sarves honly to put him on the t'other road, sure.

'Tain't often as I talks of sich matters, although I keeps a-thinkin' on 'em hever so many times. I reverences and respects, as a man hought to, them as is hinspired with a real feelin o' religion, but I can't bear the self-satisfied purfessurs as is so wrapped up in the conceit of their superior goodness, chaps as has sich a wonderful hinterest for their fellow-creeters, as always to be lamentin' the fate of the poor sinners about 'em; how werry considerate, pickin' holes in the coat o' hoomanity, disregardin' the hawful rents in their own garments which neglect is purty sure to perduce.

This 'ere harticle has become, without me knowin' of it, so mighty knowledgeable that I'm blowed if I hain't a'most ashamed on it. I feels as hif it war hout o' my line hentirely to mix or meddle with sich serious haffairs, for in hall humbleness I acknowledges the wast himportance to every man as has a soul, to find out, to the best o' his ability what's agoin' to become of it when it has wore out the clay coat nature has purwided. At all events, as fur as my limited amount o' hobserwation goes, its o' unkimmon little use to trust to houtside happeriences; it ain't always the blackest coat as hides the purest heart, nor the whitest hankecher as covers the humblest neck. 'Tain't always the yallorest features or the turnupedest eyes as hindicates the piousest hindividual, neither is it the loudest groaner or the wiolentest hair tearer as is the sincerest on the hinside—the smoothest o' happles is hoften rottenest at the core.

Therefore, hif so be as you doesn't wish to make a hexibition of your goodness, for the happrobation o' your fellow-creeters, let your kernel be sound and true, and it ain't much matter about the roughness o' the husk. The woice o' man may be deceptive, but there is a woice, a tongue within, which never lies, a chronometer of your hactions as pints to the good and to the bad without the possibility of a herror. Mind that adwiser, which is the in'ard monitor men call conscience, and you won't stand in no need of sarmons to keep you in the upward coorse.

XII.

Jack having nothing particular to do, waxes profound, and moralizes upon human nature in general, and gentility in particular, illustrating his argument by sundry similes which he thinks may be comprehended by everybody—Getting hard up for an idea, he bewails his forlorn condition, and receives consolation from the Captain, who makes a few pleasant remarks, winding up with an observation as is an observation.

To a man as takes the trouble to read it, what a heap o' knowledge lies open afore him, in the great book o' Natur', what a hendless wariety o' hincidents! what a warigated succession o' novelties. Why there ain't a minute o' time as comes along, but brings with it som'at or another, that if you keep your heyes open, will hadd a little to your store o' knowledge, aye, if its hever so sizeable, for there ain't no man so chock full o' wisdom but what he kin find room for another chunk.

To be sure some people spreads a small quantity o' sense

over an unkimmon large surface; them's the ones as thinks that they are full up an' runnin' over with gumption, but the man as really studies to scrape up knowledge, the more he gets of it, the smaller he thinks it is, until at last he's astonished to find, which is the absolute truth, that after he has stowed away all he kin carry in the hinsignificant chambers of his brain-box, that a hordinary lifetime ain't half long enough to haccumulate hanything there worth speaking of.

So you may take my word for it, always perwidin' that you cares a pin about my small twinkle o' hobserwation, that whenever you sees a self-satisfied-lookin' larned pundit comin' in Captain Grand in the way of paradin' his hinformation, it's a conwincin' proof that he hain't got much in the hinside, and is hobligated to show out a sample of the little he has, jest to keep the world from supposing that he's got none at all; whereas, the man as has confidence in the hextent of his hideas, never makes no fuss, but when the proper opportunities arrive, lets them come out nateral and quiet of their own haccord.

There's about the same distinction between the naturally genteel—although I can't say as I likes the word, for it has been so habused an' happlied to things as hasn't had no right to it, sich as a genteel shop, or a genteel hat; but that ain't the word's fault, poor thing, but theirs as twists it into them 'ere unnateral meanin's—and folks as purtends to gentility, but hasn't it in 'em. All the schoolin' in the world won't stuff sense into a man's scull as isn't porious enough to let it in; no more will all the dancin'-masters in the univarse put grace into the hactions of them as hain't got it by natur.

In the hacquirement o' knowledge as well as in the study of good manners, it's the company as you keeps that fixes what you must become—hexternally, at all ewents—and a chap could no more larn the watch-makin' business by bein' apprenticed to a carpenter, than a human bein' arrive at gentility, while hassociated with them as doesn't practice the same.

Did you hever take notice of the hawful struggles as is sometimes made by wulgar rich people to make the world know that they have a little more nor their neighbors? what heaps o' sarvents runnin' here an' there, jostlin' an' bumpin' up agin each other, bells a clangin,' woices agoin', an' everything in a delightful state of hostentatious confusion, and who's deceived by it? Not nobody. But take the real full-blooded aristocrat—in the proper sense o' the term—not the hunfair an' designin' significance gave to it, by hungry wagabones as keeps society in a state o' fermentation in order that they may live upon the dregs—and jest you mark the difference. Every thing goes smooth, easy and regular as clock-work. You see no purse-proud liberality about him; he ain't painfully hospitible and uncomfortably friendly; he shakes your hand, an' no condescension keeps his nose elewated. If he does you a sarvice, he doesn't slap it on your back, that all the world may see and pay respect to his generosity. You never see no fussiness or hembarrassment about him, bein' jest as much at home in a palace as in a cottage, before a prince or a peasant; titles or wealth doesn't raise no henvy in his heart, no more don't poverty hexcite no scorn, for as a *gentleman* he knows that he kin have no superior, hexceptin' in the practice of those hamiabilities as distinguishes that 'ere character, nor not no hinferior, hexceptin' them as departs therefrom.

'Tain't necessary to go to any degree, cast, condition, purfession, trade, callin', or livelihood whatsomedever, a lookin' out for gentlemen; you'll find 'em werry thinly scattered about the world in warious positions, like plums in a school puddin', an' about as easily reco'nized as them there palatable fruit is from the mass o' hinsipidness as surrounds them.

I'm a printin' o' these remarks by the adwice of the Cap'n hisself, as is a stannin' at my helbow, werry hanxious to be a sayin' some'at upon the matter too. Ain't you mesmet?

"Why no, Jack," says he. "The way as you have put it, must bring a bit of healthy counsel to them as takes the trouble to dive a little under the sarface o' words and fish it up. We all know that there is the same difference between gentlemen as is gentlemen, and sich as tries to keep up that apperiance, as there is between the precious metals and the himitations thereof.

"Heverybody knows that there is silver spoons and there's plated spoons, and though they may look hever so like each other, one on 'em is the true stuff to the heart's core, and the other only has a werry thin wash on the houtside. You may rub one on 'em till all's blue, and the pure metal will only shine the brighter, but scrape an acquaintance with the other, and you'll soon see the original iron stickin' out."

"That's true, old tar," says I, "true as the needle; but ain't we a wastin' time and paper in the makin' sich hobserwations? Doesn't all the world acknowledge the same thing?"

"Yes, Jack," answered the Cap'n, "in coorse they do, but it don't do 'em no harm, now and then, jest to put 'em in mind of it, but now, if you've got to the ind o' your rope, we'll turn out a spell, and get a bellyful o' fresh air."

"Aye, aye," says I, "so down goes my pen, and unkimmon glad I am, too, for the tide of my hideas has ebbed out, and left me high and dry, reg'larly stranded, a hawful onpleasin' position, Cap'n, for a craft as hengages to make certain passages."

"Not a bit on it, shipmet," says he. "'Tain't your time yet. The luck of it is that you ain't so heavily laden, but a half a tide 'll float you off bye-and-bye: so jest you give over a thinkin' about it, for it would be as easy a job to put spurs into a wooden horse, and expect him to gallop, as to try and wake up your himagination when its determined to have a nap."

"What would you advise me to do?" says I.

"Let it alone," says he. "Go out and walk, or sit down and mend your tarpaulins. The mind of man, old mesmet, is a terrible perplexin' thing, and werry like a woman; worry and hunt after it, and ten to one if it doesn't play hide an' seek with you, till you lose it altogether, but keep never mindin' for a few bells, and you'll find it come to you nateral.

"If so be as you are goin' free and full afore the wind, why crack on in coorse with all the canvas you can spread, but purwided that it chops round and blows dead ahead, why 'bout ship's the word."

So 'bout it is.

XIII.

The Captain and Jack luxuriate in the Indian Summer weather, of which they record their impressions, and contrast with the Novembers on the other side—Jack acknowledges his partiality to fog, and accounts for it naturally enough, thereby arousing the ire of the Captain, who makes disrespectful insinuations with regard to the extent of Jack's knowledge, branching off into strictures upon sectional prejudices and the unhealthy state of education generally.

The Cap'n an' me turned out bright an' early this mornin' jest for no other reason in the world than to enjoy the slice o' fairy weather as is sandwitched in between the Hautumn and the Winter, in these here werry highly-favored latitudes, what one might call the soft, beautiful twilight of the year—a kind of general sunset afore the night season sets in.

There ain't no part o' the year but what has some'a to make it pleasin', if only in the way of wariety, but it does seem as if all the months had clubbed their beautifullest bits o' sunshine, and poured it out at oncet, to give the earth a glorious holiday.

"And hain't she grateful for it?" says the Cap'n. "In coorse she is! and doesn't she make the most of it? in coorse she does. Why the werry days, drinkin' in the spirit o' joy and happiness, gets hintoxicated with delight, and goes to bed in a sort o' haze, and, as is the natur' of men and things under sich sarcumstances, gets up in the mornin' a little foggy at the first go off."

"It's what they calls here the Indian Summer, I bleeve," says I.

"Werry like," says the Cap'n, "and beautiful as it is, they tell me it's only the tail end of it we get here, but off there in the West, it would take the eyesight clean out of a chap as has bin used to the drizzly, sloppy, uncomfortable Novembers our way."

"Well now, say what you like," says I, "there's some'at comfortable even in that drizzly slop. I likes it better nor the finest sunshine you could manufactur', cos it's at home. Home! ah! that's the word as brightens the darkest, dismallest lot. I don't care who knows it. I likes that 'ere drizzle."

"In coorse you does, you henthusiastic owld stockfish, or you thinks you does, which amounts to the same thing," says the Cap'n, a jeerin' like. "That ere's one of the consequences of the wery circumscribed hextent o' hedication in our times. Hinstead o' cultiwatin' a universal love for hall mankind—for this here world hain't sich a houtrageous size as to make a fuss about little bits of it:—the fellows as has charge of our intellectuals, crams us full of sectionalities, huntil we naterally looks upon ourselves as the honly nation as has any right to elewate our figure-heads and stare the sky in the face, and ekally despises all them as had the misfortune to be born anywhere else.

"Why there hain't a schoolbook as you kin take up—leastways in my time, they're better now—but what you'll find glorification on one side, and ridicule or imperence o' some sort on the other. Ain't the youth of hevery country, that is to say sich countries as lays claim to civilization, ain't they heverlastin'ly tutored only jest for the circle as they're to rewolve within. Did you hever know the hedication of a hofficer, for instance, to take him further nor the cabin door. What is he perpetually towld to do. Why to behave himself *like* a hofficer. Now hif they'd honly stretch hout the advice, and tell him, on all hoccasions, to hact like a *man*, Latin and Greek couldn't teach him more."

"Then it's your opinion that there ain't hedication enough," says I.

"Too much, Jack, too much," says he, "but it ain't in the right coorse, nor it ain't of the right sort. There's a heap o' knowledge swallowed at them colleges, to be sure, but it's so mixed up with small prejudices and chunks o' hignorance pitched in by the perfessers themselves, for of hall the hignorance in the world' the self-satisfied, pompous hignorance of them turnip-faced pumps in spectacles is the most hamusin' to them as knows what a werry hinsignificant part of hedication as *is* hedication books is; that when a poor word-tortured devil comes out among men, he finds that he's bin feedin' upon owld pages like a moth, and the consequence is, nine times out of ten, he flies right into the flame, and hastonishes his wings. Why, sich fellers has no more right to tie down the thoughts, feelins an' haffections of hindiwiduals to one perticklar spot o' ground, no more nor if that same spot had a hexclusive hatmosphere, or went on its hown hook in the way o' rewolwin'.

"A good Providence has circled the uniwersal globe, as we ain't worthy to inhabitate, with one beautiful canopy o' hair, and hevery livin' creeter gets his share of the same, purwided that his lungs is in good horder, don't he?"

"Aye aye," says I.

"Werry well, then," says he, "if any set o' folks opens their mouths wider, to show they have a better right to breathe the general hair nor any hothers—why they'll only hurt their jaws a-stretchin', or get laughed at by the rest o' the world for makin' faces."

"How is that 'ere sort o' thing to be prewented?" says I.

"Now you puzzles me, Jack," says he. "Hedication has bin so long a-goin' on in the same owld jog-trot that them as deals therein thinks it wouldn't be safe to go faster. The mind o' man, Jack, wants judicious feelin' jest the same as the body, and sich solid hunks of jints as is cut out o' the dead languages, and bolted at the banquets of sense, must result in a reglar dyspeepsy o' knowledge. Sposin' now a chap tucks in a lot o' dinner every day, punishin' nothin' but substantial gallops o' meat, don't it stand to reason that he's only purwidin' fodder for a troop of nightmares. So it is with them as is crammed with too much hacquisition; their heads ain't bright and clear and comfortable, but they are perpetually sufferin' hunder a sort of hindigestion of hintellect."

"There ain't no chance of the things bein' haltered now," says I.

"That jest shows how little you know about it," says the Cap'n, in a way as made me feel werry hinsignificant. "It's halterin' hevery day, you grampus; the folks has found out that them 'ere colleges, conducted as they used to be, was a destroyin' the very character of the country through its supporters, that hiniquity an' hall kinds o' wiciousness was the classics as were taught, where, if a man wentured to study anything good or useful, he stood a rare chance of bein' sneered at for a fool, and that the most finished scholars were those as could make the best book at the races, drink hardest, swear loudest, and shock decency in the houtrageousest manner.

"Both the rich boy and the poor one find it difficult to avoid catching some bad characteristic from the companions by which they are surrounded; if either of them reach manhood a gentleman, and escape pure of heart and mild of manner from such association, I think, the chances are in favor of the poorer youth. Poverty forces men into crime from necessity, oftentimes against the will, but Luxury lures them into it, through hindulgence and full hinclination."

"Werry well then," says I, "The haim of your hobserwation goes to the hassertion, that there are more gentlemen in heart and feelin' to be found among the poorer classes than the rich."

"Well," says the Cap'n, a nibblin' of his hook. "Old mesmet, mayhap it may, and then again mayhap it mayn't."

"If so be, what's the hodds."

XIV.

The Captain and Jack, after an evening's amusement, indulge in a morning reflection, acknowledging the corn, and moralizing thereon profoundly.—They touch slightly on Temperance, a dry subject, which they may probably dig deeper into at some future time.—The Captain evidences his acquaintance with Greek philosophy in general, and that of Epicurus in particular, to the great edification of Jack, who waxes uncommonly thirsty, and receives an admonition in a parable which may be understood by many.

THE Cap'n an' me is a sufferin' this mornin' from a carcumstance as I'm a'most ashamed to make public, but they say "honest confessions is good for the sowl, eh Cap'n?"

"Aye, aye, Jack," says he, a forcin' the words through jest as if there was a firstrate cobweb a festooned across his throat; "hout with it, 'taint murder, you know, there's some as thinks it nigh as sinful."

Well then, here goes.—Now if so be as you're a water-drinker, and prides yerself thereon, you, I mean, as is perusin' this here line, prepare to squirm and look as if you'd bin lunchin' on lemons, bark out loud and cry hawful! but if so be, on the contrary, as you loves temperateness, and doesn't wear no horder in yer face to show the world what a hesteemable creeter you are, you'll maybe whisper to yerself, poor fellows! and pity our weakness rather than rejoice in your own strength.

But if so be, agin, as you happens to hindulge, not hoften, for that's foolish, nor hall the time, for that's beastly, but jest now and then, in a few hextra liquorin's, not rushed hinto for the mere love o' the thing, but a growin' hout of hoccasions, fruits as haint wilfully plucked from the tree o' sarcumstance, but what a body might call windfalls a droppin' into your mouth in the nateral coorse o' things, and in hobedience to the laws o' gravity—if so be as you're one o' them 'ere indiwiduals, you'll slap us imaginationally on our backs, and call us "jolly cocks."

Now it's comin'—look sharp, purfessors o' Temperance, look sorry, practizers of the same, and look any way you please, you as stretches your hinclinations, now and then.

The Cap'n and me was round the horn last night.

"Drunk, Jack," says the Cap'n, lookin' werry serious. "Hout with it honest; drunk we were, and now we're a sufferin' for it, and it sarves us right."

"Not so bad as that," says I. "I ain't a goin' to allow it."

"You can't help yourself," says he. "The man as is not sober must be drunk. There ain't no hintermediate state as I knows of; there's a meterial difference between a man and a ship in this here perticklar. A man steers by the head, and a ship by the hopposite hextremity; but in either case there must be some one at the wheel; and the minute the rudder's let go, the hull's at the marcy o' the tempest, purwidin' it blows; therefore it stands to reason, when yer sense is beginning to ewaporate, there hain't no use in your a tryin' to steer a sensible coorse."

"That's all ship-shape enough," says I. "But when the sea's all smooth, you kin tie her up and let her run alone for a spell."

"Not a bit on it, Jack," says the Cap'n, a heloquently drivin' of his hook into the table about a hinch; "not a bit on it. It's werry bad seamanship to let a wessel have her own head even for a sekind o' time. Squalls is werry unsartain—and arter a craft's on her beam ends, it's too late to cry, 'who'd a thought it?' No, no, Jack, old mesmet, when a man woluntarily surrenders the rudder o' reason, not only a walkin' away from it, but lettin' the spirit o' foolishness lay howld of it—for there's another difference between men and ships,

Jack, and a huncommon remarkable one it is; if you gives up a ship's helm, you leaves it to chance, as won't take no houtrageous hadwantage, but when reason is druv away, folly takes his place, and can't keep it long neither, not havin' no capacity, so that if reason don't come back, madness knocks his father, folly, on the head, seizes the wheel, and away goes hevery thing to Davy Jones, helter-skelter."

"Wery well, Cap'n, be it so," says I. "I ain't a goin' to argufy the case for this here reason. I hentirely agrees with you chock a block. All I wants to hinsinivate, and I does it more because I thinks I ought to diskiver somethin' in the way of a hexcuse—howld on till I'm done—I knows I'm wrong."

"Me too, me too, Jack," says he on a suddent, "I'm the worst. I ought to have showed a better hexample."

"You be blowed," says I. "Don't go for to hinterrupt me agin. I only wants to say, by the way of hapology, that I was hovertook, as you was, not bein' neither on us in the habit of hindulgin', we was hoff our guard, and the inemy hentered unbeknownst. Pooh! don't keep on a shakin' of your head; doesn't I know, jest as well as you do, that sich a lame hexcuse can't stand nohow, if so be as you comes to right hup an' down argeymint? but can't you let a fellow flatter hisself that folks 'll wink a bit at it, and suffer it to go unnoticed?"

"There's one thing, owld shipmet, as you ought to know if you don't," says the Cap'n, "and that's this, there's werry little winkin' among folks, when they're a lookin' at hother people's misdemeanors, instead o' shavin' a slice off, they generally slaps a chunk on. They takes hobserwations of other folk's follies through a hunkimmon large telescope, but they rewarses the hinstrument when they're a tryin' to dis-diskiver their hown; and do you know why they do this,

Jack? I'll tell you: it's jest a delusive way of tryin' to cheat theirselves into the belief that their misfortunes ain't nothin' in the scale when weighed agin the faults o' hothers. No, Jack; there hain't no excuse for it whatsomedever, not no how, no ways. Nature's the great horacle always, Jack. She never does nothin' without a meanin' and a motive. What do you think she stuffed these here wedges o' pain in our indiwidual heads for, this mornin? Why to make us feel that we hacted wrong last night.

"Them owld ancient philosophers knew a thing or two, Jack. Didn't they?"

"Well, I bleeve they did! I never knowd any of 'em," says I.

"Why, they tell me mesmet," says the Cap'n, a puttin' on his schoolmaster look, as is beautiful to see, in regard of the sense as looms out all hower his countenance, "they tell me, that one of them ould Greeks, with a houtlandish name, lays it down as a rule, that there's a ekal balance all through the uniwarsal world; and in my hinsignificant mite of a mind, he hain't far away from the truth ne'ther. He says, hevery haccountable man must keep a kind of debtor and creditor book within, good and evil are the figures he works with, and the haccumulation is either happiness or misery; moreover, he contends, that there hain't a single bad haction of a man's life, from the smallest mistake hup to the greatest crime, but is debited its amount of punishment. Conscience, the uncorruptible bookkeeper, puts it down, and sarcumstance, as you are doin' the business o' life with, pays you back to the werry uttermost pennyweight; but hif so be as you does the thing what's right, the greater amount of good you do, the more return you gets in comfort an' happiness."

"And a werry hexcellent sort o' philosophy, too," says I, "in respect of its makin' people think a little afore they does a wrong haction, for feared of the himmediate consequences of the same; likewise, a stimulatin' them to rightful conduct, in the hopes of a correspondin' reward soon."

But at this period o' time, my throat got as dry as a lime-burner's wig, and I was a-goin' to wet my whistle from the junk-bottle, when the Cap'n, a layin' of his hook solidly on my harm, shakes his wenerable head, and says,—"Jack!"

"Aye, aye," says I.

"Did you hever scratch an ould muskeeter bite; one as you thought was dead an' gone?"

"Werry hoften," says I, "and always found 'em burn stinginer than before."

"Take that 'ere lesson to your heart, Jack," says he, "and never attempt to wake up an ould drunk."

Ne'ther don't you.

XV.

A few more remarks on Rum and its consequences—The Captain enlightens Jack with regard to the various reasons which instigate the thirsty portions of the community to swallow the fiery temptation; he also gives some illustrations of Temperance and its professors, giving honor where honor is due, and vice versa, together with some profound observations on various subjects, having a tendency to uphold real Religion and to pull down Hypocrisy, interspersed with small bits of Poetry, Philosophy, extraordinary apothegms and other matters well worthy of investigation, perhaps.

"JACK!"

"Aye, aye!"

"That 'ere rum ain't quite out o' me yet. When a chap fills his glass too full, it must swamp the table-cloth, and it depends on the quality o' the liquor, as well as the quantity, how long the stain 'll last."

That's the werry significant hobserwation as the Cap'n

begun the mornin' with yesterday; a hobservation as I felt in duty bound to agree with, for the reason that the state of my hupper works painfully persuaded me that there warn't no mistake at all about the matter. "Cap'n," says I, a throwin' out a bait for a chunk o' wisdom, "What's the reason that folks will suck at the wagabone stuff when hexperience has towld 'em hover and hover agin, that the consequences is so onpleasin'?"

"What's the reason," says he, "warious, Jack, warious. One chap lays howld o' the liquor because he likes the taste on it—it's agreeable to his palate; another because he's low-spirited and seeks a bit of hexcitement; then agin, some fellows get jolly in company, and scarcely know that they're a drinkin' at all until their senses is under water; them is the most pardonable of all, but the private soakers as locks themselves up with the grog, and mugs themselves, alone, I'd have every selfish son of a monkey up to the gratings if I had my own way.

"There's a wast deal of hexcuse for the poor world-crushed, poverty-stricken wretch who rushes to a dram whenever he can steal a small amount from the cravings of his hunger to get it with. Charity, Jack, winks hard at that 'ere transgression, whatever the snugly-housed, self-complaisant, cellar-stocked humbugs may say to the contrary. If one of the latter well-fed fraternity meets a poor devil a little "how come you so," pooh! how he squirms and sniffs, and turns up his dainty nose, with perhaps a hypocritical hejaculation touchin' the depravity of human natur'—pickles! let them change places. Let the rich home-sensualist lose his cozey snuggery for a month—let him try and push his way through the bristling *chevaux de frize* the power of wealth has strewn around the poor man, called by high-sounding names, law, morality, nay sometimes the sacred name of religion is used, to keep the starving brother from seizing on his right—to stifle, in his grumbling internals, the envy of his overgorged relation—let him do that 'ere, then see if he won't try and quench the burning brand of care within him, with a toothful whenever he has a chance."

'Aye, but does it quench care," says I.

"No, not a bit on it, Jack," says he, "not no more nor a shower of rain could quench the stars; you don't see 'em while it lasts, but they shine out mighty bright arterwards; jest so it is a tryin' to drive out care with drams; it may make him a little sleepy for a short spell, but he's sure to wake up savager nor ever."

There's bin a deal o' good done by that 'ere temperance thing," says I, a wonderin' how he'd take it, for the Cap'n don't despise his grog no ways, neither is he shamefaced about anybody a seein' of him toss it off; there hain't no shabby underhanded slyness about him.

"There has, Jack," says he, "a wast quantity, and it's a honor an' a credit to them as adwised sich a movement, likewise also to them as follows it from the heart, real and conscientious-like, but old mesmet, there's a jolly lot o' purfessors as goes through the motions in public, and practises werry different behind their parlor doors. At the same time recollect that don't take away from the excellence of the system, if it's gone into nateral, that is to say, if a man likes to habstain hisself.

"But I hobjects entirely to their making a parade and a hostentatious play-hactin' consarn of it. There was a time when a fellow as thought he was tolerable good, was parfeckly contented to keep it to hisself, but now he must have banners an' stars an' rosettes an' diplomas, and nobody knows what, to let the world see what a piehouse creeter he is."

"Well now, that's a fact," says I, "that is a fact. There

hain't nothin', it seems to me, as some folks won't do, to have a chance of hornamentin' theirselves a trifle. If a youngster feels a little downey about the chin, he must belong to some phalanx or hassociation or debatin' society or hamateur someat or another. Arter a boy's got out o' jacket and trousers, he never rests no how until he's hid behind a big scarf, or knocked into a cocked hat."

"It's easily accounted for, old tar," says the Cap'n. "It's only one proof among the thousands that can be perduced that nobody ain't haltogether satisfied with the part he's got to play in the great drama of Hexistance. Destiny, the stage manager, casts him for the character he has to sustain, but he has the actor's privilege of grumblin' at it, whatever it is, some on 'em just for the sake of kickin' up a row, some because they are conceited enough to think they could shine in a higher line, and others, because they really are better fitted to enact the parts they see smaller geniuses struttin' about in, daily and hourly. Hall those hextravagances as you speaks of is only the hefforts as they makes to be something else rather than what they are."

"It is werry remarkable," says I, "what a tendency there is for folks to wish themselves in amost hany other station than that in which God's wisdom placed them."

"And unkimmon foolish it is, Jack. The worst of it is, we all know that it is so, jest like what we were talkin' about in the respect of drinkin'; we knows it's wrong, yet at it we goes agin, arter the headache's hover. As to henvyin' people as is better off nor ourselves, and wantin' to be in their places, what do we know of the number of concealed sorrows as is tearin' away his heart, notwithstandin' the smilin' lips as is turned to the world. At best it would only be hexchangin' discontents, for take my word for it, he wants to be a step higher nor he is; and the further up you are, the more fierce is the desire to reach the top. A man as lives at the bottom of a mountain he couldn't climb without wings, lies down in comfort, and never thinks of the summit, but if there's hever so difficult a pathway, there 'll be much waste of time and breath, much hagitation, toil and trouble before the top is gained."

"Yes, Cap'n, and how few is satisfied when they get there," says I. "Indeed, how few of the millions as are groanin' and sweatin' and laborin' hever comes within hailin' distance of their hexpectations at all."

"Aye, aye, Jack," says he, "and then the kickin' and bitin' and strugglin' not to elewate themselves, but to prewent those around from goin' ahead, ha! ha! I thinks I sees 'em Jack, in a sort o' wison, some dartin' off in a hurry; they'll soon get winded and loose ground; some slow and steady; some, instead of smoothin' their own road, plantin' thorns in the way of those who are coming after—they forget that in retracin' their steps they'll only lacerate their own feet; to make amends, there are others, self-sacrificing, pure, noble-hearted lovers of their species, who disdainin' their own advancement, cheer and help along the weak, or the crippled, sowin' flowers in the path of the wayfarer,—flowers upon whose winged odors the soul of the benefactor is wafted to the realms of heverlastin' happiness an' joy."

"I wish some on 'em would make theirselves known to me," says I, "jest that they might lend me a hand to get my little boat through the shallows. I never sees none on 'em."

"No, nor never will Jack," says he, the logical ould warmint, "and for this here reason, the minut a man talks about, or makes a hexebition o' his piety, and so forth, you may jest take your oath that it's not the real harticle. Spurious goods, Jack, spurious goods."

"And yet they'll pass the world's custom house reg'lar enough," says I.

"In coorse they will, Jack; hif the formal duties is paid, that's all they care about," says he; "not only will they pass on the books, but when man's uniwarsal creditor, Death, walks in and breaks up the hestablishment, they'll be registered among his assets as bonyfiddy wartues, and werry probably be hinscribed upon the tombstone, as sarves for the certificate of his good behavior."

"If so it is, why so let it be."

XVI.

The Captain peruses one of the "influential dailies," and upon reading the latest intelligence from Europe, shows much irritability, railing "in good set terms" against Austria, with a slight allusion to Ursa Major; he and Jack converse about various matters connected with the present state of Europe, its civilization and policy, the Hungarian refugees, magnanimity of the Turks, and do a foolish thing by administering a deserved rebuke to those to whom it will do no good.

As the Cap'n was a lookin' over the newspaper this mornin', for one of them 'ere "hinfluential sheets" is perfeckly hindispensible to us at breakfast—jest as he was in the hact of swallerin' a basin of bohea, he dashed down the paper, and nibblin of his hook as he halways does when he's hout o' sorts, "Jack," says he, werry savage for him, "they purtend that this here is a hage of henlightenment and hintellect, and all them there capers. Humbug! Look at that there paragraft." With these words he directed my heyes to a bit o' news as made my weskit tight, for the swellin' of my heart, as I read it. It was an account of the willinies of them 'ere Haustrians in regard of butcherin' the women an' children, together with shootin' and hangin' and torturin' the brave people as they warn't hable to subdue single-handed.

Well, I looked hinto the Cap'n's heyes when I'd finished the hawful relation, an' it was a glarin' on me as if I was a kind of haccomplice in the rascality by not burstin' out into a roar of hindignation; but the fact was, I hadn't got hover the pity for the murdered, whereas he had, and therefore had the adwantage o' me there.

"You stony-hearted, sea-farin' statue of a nable sailor, why don't you hexpress an opinion? Ain't it houtrageous? ain't it hatrocious? Speak hout, you porpoise, or I'll fling the cup at your lubber's head."

"In coorse it is," says I, werry suddent, for I knew well enough I might expect the chaney somewhere about my figure-head if I didn't answer quick. The Cap'n bein', like a'most all hother heasy-goin' folks, mighty hobstrepulous, when the stick of provocation was long enough to stir up his temper.

"In *coorse* it is;" says he; "there can't be a livin' tongue as hinterprets the language of a humane heart, that won't say the same out loud. It may begin with a whisper first, but it must hincrease to a hurricane afore long. Jack, I wouldn't henvy the man, whatever country he might belong to, as could read that 'ere haccount without wishing the condemnation and punnishment of eternal justice to be poured out upon the scoundrel brood; and it will come, mesmet, depend upon it, it will come. If God's vengence surely overtakes the life-taker—how can it overlook the slaughterers of a nation."

"It aint like reading the hoccurrences of the present time nohow," says I.

"That it aint," says he, "at all ewents not in civilized Europe, as it is so everlastingly a boastin' of its refinement and humanity. Why, Jack, hif sich a tale was told of a pack of New Zealanders, or hany other hunnatural savages, don't you suppose that all the so-called Christian world would jine together and hexterminate the wretches. Yes, that they would, and sarve them right, too, and yet come to the justice of the thing: in their case they would be honly follerin' the hinstincts of their brutal natur' and the requirements of their dark hidolatry; but in the other, heverything that they have been taught to believe good and proper is trampled under foot, and the werry rites of a religion which preaches "peace to all men" shamefully burlesqued by being called into requisition for the purpose of glorifying wholesale murder.

"Aint nobody goin' to take no notice of it," says I.

"Jack, old mesmet," says he, "it aint necessary;" then respectfully a pullin' of his hat, he went on werry serious: "There's a power above," says he; "a judge as holds the balance of good and evil; wait—when the scale of their hiniquity is full, and it must be gettin' near it now."

"It's unkimmon large if it aint," says I.

"Then," says he, "the weight of sure coming justice will be dropped into the other side, and what'll become of the wrong doers? why destruction everlastin' must overwhelm them, for if there aint an after life of sufferin' for a present one of iniquity, it wouldn't be exactly fair to sich of us poor creeters as strives to do the proper thing to heverybody. They'll catch it, Jack, some of these fine days, see if they don't; and then won't humanity open its mouth and laugh, until the heavens ring again with the rewerberation o' joy.

"Aint England and France a-goin' to take it up?" says I.

"Pooh! They pretended to do some'at the first go-off, but what did it amount to?" says he, with the contemptuousest expression as he could call up to his benevolent phizog. "What did it hamount to?" I says again, jest so much bladher. "Why didn't they back up that 'ere trump of a

Turk as taught the Christians the duty of men. No! not a bit on it; them there stars and ribbons met together, and policy rode over humanity, as it almost always does. Why, it would scarcely be credited if it was in a book: that Christian Europe sot quietly down, while the remains of a brave band of free souls were offered the choice between given up their faith or their lives. No, sir! They'd look upon it as a Baron Munchausen lie; but it aint. They know, the blood-suckers, how to torture a man's heart—when tender women and children are hangin' upon the life's breath of a man, why in coorse he must brave the hindignation of bigots, who would rather he should die, stifling the voice of natur' in the shouts of the cold-hearted zealot; what do they care about the home destroyed and hearts desolated? No! their hexclusive hopinions must be substantiated by blood, and the hobstinate fools, they glorify with the sublime title of martyrs, die in a delusive hextasy.

"Some on 'em has turned Turks, aint they?" says I.

"What could the poor creeters do. Ain't I a tryin' to find an hexcuse for them now; Bem, they say, has put a syllable or two to his name, and hadded a tail or two to his title; but what has that to do with the inard feelings, thoughts and hinclinations of the man his self; they can't change his natur', with his name, neither can they change his religion with the rites. Everlasting wisdom and Justice looks to the heart,—thank God for it—and not to houtside show. He knows and weighs the secret of the soul, depend upon it, Jack; men are not judged by the manner in which they *perform* their devotions, but the spirit that hinstigates them thereto; this man who faces the dismay and horror with which priest-ridden people regard the stepper aside from their particular path—this man who conceals the barbed arrow in his own heart—for who doubts but that he would rather die a thousand deaths, than live infamous in the eyes of a few, and even to preserve a life dearer to all others than to himself, he is the martyr who deserves immortal honours."

"The hover pious folks will be down on them hawful, eh, Cap'n?" says I.

"In coorse they will, has in dooty bound," says he. "There's a some'at so hexcruciatin' in the phrase 'he's turned Turk,' why it sounds worse nor to say 'he's turned Jew,' and yet compare both on 'em and where'll our Hebrew friend be; but what o' that? don't Christians confabulate comfortably with them? In coorse they do, to be sure they have an ould score to pay off—but its goin' by installments; the chosen people have always bin celebrated for their skill in business transactions hever since the hosier peeling affair, not to say a word about the mess o' pottage, so they have bought the privileges, and for a purty large sum, or history hexaggerates considerable; wealthy people is wery respectable companions, and I rather think in this stage of the world's biography, the cloak of charity ain't a circumstance to the capaciousness of money's garment in respect of coverin' sins."

"Ain't it the women, Cap'n," says I, "as swells the houtcry agin' the Turks, as regards that 'ere polly bigamy?"

"Well mesmet," says he, a laughin' like a good 'un, "mayhap it is; at all events, they certainly has some cause to complain, they haint got their fair share of priveleges no how; but the march o' hintellect will soon remedy hall that 'ere in time."

XVII.

The conversation turns upon Fashion, its vagaries and its votaries, its absurdities, impertinences and inconsistencies—The Captain brings a heavy charge against nature, and draws comparisons unfavorable to the male portion of humanity—Jack endeavors to account for sundry phenomena, and puts his foot in it—The Captain eulogizes clean faces, and decidedly sets his own against whitewash, whereat Jack presumes personally to address the ladies on the subject of cosmetics.

The Captain and me turned out this arternoon for to have a cruise up the Broadway channel; it was the time o' day as the titivated doors of nothin' calls mornin'—bless their hunsophistic naters, they knows as little about that there hexilira-tin' period, as they does about jometry, and it is really surprisin' to see the creeters lookin' as fresh as paint, 'specially the feminine hornaments o' creation, jest as if they had their reg'lar spell o' that 'ere 'sweet refreshment sleep,' as the poet says—I ain t sure which ne'ther does it sinify—when hevery body knows, leastways hevery body as knows hanything knows, that the sad, silent hours o' the night, as likes to glide away in secret while men's heyes is closed, are stared right out o' countenance by them there fashionable peepers—for it's one of the werry choicest and universalist privileges of the top sawyers, to look at hevery thing, heven the most modestest and sacredest, with lids wide open—likewise to talk loud in public hassemblies—that their peculiarly modish practice hain't got into church yet—but there's a kind of howdacious whisper hecos through them hedifices now, as shows that it's a comin'. Upon my hintimatin' that hidea o mine to the Cap'n—

"Jack," says he, "you're right, old salt, quite right. Hif a fellow wants to see the onrulyest and worst-manneredest crowd as could be collected together—he has honly to inwestigate a first-rate fashionable hassemblage. Let a poor devil of a stranger show his phisog among 'em—one as don't belong to their 'sets'—hit's their own word, Jack, and a good un too—Lord, won't hall the heyes in the place flash out at him, 'What brings you here?' as plain as a speakin' trumpet? If so be as the hintruder has narve enough to stand the heyes, why the tongues goes at him werry hunceremonious, huntil the miserable wictim of sarcumstances looks like a stupid, and hultimately sneaks hoff, 'ready to jump sky high for joy that he's got hout o' the harctic hatmosphere."

"That there Fashion," says I, "is a hard taskmaster."

"It ain't nothin' else," says he; "moreover, if a chap binds hisself thereto, he voluntarily gives up his liberty to a life-long apprenticeship."

Just at that moment there came bearin' down afore us one of them 'ere hengine-turned, capped and jewelled speciments of she humanity as seems to be specially hordained for the consumption o' welwets and hother hextravagancies—a high-finished creeter as you would no more hassociate with the makin' of a puddin', or the doin' of yany thing at all useful, no more nor you could think of a jolly feed and a boardin' house dinin' table at the same conjunction o' time. The Cap'n and me made a dent in a shop door a steerin' out of her coorse, but she never haltered it a point—no, nor would'nt —if we'd a kep on, she'd a run us down jest as sure as my name's Jack.

Well, when she passed on, a jerkin' of her purty head like a pigeon pickin' peas, the Cap'n lifted off his tarpaulin, and giving his owld bald a hunnecessary scratch with the hook, looks arter her wake, but didn't say nothin'. I knew there was a chunk a comin', so I kep' quiet,—and it did too.

"Mesmet," says he, "did it hever strike you as some'at

werry remarkable, that us hemales of the humane specie was treated rather bad by Mother Natur—aye, Jack, worser nor the beats. Why there hain't a bird as flies but has the adwantage of us."

"How so, Cap'n?" says I, a feedin' of him cunnin'.

"How so? why in the regard of hexternal hornament. Look at the brutes, as don't care about it—hasn't the sense to hestimate it—an' tell me which is the finest-lookin' and most ornamentedest speciments—why the gen'lmen hanimals in coorse; then go among the birds, and you'll find that the he's has it all to nothin' in respect o' plumage—while us poor, ill-used man folks is snuffed hout altogether by the superiour skill and workmanship ewinced in the manafactur' of the feminines, 'tain't exactly the Stilton no how. I goes for ekal rights and democratic principles, to the end o' the chapter."

"Don't you think?" says I, "that there's a good deal in the 'dresses an' decorations,' as the showpeople has it. The women ain't such gump heads as to enwelope their hanatomies in the clumsey, slovenly, wagabone, no-shaped hatrocities as them high priests o' fashion the tailors insists upon the men hidin' themselves hunder. Hevery change it seems to me only gets us deeper in the hocean of hugliness; jest look at them specimens 'afore us now. You can't see no feet nor not no hands, hevery helegant full dressed hindividual now, looks as if he had his big brother's coat on, somebody else's pantaloons, and his great grandfather's weskit; but do you hever see the shemales a disfiguratin' themselves? not a bit on it; they're all trim and tight, and set off to the greatest adwantage. 'Tain't a fair shake Cap'n; jest go and take the curls away, and the hear-drops, necklaces, bracelets and finery, shut up Stewart's and banish Professor Gouraud, and where'll they be then?"

"There is a some'at in that Jack to be sure," says he, "but at the same time you ain't a goin' to flatter your hugly mug, that it's carved out in the same sort o' way, not a bit on it—there haint no differ in the material, but we're chopped out o' the rough log, without some on us havin' the mark o' the haxe scraped off, but they are planed up and sand-papered down, weneered an' warnished up to the nines."

"And yet they haint satisfied with that, least-ways a jolly lot on 'em haint," says I. "But lays on the whitenin' stuff a himprovin of nater."

"Which is wery habsurd to suppose that they do do, mesmet," says the Cap'n. "Ah! Jack, gi' me the lively bright nateral cheek, with the down a lieing on it like the sunny side of a ripe peach, full o' healthy moisture—sweet, crisp and dewey as an unplucked rose-leaf of a summer's morning;—them's the faces for me, old tar, glowing with real unmistakable life and loveliness, conscious of legitimate soap and water, fresh, wholesome, clean and kissable, not the doll-baby, lime-burnt, dried up, harsh, and altogether unsatisfactory masks as you sometimes meet with;—them there chalky countenances, that if a chap was to attempt for to kiss them, would pucker his lips into a hinwoluntary whistle."

Now that 'ere's wisdom if you like. I didn't say so to him cos there was no hoccasion for it, but I says to you now, that I hentirely agrees with the Cap'n, and moreover not that, I conscientiously b'leeve that there ain't a man as walks, but will coincide with us in our hopinion.

Therefore, if so be as it is so, my dear darling of the blessedest sex, don't go for to do such a presumptuous thing as to try your hinexperienced hands in the face-making line agin' that ould hartist, natur'; you see you hain't bin a practisin' of it honly for a few years at most, but the other hindiwidual has worked at it since the beginnin' o' the world.

And so, hopin' that you'll hacknowledge the habsurdness of the hattempt, do for gracious sake wash off the chalk, and let us see a little more of the human face dewine.

XVIII.

The Captain delivers sundry pertinent, although perhaps not over characteristic remarks—which the author acknowledges with deference, for the propitiation of the critics, should such condescend to peruse his hasty and impossible-to-be-well-digested observations—upon the "present horror of the time"—Jack describes a sudden change in the Captain's temperature, and satisfactorily accounts for the same—They then discourse upon very serious and opposite subjects, winding up with an opinion which is confidently expected to be acknowledged as an opinion.

"MURDER!

"What a thrill of horror that there word of two syllables calls up, by merely spelling of it hover, but when it's caught up and shouted by thousands o' woices until it echos through the werry hatmosphere, so that hevery moaning wind-gust seems to wail it into your ear, it's hawful; just at this present moment o' time, the scent o' blood is on the air; Murder holds Carnival, an unnatural shadow stands within the path of thought—unnatural because cast from no ray of light, but all stark, and black, and spectral,—while the bright, beautiful, God's earth, seen through the fearful medium sarcumstance has placed before the eyes of man, shows red and angry, as though the world's glorious sun had quenched itself within a sea of crimson.

"Howsomedever, one man's poison is another man's meat, as the saying is, and the terrible doings of the last few weeks, has given a respite to the fagged-out brains of the newspaper feeders, as had nothing but Hungary to cut into for the benefit of their readers, and it is astonishin' what a woracious happetite that there dewourin' public has in the way of news; how it feasts its heyes upon a rich bit of horror, and swallows down a dish of nastiness with the woluptuous relish of a gutter-ploughing hog."

Them there's the solid hobserwations the Cap'n made this werry blessed mornin', as he was a crackin' of his second hegg, which didn't turn out hover an' above palatable, by reason of its bein' rather chicken-hearted. Whereat he up and spoke in disrespectful terms of the half-hatched habomination, likewise of its himmediate hancestors. I makes this here hexplanation by way of haccountin' for the biliousness of the few remarks as I have jest quoted.

But bless his owld hook and eye—when he's done a nibblin' of one, good temper shines out o' the other. His bit of cross humor is only a squall, purty sharp and suddent, but hover in a hinstant, whereas some fellows blows a reg'lar gale o' hanger as drives you out of your recknin', or enwelopes you in a fog o' sulk you can't see your way through no how. As soon as I seed the nateral smile a playin' about his jolly ould countenance, as if there was a sort of mirthquake a running under his cheeks, and tryin' to force its way hout some of it findin' went at his heyes, as sparkled all hover with a kind of sunnv spray. I knew that I might wenture a hopinion, and so I lets fly one at him, slap, in these here identical words:—

"Cap'n," says I, "haint it werry surprisin' that great crimes, like misfortunes, never comes singly, but whenever you hears of somethin' hout of the way bad' you're a'most sure to find some hothers of a similar character?"

"Well, that has struck me, Jack," says he, "in a hunthink-about-it-sort of a way, but I haint never tried to go into the real bearin's of it; that there sarcumstance is most hevidenced in the matter of men's making away with themselves. There has been, afore now, fashionable ways of gettin' rid of the load o' life, and let hany horiginal genius find out a novelty in the way of makin' his hexit, there'll be sure to be a suicidal hepidemic right hoff. When that there young female thought proper to fling herself from the top of the Monument in London, didn't the love-sick or gin-sick noodles dash in the place where their brains ought to be, in that there high style, until the hauthorities netted it over like a hammock?"

"To be sure they did," says I. "The bridges were unkimmon fashionable at one time for jumping-hoff places; what is it, I wonder, as drives people to do sich desperate things?"

"Warious causes, Jack," says he. "In the young 'uns, it's love; and I tell you, a sharp attack of that 'ere complaint confuses a feller's brains considerable, 'specially if the hobject aint get-at-able; a hobstruction in sich a current dams up the senses mighty quick, if they don't happen to be jolly strong."

"Aye, that's likely enough," says I; middle-aged ones. I can't satisfactionally to myself haccount for a man as is a full-grow'd man a cuttin' off his own thread, and lettin' hisself tumble down into the blackness of uncertainty."

"Ah, Jack, old messmet," says he solidly, "them 'ere matters is habove our comprehendin'. My private hopinion is, that the two greatest causes of the hinsanity, as usually precedes that there life-quelling hextremity, is perduced heither by not givin' the brains enough to do, or by overtaxin' of them too much. You never hear of sich a thing takin' place among people as labors with their muscles to scrape a small livin' hout of stony fortune, but the hover-fed, lazy-headed do-nothings, lets their hintellects fatten upon luxurious hidleness, until it smothers itself in a fit of hapoplexy; but of all the cases of the kind, as we hears on, nothin' is so touchin' to the feelings o' mankind as to see the decay an' desolation of the great author-minds, who in the full healthiness of their faculties have hinstructed or amused the world. Ah! it's a sorrowful thing to witness the hextinguishin' of sich brilliant fires, and to know that the flames that have consumed them, were self-lighted for to benefit those who gloomed through the darkness of hignorance or of sad heart."

"It is, Cap'n, no doubt," says I. "But who knows what hidden stabs or cankers, what single wrong or sum of small disquietudes had worried sense until it found no resting-place; who knows what world storms have roared and raged about the bark of life, until it plunged madly into quick destruction, or sense gave up the helm, and left the shattered wreck to drift rudderless about the hocean of hexistence, at the marcy of the winds and waves."

"Old mesmet," says the Cap'n, "the world is werry wicious agin' the criminals as takes life in a wiolent manner. But there are worse murderers than they are, domestic destroyers, slow poisoners of all that is wholesome in life; who taint the hatmosphere of home itself, which should be so pure and healthy, with a moral infection that eats into the heart, there are those in the world, Jack, and I have known such, sleek-seeming, well-considered counterfeits of humanity, upon whose murderous track death has as surely waited as upon the assassin's knife, and men have known them also, well—have marked and numbered every change upon the victim's face and spirit, have seen the secretly tortured frame give way, in passive silence, until the soul, dissolved from its earthly partnership by the tardy, but most certain poison of unkindliness, seeks its creator, and, if any of the woman's spirit should yet imbue its nature, regretfully avow that through a once loved hand, the spark of life was quenched; for no fictitious sorrow will avail the household killer there, no eyes overflowing with false tears, no sable garments or extensive crape but classed with the vilest of the crew, his brother demons will shriek into his ear, 'behold a murderer!'"

That there's werry high-flown, but that ain't anybody's business.

XIX.

Jack having seen a lecture by the Rev. Henry Ward Beecher, wherein he comes down upon his friends the players like a thousand of brick, waxes exceedingly wroth, and while under that very rational, and he thinks, pardonable excitement, loads an epistle against the Rev. Gentleman, which he incontinently fires point-blank, hoping thereby, to patch up the Rev. Gentleman's manners a little, however small effect it may have on his morals.

THERE ain't nothin' on this here blessed earth as biles up the tea-kettle of my temper so suddent, as the blazin' gas of *cant*, and there seems to be a wonderful manufacturer of that 'ere harticle among us, judgein' from a fiery speciment I saw this morning, a blackenin' the columns of a respectable newspaper called the "Sun;" but as there is hoften to be hobserved dark spots upon the real shinin' luminary, so I s'pose it is but nateral to expect similar dirtinesses upon his hintelligent namesake.

There is a hinsane indiwidual somewhere at large, as rejoices in the name of HENRY WARD BEECHER. There aint nothin' remarkable about the cognomen, except that he tacks afore it the hunexplainable hepithet of *Reverend*. Now, if that means anything, it is, that the owner of the title, by the simple reason of having that 'ere handle,—no matter how he got it, or whether he has any right to it,—distinctly taxes us for our reverence.—But oh! unerring wisdom, to whom the specious veil is rent from every hollow heart, thou knowest how many hearths have been made desolate, how many myriad souls have been destroyed, by placing too much confidence in that mere man-fashioned word. Do we ever take up the papers that the fact don't stare us in the face? Is not the caption almost stereotyped upon the world's memory—*Another Clerical Scoundrel.* And yet shall we condemn all, even for the many? No, Charity forbid. We deplore the circumstance which gave such fatal direction to their life-road—we regret the temptation which lay in their path:—we pity the weak humanity which yielded to it,—and we implore their yet undiscovered fellows to pause in their career of guilt: Guilt, the more atrocious, as the heart of domestic love and peace, and happiness, lies as an open book before them: Guilt, the more tremendous, as the soul, blindfold, is delivered up to the *reverend* guide, who should lead it upward, toward the after hope of *all*, the radiant sphere of everlasting happiness, not angel-voiced, but demon-hearted, plunge it into the never-ending abyss of torture.

I haint got the gift o' horotory, like the self-satisfied, vain young gentleman aforementioned—ne'ther can I string long-winded sentences together which means nothin' but sound, and yet in my hown plain matter-o'-fact way, I'd like to have a word or two with him: and I will too.

Rewerend Sir—

You have thought proper, hout of the overplus of your righteousness, to bestow a thought or two upon a community of people as I happen to have a thorough acquaintance with; I means the hactors, lumpin' them up werry properly with "gamblers, racers, horse-jockeys," and hall sorts o' ragga-muffinism—as heverybody knows, they're one family, jest the same as all the religious-mongers—your Jumpers and Whistlers and Mormons, and the thousand and one offshoots from the real pure fount of Christianity, which we truly reverence, are to be classed together under one common head.

Now, my conceited, but reverend friend, you commence your wordy wind-bag of a horation, by asking a mighty silly question. You ask werry sagaciously "if prayers wouldn't be discordant in a theatre?" Why, in coorse they would; that is to say what you—no—I won't say you: because there is a shadow of a chance that you may be sincere in your hallucination, a softness of the hintellect is a calamity, not a crime, and I respects the man who speaks hout honest from the heart whatever he may say—but what some of the skin-deep disciples *calls* prayer—a few set phrases grumbled out through a pair of lantern jaws, while their mental harithmetic is a contemplatin' the collection, or it may be concoctin' a trifle o' willainy—*they* would be hout of place, certainly: but, reverend sir, if you don't know the principles of the religion which you *talk* so much about, suffer a poor sinner like me to tell you that one can *think* a prayer, deep and silent, within the recesses of the heart, which would be more efficacious than all the hypocritical bellowings that ever echoed through a conventicle. I want only to hilluminate the darkness of your ignorance in another particular. You seem to think, poor benighted teacher, that all those sacred matters are monopolized by such as you: and that those "miscreants," as you charitably call the poor players, who humbly acknowledge their urgent need, are pre-doomed, by your merciful account, to "whistle towards the gates of Hell." Now, sir, we have very fortunately the word of one mightier than thou, that "There is joy in Heaven over one sinner that repenteth," and so with all proper respect for your *Reverence*, we'll continue to believe that word in preference to yours, and despite your high-sounding malediction, will yet venture to look forward with humbleness and *hope.*

Amongst a number of other similar stupidities which have been flung against the hobject of your mild and gentle abuse, you venture upon a question, which from the very fear of provoking comparison, I should have thought you too politic to touch upon; with all the simplicity of presumed or assumed ignorance, you ask, "Why don't the teachers learn their own lessons?"

Why indeed? Ask your reverend compatriots the fatal fruits of whose teaching I slightly hinted at a little way back; there is an old but werry happropriate proverb as says: "Those who live in glass houses, shouldn't throw stones;" but, inasmuch as it is beyond the limit of man's power to judge his fellow, we leave the crime and criminal to the judgment which is to come, imploring for the erring mortal *mercy* and not justice.

I regret to say, Reverend Sir, that I must accuse you of having made another most egregious mistake in asserting, with your peculiar self-satisfied dogmatism, that "The Church is the mortal enemy of Theatres." Now, sir, the spirit of universal charity and all pervading love which I consider to be the groundwork of Christianity is not the "mortal enemy" of anything; it comes not with the sword, but with the olive branch; it seeks not to revenge, but to reform. Your sanguinary words breathe nothing but extermination; it would seem as though they were uttered by a mailed champion of the Church Militant, when it was deemed necessary to reverse the command of its "meek and lowly" founder, and to baptize their proselytes in blood.

I must also, my eloquent friend, admonish you that your language is "very tolerable, and not to be endured." You make use o' words as would disgrace a hungry fisherwoman; no decent-minded father would let his daughter read them. Why, sir, on the stage, as you say, in sich a sink o' hiniquity, the mildest of the habusive terms you scatter through your gentlemanly lecture, would meet the merited hindignation of all present. There is another simple truth I would like you to know, and that is, Actors and Actresses, "miscreants" though you may consider them, are yet *men* and *women*, bearing within their hearts the strong feelin' of affection for their kindred, and insolence, even though coming from a *reverend* mouth, is apt to provoke indignation, and indigna tion has lain its cudgel upon the back of many a *reverend* slanderer before now—not that you need have any fear—for your unchristianlike and vindictive tirade of mouthing non-sense would provoke nothing but pity for its overweening vanity, did it not excite a thrill of horror from its fearful blasphemy. For a "miserable worm" like you to arrogate supernal power, and hurl your anathemas against a whole community at this age of the world's history, is simply folly.

Who invested you with the attributes of Divinity?

How dare you interfere your presumptuous hand between a mortal soul and its Mediator?

Seriously and soberly, my Reverend railer, I would advise you to reflect, and see how far the *Ignis Fatuus* of a suppo-sitious holiness has seduced you from the true path. Advise, and admonish. Point out what you consider the right path, if you will; but in the plenitude of your usurped authority, meddle not with the "immortal essence;" leave the soul of your brother sinner to its Creator, and, minding the awful of the admonition, "Judge not, lest that ye be judged."

'Taint hoften as I hindulges in such matters, inasmuch as I thinks 'em of too much himportance to be treated in hany way in the slightest degree happroachin' to levity; but I do hinsist upon hendeavorin' to raise my little shield again' that impudently confident, sinless professor, who not only "throws the first stone," but keeps continually a peltin' of us, in sich a houtrageous manner, I must confess the Reverend genl'man writes unknown strong, as far as the brimstone flavor goes; but upon takin' a business-like view o' the whole affair, I can't help thinkin' that the "halmighty dollar" shines through the thin veil of cant and vituperation, like "the sun on a morass," it ain't the "corruptin' influence," it ain't the hawful "waste of time," it ain't the hatrocity of mirth, or the sinfulness of smilin', but it's the heaps of "GOLDEN COIN" which would, no doubt, be better hemployed, lining the pockets of the "faithful."

Oh! for shame, *Reverend Henry Ward Beecher.* So you are nothin' but "Brummagem" arter all, a polished counterfeit, a highly plated spoon; rub off your flimsy surface of Religion, and lo! the base metal of cupidity and selfishness peeps through.

And so farewell my Reverend friend, had your arguments been worthy of refutation, I would have treated them in a more serious manner; as it is, I take leave of you with no worse a wish, than the hope that the light of *real* knowledge will yet be able to penetrate the dense fog of your self-sufficiency, and enable you to realize the immensity of your presumption, in daring to arraign the economy of Heaven, by pre-condemning those who are but "*striving to do their duty in that state of life to which it has pleased God to call them.*"

XX.

The Captain and Jack are disturbed at breakfast by an unexpected, though not unwelcome intruder, whose unseasonable appearance forms the ground-work for some pertinent discourse—The Captain affects the philosopher, and draws a parallel between men and flies, which tends to warn the former against undue indulgence, becoming more and more profound, he waxes eloquent; and taking a leaf out of "Carlyle," makes himself foggy to the common understanding, by being fashionably abstruse, for which, it being the prevailing "error of the moon," he considers himself to be in every way excusable.

THERE was a triflin' sarcumstance took place this mornin,' while the Cap'n and me was a henjoyin of our quiet breakfast, by ourselves,—for be it known to all whom it may concarn, or otherways, that we buys our own prog, cooks it to our own likin', and heats it comfortable. We hain't got no greedy-eyed boardin' house Hargus a limitatin' our happetites, by watchin' the mouthfulls, or a sloppin' of our hinsides with werry duberous coffee, flavored on the *hum*eopathic principle, which they tells me is the new and superior style of physic; and there hain't nothin' leastways, as I knows of, in the way of physical henjoyment, as can compare to the sense o' hindependence, with which a fellow with his palate sharpened by a few hours' hair an' hexercise, tucks hinto a jolly feed, with nobody guagin' the hextent of his swallow, or a twistin' o' their hunsatisfactory muscles at the disappearance o' hevery chunk.

Well—as I was a-goin' to remark—a mere triflin', hough I must say, rayther hunexpected sarcumstance, happened durin' our meal, as sarved for a peg, whereon the Cap'n hung hobserwations by the hat full. It was the presence of a wisitor to our table, as one is hapt to be savage with in summer time, in regard of their bein' too numerous, but as you are likely to treat with respect and hattention in the winter, inasmuch as it's a solitary stranger, and a mysterious representative of the past,—A Fly.

A real hundoubted, no mistake, lively, sugar huntin', milk stealin', himpertinent fly. Sharp sleet was ringin' agin' the window pane; yet, there was that hunaccountable hinsect a buzzin' round, and pokin' his hindia rubber tellyscope of a proboskiss hinto hevery thing about. The Cap'n and me watched the fellow's capers with perfect hadmiration for as good as a half-an-hour: now he'd make a dive hinto the sugar-bowl, but wouldn't stay there long, bein' hevidently a west-hend fly, and we uses "brown;" then he'd light gingerly a top o' the milk pot, walk down the side like François Ravel, and take a snout full of the cream, retire a little for the sake of digestion, I s'pose, and plunge into it agin.

Arter he'd backed and fi'led, enough for the present purposes, away he'd start on a healthy hexcursion, mayhap wisit the Cap'n's nose—a hunkimmon favorite restin' place for them there specieses,—but I halways remarks that they starts hoff suddent, jest as if they'd singed their toes—when the wagabone had a turn round the room, hinwestigated the chimbley hornaments, and left his hautograft on the ceilin', back he'd come agin to the heatables, have another shy at the sugar, another dip hinto the milk, and, not satisfied with what he knew by hexperience was pleasant and palatable, like a reg'lar hepicure, he'd make hunsuccessful hexperiments on the butter, or scald his flexibility in the hot tea.

It so turned out, that while the gormandizin' blaggard was on one of those foragin' hexpeditions, that somehow he lost his balance and tumbled head over heels right slap into the Cap'n's cup.

You should a seen the Cap'n, bless his benevolent ould hull; I didn't know what he was thinkin' on—but may I never see salt water agin if he didn't shout out,

"Man over board!"

And I'm blessed if he wasn't a'most as much concarned as if it had been a hooman bein' as he put his hook into the cup and fetched up the half drownded hinsect high an' dry, tumbled him over hinto the palm of his hand and breathed on him to bring back his witality.

"That sarves you right," says he, as the chap began to wash his face, and find out the hextent o' damage as was done to his legs and wings. "It sarves you quite right you hunreasonable warmint; you wouldn't be content with plenty o' good milk and sugar, your proper nateral fly food, but you must dip your beak in the hot tea, eh! and what have you got by it? answer me that, what have you got by it? I say, —a wet skin; you fool, and mayhap the rheumatics in your legs to-morrow, if this weather continues—think o' that Jack," and he turned his sensible heyes upon me—" think o' six legs, and the rheumatics in them all."

"It'll be a lesson to that there fly as long as he lives," says I.

"Will it?" says he. "I'll lay any wager that the minute he has the use of his wings he'll be at it agin."

An' sure enough, when the hungracious willain was in flyin' horder, before you could say Jack Robinson he was a wrigglin' about in the werry same cup. The Cap'n hacted the part of a Humane Society to him once more, a sayin' to me as he hooked him out.

"Call this here fly a man, and that there tea hunlawful and forbidden hindulgences, then overhaul your hintellect wigorous, and when found make the happlication."

That there last plunge took the conceat out o' the hinsect tolerable, and so arter he'd made hisself respectable, he was perfectly well satisfied with takin' short walks about the tablecloth, a nibblin' at a crumb, or suckin' of a damp spot, hevery now and then, having to kick the consequences of his warm bath off his wings, or clean his legs on the patent corkscrew principle.

Howsomedever, he seemed to consider hisself quite at home, and consequently hacted haccordin'. It was jest at this time that the Cap'n looked at the hintruder werry solid for a minute or two, and then said to me with a woice o' melancholy:

"That there fly," says he, "is a hobject o' pity, and it don't take nothin' from the sensibility of a man to feel for its lonely condition. Born to live and die in the warm hatmosphere o' summer, what brings it here amidst the bitter cold o' winter. Is it a hold patriarch o' the last generation, as has houtlived its kind for hages, in the fly computation, whose years are minutes and whose hexistance is a single season, or is it one of the generation as is to come, sent into the world a hequal length o' time too soon.

"Ah, Jack, how often do we find parallel cases among men; there's some who think and feel and hact as though they were hatched in the very nest of hintolerance and bloody deeds, clingers to bygone mummeries and monstrous crimes, done then, in holy names—Old World worshippers, to whom the sword and the shackle are more consonant than the hanvil and the plough—Crutches for decrepit prejudices who see more beauty in those hancient deformities than in the hale structure of the present time—Promoters of sectional discord, who would rather keep alive the brand of hatred for 'opinion's sake,' than help along the universal brotherhood of love, to which the world is slowly, but most suredly tending.

Other men there are, whose impulses are jest as much before the time in which their feelings will be general, Pioneers as it were of a new caste of thought, who move amidst the present race of neutral people, and belong as little to them as though they were droppers in, from some adjacent planet.

"But see, Jack, the fly is gone and the breakfast cold, a plain proof that the real Now must be attended to, before the speculative FUTURE."

It strikes me werry forcible that the Cap'n must a ben' readin' one of the new light uncomprehendable books, as is writ every now and then by the word-philosofers, but what does it si'nafy? what's gone is gone, and what's comin' will come, fast enough to trip up many heels though it will find *some* who still will run before it.

XXI.

Jack begins in a hail storm, which gives him occasion to express his gratitude, for shelter, intending to convey a word or two of advice to the wearers of "purple and fine linen," as to the criminality of neglecting their poorer relations in the great family of man, especially during this element season; but an adverse current of thought springing up, he is obliged to follow its direction and go upon another tack—The Captain and he therefore discuss sundry and several subjects upon which they take leave to differ from the world's opinion considerably.

Broo! how the wind howls Cap'n, as if some unseen tormenter was a lashin' of it into fury. Jingo! there's a great bang right up agin' the window, as if entreatin' of us to let it come in and stow itself away somewhere from the pitiless pursuer. Now, the hail sleet with its thousand points, cracks sharply agin' the pane, no doubt a stingin' the cheek of the wayfarer, like a legion of lilliputian harrows; this here's a night as forces a fellow to hestimate the walue of honest doors and hair tight windows.

"That is it, Jack," says he, with a blessed look o' gratefulness a playin' about his ould countenance: "when we can hafford to pay for sich luxuries, not that I'm agoin' to complain, Jack, I hain't sich a hungracious wagabone; but honor bright, look at that 'ere gap in the window, and them there wentilators all round the door; oughtn't the landlord as leases them conweniences for rheumatism, be hanswerable for the consequences thereof? In coorse he should, and is—morally; but what does he care about that? to be sure legally there's a remedy, but what o' that 'ere? No poor man can hafford to hindulge in sich hexpensive hamusement: the ould sayin' is werry true, though it hain't always taken in the right meanin." "Necessity has *no* law," ne'ther has it, no how; the money-maker's morality is a sort o' werry coarse net work, the dollars drop through and don't fray it a bit; there's a great many things, old mesmet, as the public doesn't see in the right light yet; there's more crimes in the world than those whose horrid names makes hevery body shudder—crimes as are so whitewashed hover, gilded an' galvanized, that their blackness is hidden in the dazzlin' blaze;—criminals, there are too, as walks about comfortable, and looks men in the face without winkin'; criminals as hain't awake to the knowledge of the fact, but dress in black, and look demure: goes reg'lar to church, says their prayers, and flatters theirselves that they are patterns o' piety. Jack, old shipmet, how the arch deceiver of souls must grin with delight, when he contemplates sich masqueraders."

"Aye, aye," says I, seein' that he expected me to say somethin', though I didn't ezactly know the coorse he was a steerin'; but kalkilated sartain that he'd bring up somewhere on the coast o' wisdom.

"Now for the sake o' hargument," says he, a takin' off his tarpaulin, and settin' hisself down in earnest; "jist honly for the sake o' hargument, if one man loses his life through the hinstrumentality of another, it's murder, hain't it?"

"That's what they calls it," says I.

"Werry well, then," says he. "It doesn't si'nafy by what means, whether pizon or pistol, so as death hensues, it would be murder; and men would elewate their heyes an' groan, and whisper terrible words to each hother. But now, s'posin' a rich man owned a lot o' houses, which he rented out to poor folks for considerable more nor they were worth,—for poverty actually pays more than wealth for hevery thing, as I shall explain by and by:—but to come back to my hargument. If it should happen, heven in one of them, that a human being, through the criminal neglect of sich landlord, chanced to catch a disease which ended in his death, what would the public say then? not a word. But no one can dare to tell me, that the murder hain't as much a murder in one case as in the hother. Nay, more so: for the first, appalling though it may be, might result from insult or provocation, to no personal adwantage. But the hother is a sordid and contemptible weighing of men's lives agin a piece of dirty money."

"I never seed it in that way afore, Cap'n," says I. "Ne'ther do I b'leeve you can get any o' the wealthy house-owners to take off their spectacles for the purpose of lookin' into it so closely."

"I hain't sich a fool as to think they will, Jack," says he; "but if so be as they did, it would be better for the wholesomeness of their sleep, nor if they reclined on poppy pillows."

"I agrees with you hall out, Cap'n," says I. "But you made a hobserwation jest now as I'd like to hear you gi' me some proof on—respectin' the poor payin' more than the rich."

"Why, you think for a sekind o' time, old tar, and you won't want no hexplanation o' that," says the Cap'n: "for hinstance now, the rich man can go to the first market and get his meat by the cart load, thereby awoidin' of the many slices as is chucked on as it progresses from the carcass to the jint, and from the jint to the chop, in hevery stage o' the road poverty hout of its small means having to pay toll to speculation or to havarice; if so be as you agrees to the truth o' that—and you can't do nothin' else,—why, in coorse, the same holds good in hevery harticle of necessity, and therefore it is I say, that the poor man is taxed back, belly, and boots, a thousand times more nor the wealthy: haint it so Jack?"

"Why, Cap'n," says I, "you puts it afore me in such a conwincin' way, it's as clear as the ship's light in fair weather, but it's werry strange that nobody don't think o' these things."

"Ah, Jack, old chap," says he, "this here pert and pragmatical world, fancies itself grey in wisdom, whereas it hain't hout of its long-clothes yet: look at the jolly lot of Dombeyfied professors as it builds up colleges for some on 'em pokin' their noses up skyways, a henlightenin' of our wonderments by tellin' us about the domestic heconomy of the planets; others agin' with their eyes along the ground pryin' hinto the secret history of the weeds and flowers: single hidea hunters as has no knowledge of the wants and requirements of their fellow-beings, but to balance that, they can tell you the difference between a male and a female polyanthus, and give you crack jaw names for every tuft of grass you put your foot on, and yet, when they 've filled up their little pinnance o' heducation, they looks at it through the maknifyin' glasses of their own importance and sets it afloat upon the hocean of life, marked A 1!"

"It 's my hopinion, Jack, that if the hanimated finger-posts as pints hout the road o' hinstruction would honly condescend to either come down a trifle from the helevation, or get up a little from their depression, jest so much as 'll bring the hindex within the range o' mankind, and instead of spending all this time star gazin' or weed dissectin' study to give their pupils a thorough knowledge of their duty to their struggling fellows first—to himpress upon their minds that the beginning and hendin' of all knowledge is Humanity; to admonish them that their first care should be to write their names legibly upon the page of hexistance, then afterwards put in the flourishes if they 've a mind to;—let them do that 'ere, Jack, and though there might be fewer scholars, there would more MEN."

That 'ere's the Cap'n's hopinion, and moreover, it's mine. I don't care who knows it,—therefore, if so it is—why, so let it be.

XXII.

The Captain and Jack embark upon a scientific excursion, intending to investigate the mysteries of Daguerre, but some how manage to get into a dangerous extremity, illustrating thereby one of the criminal chapters in the City's passing page of history, almost as well as any of its modern Illuminati—The Captain exhibits a wonderful deal of courage and self-possession during a most severe and unexpected trial, escaping from a scene of horror with considerable cunning, whereat Jack wakes up the slumbering authorities with a dig in the ribs, by the way of information and advice.

As the Cap'n and me was a dubitatin' what we'd do with ourselves, this mornin', he suddenly started up, and says,

"Jack!"

"Aye, aye," says I.

"S'posin' we goes and gets our phisogs took off," says he.

"How?" says I.

"Why, by the new light system. Them there Derogatory-types," says he.

"Werry well," says I. So off we went, in search of what they calls a hoperator. 'Twarn't long afore we bore down on a sign as give us to hunderstand sich things was a-doin' hup stairs; hup stairs we travelled, accordin'ly,—a wonderful high house it was, with stories enough to make a "Friendship's hofferin'." Howsomedever, arter two or three restin' spells, we found ourselves right smack up at the sky-parlor, and a little beyond.

We had to take our time, in coorse, so down we sot, in a terrible light room for a bashful human, there bein' a whole heap o' people a settin' as stiff as a lot o' Hegyptian Mummies, —as for the Cap'n, he'd scarcely look up off the ground, he was so took aback. Soon there came in a hard-lookin' chap, with a countenance like a ship's block, as had the measles bad, and he bowed and scraped—'specially to the feminines, the heartful scoundrel—as consisted of two elderly females, dressed up to the nines, together with a squad of smaller speciments, hall curls and conceit.

When we'd ben there about an hour-and-a-half, the last batch o' candidates for hexecution havin' bin drafted off, the Cap'n uplifted his woice for the first time, and says he,

"Jack, old tar, shall we lie to, still, or 'bout ship?"

I was towld this here description o' pictur' takin' was done in a giffy, and see how we've been a wastin' o' the blessed moments as never kin come back to us. Come along, my name's O. P. H.

Jest at that time in comes the lignum-witey faced hoperator, and

"Now, gen'l'men," says he, "I'm ready." With that the Cap'n diwested hisself of the tarpaulin, and runnin' o' his hook through his hair, for to give it a becomin' twist, hover the bald, purceeded along with me to the hartist's sanctum snorum, both on us wonderin' how a feller could take your face off in a few sekinds o' time, as we'd heard they could.

When we got hinto the place, I looked round, but I couldn't see no paints nor brushes, nor not no harticles as you hexpects to see in a hartist's hestablishment; there warn't nothin' but a bit o' a box on three legs, with a sort o' hover-grown gun-barrel a peepin' out o' the middle, and on a table a whole cargo o' strong-smellin' physicy looking combustickles.

The Cap'n was a hangin' back, scared a trifle, I should say, by my own feelin's,—for there warn't anybody in the hestablishment but us, and the not hover pleasin'-faced indiwidual as busied hisself about the dangerous-lookin' machine, hover in a dark corner. You see we'd been readin' some of them 'ere hawful books about the City and its diabolicals, and warn't altogether sartain that we hadn't got into a tight corner hunawares.

The Cap'n was the first to be hoperated hupon, and then he got a start in right earnest. The smilin' willan of a hoperator sot him down in a cheer, and as soon as he'd fixed his wenerable head by a screwing it on to a crooked piece of hiron, as it seemed to me, he goes to the hinfernal machine, and pints it slap at the Capn's heyes—this was too much for him.

"Awast mesmet," he cried hout, a shielden' of his heyes with the hook; "Just turn the muzzle o' that 'ere thing a little aside; I ain't a goin' to stand no sich capers as that. I knows yer city tricks well."

Would you believe it, the fellow laughed like a good 'un at the Cap'n, for he had pluck enough not to flinch 'afore the danger, though he did wink a trifle.

"You're not afraid, sir?" says the hindiwidual.

"Afraid," says the Cap'n, a given' of his nose a contemptible toss; "that there hisland doesn't lie in my geehography; but it rather *is* cool to be looking into the barrel of a new fangled, thingamy, and not know what the creeter's loaded with."

"It ain't werry dangerous," says the fellow who was hevidently henjoyin' the Cap'n's distress o' mind.

"What's in it, anyhow?" says the Cap'n.

"Some'at as 'ill take your head off without hurting you in the least," says the other, with a nasty sort of a grin.

"That would be capital hexecution and no mistake," says the old tar, a laughin' woraciously at his own joke, being more at his hease, by reason that the mouth o' the hinstrument was covered with a brass plug; besides which it's a good way to swindle yourself into the belief that you're not frightened.

I was just beginning to wonder why the chap didn't begin to chalk out the Cap'n, or how he was a goin' to picter him at all, he bein' so busy with that there mysterious box, and not makin' no hapology to ne'ther of us for the delay, when the ruffian politely hinsinuated that I had better walk hout, which I did, but took care to keep my heye and here at the door-crack.

"Now, for it," I heard him say, "are you prepared?"

"In coorse I am," says the Cap'n, as patient as a lamb, "awaitin' on your conwenience."

"Don't you wenture to stir, then," says he.

"Whatsomedever happens, I'm resigned," says the Cap'n, seein' the chap had his hand on the brass cowerin', and not knowin' ezactly how to ward hoff the comin' catastrophe.

"Not a word," says he. Off came the plug, away went the hoperator, as hif to awoid the hexplosion, and there sot the courageous old wictim hexpectin' of it to fire some'at at his nose hevery sekind.

It must a been a hawful situation, judgin' from my own feelin' houtside. But the wagabone had some natur' left, for jest as I was a makin' up my mind to rush in and keel him hover and his machine together, he thought better of it, hinasmuch as he went hisself and shut up the thing, werry much to the Cap'n's relief, and no more to mine, bein' now conwinced that we'd stumbled upon one of them horrors as was so wiwidly depicted by the city historians, as we'd been a readin'. Arter a few minutes of terrible suspense, what should I see but the Cap'n a movin' soft and cautious across the floor, like a big cat towards a canary, a hopenin' the door quiet, and stealin' hout sagacious.

"Hush, Jack, old shipmet," says he in a whisper, "make no sound;" then he crept silently away down one flight o' stairs, cut like blazers down the rest, and never breathed a comfortable breath until we were three or four streets hoff from the place.

When we felt ourselves safely away from the danger, I asked the Cap'n how he'd guv the rascal the slip, when he squeezed my hand as heloquent as a bushel of halphabets, as much as to say, "Thank Heaven, we're here, and,

"Jack," says he, "we've had a huncommon narrow hescape. When I seed the warment a divin' into a black cubboard of a concarn, hevidently for the purpose o' procurin' a fresh load o' combustickles, the first one having missed fire, I started quick. What's the use in fellows gasin' and purtendin' to hexpose the mysterious crimes o' this here metropolis, and never to say nothin' about that diabolical inwention?"

"It was a mercy it didn't go hoff," says I, "whatever it was stuffed with."

This I will say, and it's a dreadful thing to contemplate upon, that of all the poor wretches who went into the fearful den, *not one of 'em came out agin*—as I could see. I mentions this fact in horder that it may come to the hears of the hauthorities, so that if so be as they have any time on hand that they can dewote to the hinterests of the public, that they may be hinduced to take the subject into their serious consideration, and hendeavor, as in duty bound, to prewent their fellow-creeters from bein' taken hoff in such a houtrageous manner, in the werry face of the broad day-light.

XXIII.

Jack gets up with a pair of pleasant companions, the toothache and rheumatism, and as is usual in nearly all such cases, fancies himself the most ill-used individual in the world, for which unreasonable thought he is very properly rebuked by the Captain, who by force of argument and illustration, succeeds in impressing upon Jack that there are worse things to be endured in the world than even toothache—Jack demurs, but ultimately comes over to the Captain's opinion with a tolerably good grace.

I TAKES a little mite o' credit to myself for the sarcumstance, that I'm never above receivin' a lesson, howsomedever it arrives, or whosomedever is the carryer. It was only this very mornin', as the Cap'n took me to task with considerable severity (for him), because I was foolish enough to kick up a fuss about small annoyances when—but mayhap I'd better relate the conwersation as near as I can remember it.

Well, it so happened that, what with a hollow tooth as amused itself by darting a long needle into my jaw bone every sickond, like a continuin' pulse o' hagony, combined with a biting rheumatism mumblin' at my shoulder, I called wainly upon sleep to shut off the pain; hevery now and then I'd go off into a sort of stupidity, only to be tortured into wide awakeness, by the combined exertions of them two "heirs o' flesh."

You may werry well imagine that I rose early, and not in the delightfullest of humors, so that when the Cap'n turned out, he diskivered your humble, in a blessed state o' disgust with hevery thing, from a half an inch high up'ards.

Ill-conditioned brute as I was—why, even the Cap'n's jolly, healthy ould countenance, jest fresh from cold water, and a shinin' like a new button, instead of hexcitin' my hadmiration, as it ought to have done, filled me full o' hill nature and henvy, and I s'pose made me look like a griffin, for the Cap'n says to me,

"Hollo, Jack," says he. "Whose head have you got on your shoulders? eh, mesmet? you look as if you'd swallowed a vinigar cruet."

"Mayhap I have," says I, wicious as I could muster the hexpression, "and if you'd been a groanin' all night with the rheumatics atop of a toothache, you wouldn't be quite so smilin' yerself."

"Toothache is bad," says he, "and moreover, so is the rheumatics, when they grabs you hard; but Jack, old tar, there's a som'at worse nor either, and that is bad temper. What right have you to think that you're to be passed over when a chunk o' sickness is to be distributed. Why, Jack, I'm ashamed on you."

"How can a feller help it," says I; "its werry easy for a hearty, hale man to get up and preach patience to them as is sufferin'. I only wish that you could feel that there twinge, if it was only for a minute o' time."

"If it would take it away from you, Jack, I'd endure it for a spell, willingly."

"You would, Cap'n," says I, a shakin of his friendly hand; "you would, I know it well, and I'm a hippopottamus for what I said jist now."

"'Twarn't you, Jack," says he, mild as a wirgin; "it was the toothache and the other thing as was a speaking through your pains, old shipmet; I knows how difficult it is to keep a sharp dig of pain from rousing up ill-temper, if it should be any where near the sarface, and there aint anybody as hasn't got some stored away, in one place or another, but mark this, Jack, the greatest enemy to a man's self—to his comfort and well-doin', is his bit of bad temper, and if his better nature should succeed in puttin' it down and keepin' it prisoner to good feelin' and proper reason, it would be a victory that he might be prouder of than if he had won a battle."

"I acknowledges all that, Cap'n," says I, "but I feels as if I aint sufficient of a philosopher to hargue myself into hinsensibility; reason and hargument consists of nothin' but thought and words; they couldn't stick a pin into you, nohow, ne'ther on 'em, whereas this here rheumatism saws away at a chap's werry marrow, and the toothache bores a hole in his comfort, and no mistake at all about the matter. There may be folks in the world so unkimmon sensitive, that hard words would hurt 'em more nor a thick stick, but I aint one on 'em."

"Ne'ther am I, Jack," says he, in a manner o' speakin'; "but there's sich a thing as *mental* pain as well as bodily, and it's a toss up which is the hardest to hendure without a kick."

"Pooh!" says I, a braggin' like a fool upon my style o' sufferin'. "There aint no sich a thing as mental pain; it's only a wisionary annoyance, as is inwented by poets and sich-like sentimentally useless hanimals."

"Indeed," says the Cap'n, "now let us see if you are sich a cat-fish as you say. You and I are friends—aint we?"

"That we are, Cap'n," says I, a shaking a himitation o' rheumatism hinto his hand, with the squeeze I gave it; "and, moreover, ain't agoin' to be hany thing else till this hould hull is stranded on the beach of hoblivion."

"Werry good," says he. "Well, now, if so be—mind, I'm only puttin' a case—if so be as I was to cut adrift from you?"

"What?" says I, a startin' up with the hidea, quick.

"Listen to me, Jack. I say if I were to part company, and steer my bark o' life in a hopposite direction, and, moreover, nor that, say somethin' unpleasin' to your feelings at sheerin' off, which would you rather occurred, that there separation, or a touch of toothache? and" ——

"Shut yer mouth, you ould reprobate," says I, a stoppin' o' his speech, "which would I rather? you stony-hearted ould rhynoceros. Why, I'd traffic on toothache all my life, and keep a mouthful o' them on hand by way o' sample, sooner than a real wrong word should pass between us."

"In coorse you would, you grampus," says he; "and in doin' so most beastifully you cuts the rope that holds your argument, and proves werry significantly that there's worse things to hendure in the world than the fieriest toothache that ever made a man grumble."

"Cap'n," says I, as penitential as a baby, "I wish the blessed thing would give me an additional screw up, jist for you too see how I'd laugh at it now."

"Ah, Jack," says the ould salt-water Solomon, "it's disgraceful to human natur' to growl and lose temper at petty annoyances, when there are sich huge calamities around us; let the pampered, delicately-ribbed speciments of hornamental humanity, as complains if there's a draft in their carriages, think for a hinstant upon the terrible misfortunes that are constantly occurring to their less lucky fellow-creatures; and instead of grunting over their own little grievances, they will more probably learn to sympathize with the great woes and sufferings of others."

THE END.

www.ingramcontent.com/pod-product-compliance
Lightning Source LLC
LaVergne TN
LVHW020101110826
845151LV00001B/42

* 9 7 8 1 4 2 5 5 4 4 6 7 6 *